THE HOLY SPIRIT

THE HOLY SPIRIT

by

Arthur W. Pink

BAKER BOOK HOUSE
Grand Rapids, Michigan

Library of Congress Catalog Card Number: 70-107078

ISBN: 0-8010-6850-9

First printing, June 1970
Second printing, February 1972
Third printing, March 1974
Fourth printing, November 1975

PHOTOLITHOPRINTED BY CUSHING - MALLOY, INC.
ANN ARBOR, MICHIGAN, UNITED STATES OF AMERICA
1975

CONTENTS

1

The Holy Spirit

IN the past having given consideration to the attributes of God our Father, and then to a contemplation of some of the glories of God our Redeemer, it now seems fitting that these should be followed by this series on the Holy Spirit. The need for this is real and pressing, for ignorance of the Third Person of the Godhead is most dishonoring to Him, and highly injurious to ourselves. The late George Smeaton of Scotland began his excellent work upon the Holy Spirit by saying, "Wherever Christianity has been a living power, the doctrine of the Holy Spirit has uniformly been regarded, equally with the Atonement and Justification by faith, as the article of a standing or falling church. The distinctive feature of Christianity as it addresses itself to man's experience, is the work of the Spirit, which not only elevates it far above all philosophical speculation, but also above every other form of religion."

Not at all too strong was the language of Samuel Chadwick when he said, "The gift of the Spirit is the crowning mercy of God in Christ Jesus. It was for this all the rest was. The Incarnation and Crucifixion, the Resurrection and Ascension were all preparatory to Pentecost. Without the gift of the Holy Spirit all the rest would be useless. The great thing in Christianity is the gift of the Spirit. The essential, vital, central element in the life of the soul and the work of the Church is the Person of the Spirit" (*Joyful News*, 1911).

The great importance of a reverent and prayerful study of this subject should be apparent to every real child of God. The repeated references made to the Spirit by Christ in His final discourse (John 14 to 16) at once intimates this. The particular work which has been committed to Him furnishes clear proof of it. There is no spiritual good communicated to any one but by the Spirit; whatever God in His grace works in us, it is by the Spirit. The only sin for which there is no forgiveness, is one committed against the Spirit. How necessary is it then that we should be well instructed in the Scripture doctrine concerning Him! The great abuse there has been in all ages under the pretense of His holy name, should prompt us to diligent study. Finally, the awful ignorance which now so widely prevails upon the Spirit's office and operations, urges us to put forth our best efforts.

Yet important as is our subject, and prominent as is the place given to it in Holy Writ, it seems that it has always met with a considerable amount of neglect and perversion. Thomas Goodwin commenced his massive work on *The Work of the Holy Spirit in Our Salvation* (1660)

7

by affirming, "There is a general omission in the saints of God, in their not giving the Holy Spirit that glory that is due to His person and for His great work of salvation in us, insomuch that we have in our hearts almost forgotten this Third Person." If that could be said in the midst of the palmy days of the Puritans, what language would be required to set forth the awful spiritual ignorance and impotency of this benighted twentieth century!

In the Preface to his Lectures on "The Person, Godhead, and Ministry of the Holy Spirit" (1817) Robert Hawker wrote, "I am the more prompted to this service, from contemplating the present awful day of the world. Surely the 'last days' and the 'perilous times,' so expressly spoken of by the Spirit, are come (I Tim. 4:1). The flood gates of heresy are broken up, and are pouring forth their deadly poison in various streams through the land. In a more daring and open manner the denial of the Person, Godhead, and Ministry of the Holy Spirit, is come forward and indicates the tempest to follow. In such a season it is needful to contend, and that, 'earnestly, for the faith once delivered unto the saints.' Now in a more awakened manner ought the people of God to remember the words of Jesus, and 'to hear what the Spirit saith unto the churches.' "

So again, in 1880 George Smeaton wrote, "We may safely affirm that the doctrine of the Spirit is almost entirely ignored." And let us add, Wherever little honor is done to the Spirit, there is grave cause to suspect the genuineness of any profession of Christianity. Against this, it may be replied, Such charges as the above no longer hold good. Would to God they did not, but they do. While it be true that during the past two generations much has been written and spoken on the person of the Spirit, yet, for the most part, it has been of a sadly inadequate and erroneous character. Much dross has been mingled with the gold. A fearful amount of unscriptural nonsense and fanaticism has marred the testimony. Furthermore, it cannot be gainsaid that it is no longer generally recognized that supernatural agency is imperatively required in order for the redemptive work of Christ to be *applied* to sinners. Rather do *actions* show it is now widely held that if unregenerate souls are instructed in the letter of Scripture their own will-power is sufficient to enable them to "decide for Christ."

In the great majority of cases, professing Christians are too puffed up by a sense of what *they* suppose they are doing *for* God, to earnestly study what God has promised to do for and in His people. They are so occupied with their fleshly efforts to "win souls for Christ" that they feel not their own deep need of the Spirit's anointing. The leaders of "Christian" (?) enterprise are so concerned in multiplying "Christian workers" that quantity not quality is the main consideration. How few to-day recognize that if the number of "missionaries" on the foreign field were increased twenty-fold the next year, that that, of itself, *would not ensure* the genuine salvation of one additional heathen? Even though every new missionary *were* "sound in the faith" and preached only "the Truth," that would not add one iota of spiritual power to the missionary forces, without the Holy Spirit's unction and blessing! The same principle holds good everywhere. If the orthodox seminaries and the much-advertised Bible institutes turned out one hundred times more men than they are now doing, the churches would not be one whit better off than they are, unless God vouchsafed a fresh outpouring of His Spirit. In like manner, no Sunday school is strengthened by the mere multiplication of its teachers.

O my readers, face the solemn fact that the greatest lack of all in Christendom to-day is the *absence* of the Holy Spirit's power and blessing. Review the activities of the past thirty years. Millions of dollars have been freely devoted to the support of professed Christian enterprises. Bible institutes and schools have turned out "trained workers" by the thousands. Bible conferences have sprung up on every side like mushrooms. Countless booklets and tracts have been printed and circulated. Time and labor have been given by an almost incalculable number of "personal workers." And *with what results?* Has the standard of personal piety advanced? Are the churches less worldly? Are their members more Christlike in their daily walk? Is there more godliness in the home? Are the children more obedient and respectful? Is the Sabbath-day being increasingly sanctified and kept holy? Has the standard of honesty in business been raised?

Those blest with any spiritual discernment can return but one answer to the above questions. In spite of all the huge sums of money that have been spent, in spite of all the labor which has been put forth, in spite of all the new workers that have been added to the old ones, the spirituality of Christendom is at a far lower ebb to-day than it was thirty years ago. Numbers of professing Christians have increased, fleshly activities have multiplied, but spiritual power has waned. Why? *Because there is a grieved and quenched Spirit in our midst.* While His blessing is withheld there can be no improvement. What is needed today is for the saints to get down on their faces before God, cry unto Him in the name of Christ to so work again, that what has grieved His Spirit may be put away, and the channel of blessing once more be opened.

Until the Holy Spirit is again given His rightful place in our hearts, thoughts, and activities, there can be no improvement. Until it be recognized that we are entirely dependent upon *His* operations for all spiritual blessing, the root of the trouble cannot be reached. Until it be recognized that it is "Not by might, [of trained workers], nor by power [of intellectual argument or persuasive appeal], but by *MY SPIRIT*, saith the Lord" (Zech. 4:6), there will be no deliverance from that fleshly zeal which is not according to knowledge, and which is now paralyzing Christendom. Until the Holy Spirit is honored, sought, and counted upon, the present spiritual drought must continue. May it please our gracious God to give the writer those messages and prepare the hearts of our readers to receive that which will be to His glory, the furtherance of His cause upon earth, and the good of His dear people. Brethren, pray for us.

2

The Personality of the Holy Spirit

IF we were asked to state in a comprehensive form what constitutes (according to our views of Scripture) the blessedness of the Lord's people on earth, after His work of grace is begun in their souls, we would not hesitate to say that it must be wholly made up of the personal knowledge of and communion with the glorious Trinity in their persons in the Godhead; for as the church is chosen to be everlastingly holy and everlastingly happy, in uninterrupted communion with God in glory when this life is ended, the anticipation of it now by faith must form the purest source of all present joy. But this communion with God in the Trinity of His Persons cannot be enjoyed without a clear apprehension of Him. We must know under Divine teaching God in the Trinity of His Persons, and we must also know from the same source the special and personal acts of grace by which each glorious person in the Godhead has condescended to make Himself known unto His people, before we can be said to personally enjoy communion with each and all.

We offer no apology, then, for devoting a separate article to the consideration of *the personality* of the Holy Spirit, for unless we have a right conception of His glorious being, it is impossible that we should entertain right thoughts about Him, and therefore impossible for us to render to Him that homage, love, confidence, and submission, which are His due. To the Christian who is given to realize that he owes to the personal operations of the Spirit every Divine influence exercised upon him from the first moment of regeneration until the final consummation in glory, it cannot be a matter of little moment for him to aspire after the fullest apprehension of Him that his finite faculties are capable of; yea, he will consider no effort too great to obtain spiritual views of Him to whose Divine grace and power the effectual means of his salvation through Christ are to be ascribed. To those who are strangers to the operations of the blessed Spirit in the heart, the theme of this article is likely to be a matter of unconcern, and its details wearisome.

Some of our readers may be surprised to hear that there are men professing to be Christians who flatly deny the personality of the Spirit. We will not sully these pages by transcribing their blasphemies, but we will mention one detail to which appeal is made by the spiritual seducers, because some of our friends have possibly experienced a difficulty with it. In the second chapter of Acts the Holy Spirit was said to be "poured out" (v. 18) and "shed abroad" (v. 33). How could such terms be used of a Person? Very easily: that language is *figurative*,

10

THE PERSONALITY OF THE HOLY SPIRIT

and not literal; literal it cannot be for that which is *spiritual* is incapable of being materially "poured out." The figure is easily interpreted: as water "poured out" *descends*, so the Spirit has come from heaven to earth; as a "pouring" rain is a heavy one, so the Spirit is freely given in the plentitude of His gifts.

Having cleared up, we trust, what has given difficulty to some, the way is now open for us to set forth some of the positive evidence. Let us begin by pointing out that a "person" is an intelligent and voluntary entity, of whom personal properties may be truly predicated. A "person" is a living entity, endowed with understanding and will, being an intelligent and willing agent. Such is the Holy Spirit: all the elements which constitute personality are ascribed to and found in Him. "As the Father hath life in Himself, and the Son has life in Himself, so has the Holy Spirit: since He is the Author of natural and spiritual life to men, which He could not be unless He had life in Himself; and if He has life in Himself, He must subsist in Himself" (John Gill).

1. Personal properties are predicated of the Spirit. He is endowed with *understanding* or wisdom, which is the first inseparable property of an intelligent agent: "the Spirit searcheth all things, even the deep things of God" (I Cor. 2:10). Now to "search" is an act of understanding, and the Spirit is said to "search" because He "knoweth" (v. 11). He is endowed with *will*, which is the most eminently distinguishing property of a person: "All these things worketh that one and selfsame Spirit, dividing unto every man as He will" (I Cor. 12:11) — how utterly meaningless would be such language were the Spirit only an influence or energy! He *loves*: "I beseech you, brethren, for the Lord Jesus Christ's sake, and for the love of the Spirit" (Rom. 15:30) — how absurd would it be to speak of the "love of the Spirit" if the Spirit were nought but an impersonal breath or abstract quality!

2. Passive personal properties are ascribed to the Holy Spirit: that is to say, He is the *Object* of such actions of men as none but a person can be. "Ye agree together to *tempt* the Spirit of the Lord" (Acts 5:9) — rightly did John Owen say, "How can a quality, an accident, an emanation from God be tempted? None can possibly be so but he that hath an understanding to consider what is proposed unto him, and a will to determine upon the proposals made." In like manner, Ananias is said to "*lie to* the Holy Spirit" (Acts 5:3) — none can lie unto any other but such a one as is capable of hearing and receiving a testimony. In Eph. 4:30 we are bidden not to "*grieve* the Holy Spirit" — how senseless would it be to talk about "grieving" an abstraction, like the law of gravity. Hebrews 10:29 warns us that He may be "done despite unto."

3. Personal actions are attributed to Him. He *speaks*: "The Spirit speaketh expressly" (I Tim. 4:1); "he that hath an ear, let him hear what the Spirit saith unto the churches" (Rev. 2:7). He *teaches*: "The Holy Spirit shall teach you in the same hour what ye ought to say" (Luke 12:12); "He shall teach you all things" (John 14:26). He *commands* or exercises authority: a striking proof of this is found in Acts

13:2, "The Holy Spirit said, Separate unto me Barnabas and Saul for the work whereunto I have called them" — how utterly misleading would such language be if the Spirit were not a real person! He *intercedes*: "The Spirit itself maketh intercession for us" (Rom. 8:26) — as the intercession of Christ proves Him to be a person, and a distinct one from the Father, unto whom He intercedes, so the intercession of the Spirit equally proves His personality, even His distinct personality.

4. Personal characters are ascribed to Him. Four times over the Lord Jesus referred to the Spirit as "The Comforter," and not merely as "comfort"; inanimate things, such as clothes, may give us comfort, but only a living person can be a "comforter." Again, He is the Witness: "The Holy Spirit also is a witness to us" (Heb. 10:15); "The Spirit itself beareth witness with our spirit that we are the children of God" (Rom. 8:16) — the term is a forensic one, denoting the supplying of valid evidence or legal proof; obviously, only an intelligent agent is capable of discharging such an office. He is Justifier and Sanctifier: "But ye are sanctified, but ye are justified in the name of the Lord Jesus, and *by the Spirit* of God" (I Cor. 6:11).

5. Personal pronouns are used about Him. The word "pneuma" in the Greek, like "spirit" in the English, is neuter, nevertheless the Holy Spirit is frequently spoken of in the masculine gender: "The Comforter, which is the Holy Spirit, whom the Father will send in my name, he shall teach you all things" (John 14:26) — the personal pronoun could not, without violating grammar and propriety, be applied to any other but a person. Referring again to Him, Christ said, "If I depart, I will send *him* unto you" (John 16:7) — there is no other alternative than to regard the Holy Spirit as a Person, or to be guilty of the frightful blasphemy of affirming that the Saviour employed language which could only mislead His apostles and bring them into fearful error. "I will pray the Father that he shall give *another* Comforter" (John 14:16) — no comparison would be possible between Christ (a person) and an abstract influence.

Borrowing the language of the revered J. Owen, we may surely say, "By all these testimonies we have fully confirmed what was designed to be proved by them, namely, that the Holy Spirit is not a quality, as some speak, residing in the Divine nature; not a mere emanation of virtue and power from God; not the acting of the power of God in and unto our sanctification, but a *holy, intelligent subsistent,* or person." May it please the Eternal Spirit to add His blessings to the above, apply the same to our hearts, and make His adorable person more real and precious to each of us. Amen.

3

The Deity of the Holy Spirit

In the last chapter we endeavored to supply from the testimony of Holy Writ abundant and clear evidence that the Holy Spirit is a conscious, intelligent, personal Being. Our present paper concerns the nature and dignity of His person. We sincerely trust that our present inquiry will not strike our readers as being a superfluous one: surely any mind which is impressed with a due reverence for the subject we are upon, will readily allow that we cannot be too minute and particular in the investigation of a point of such infinite importance. While it be true that almost every passage which we brought forward to demonstrate the Spirit's personality also contained decisive proof of His Godhead, yet we deemed the present aspect of our subject of such moment as to be justly entitled to a separate regard — the more so, as error at this point is fatal to the soul.

Having shown, then, that God's Word expressly and unequivocally teaches that the Spirit is a person, the next question to be considered is, Under what character are we to consider Him? What rank does He occupy in the scale of existence? It has been truly said that, "He is either God, possessing, in a distinction of person, an ineffable unity of the Divine nature with the Father and the Son, or He is the creature of God, infinitely removed from Him in essence and dignity, and having no other than a derivative excellence in that rank to which He is appointed in creation. There is no medium betwixt the one and the other. Nothing intermediate between the Creator and created can be admissible. So that were the Holy Spirit to be placed at the top of all creation, even as high above the highest angel as that angel transcends the lowest reptile of animated life, the chasm would be still infinite; and He, who is emphatically called the *Eternal* Spirit, would not be God" (R. Hawker).

It will now be our endeavor to show from the Word of Truth that the Holy Spirit is distinguished by such names and attributes, that He is endowed with such a plenitude of underived power, and that He is the Author of such works as to altogether transcend finite ability, and such as can belong to none but God Himself. However mysterious and inexplicable to human reason the existence of a distinction of persons in the essence of the Godhead may be, yet if we submissively bow to the plain teachings of the Divine Oracles, then the conclusion that there subsists three Divine Persons who are co-essential, co-eternal, and co-equal is unavoidable. He of whom such works as the creation of the universe, the inspiration of the Scriptures, the formation of the humanity of Christ, the regeneration and sanctification of the elect, is, and must be, GOD; or, to use the language of II Corinthians 3:17 "Now *the Lord is that Spirit.*"

1. The Holy Spirit is expressly called God. To Ananias Peter said, "Why hath Satan filled thine heart to lie to the Holy Spirit?" and then in the very next verse, he affirms "thou hast not lied unto men, but *unto God*" (Acts 5:3, 4): if, then, lying to the Holy Spirit be lying to God, it necessarily follows that the Spirit must be God. Again, the saints are called "the temple *of God,*" and the reason proving this is, that "the Spirit of God dwelleth in you" (I Cor. 3:16). In like manner, the body of the individual saint is designated "the *temple* of the Holy Spirit," and then the exhortation is made "therefore *glorify God* in your body" (I Cor. 6:19, 20). In I Corinthians 12, where the diversity of His gifts, administrations, and operations are mentioned, He is spoken of severally as "the same Spirit" (v. 4), "the same Lord" (v. 5), "the same God" (v. 6). In II Corinthians 6:16 the Holy Spirit is called "the living God."

2. The Holy Spirit is expressly called *Jehovah,* a name that is utterly incommunicable to all creatures, and which can be applied to none except the Great Supreme. It was Jehovah who spake by the mouth of all the holy prophets from the beginning of the world (Luke 1:68, 70), yet in II Peter 1:20 it is implicitly declared that those prophets all spake by "the Holy Spirit" (see also II Sam. 23:2, 3, and compare Acts 1:16)! It was Jehovah whom Israel tempted in the wilderness, "sinning against God and provoking the Most High" (Ps. 78:17, 18), yet in Isaiah 63:10 this is specifically termed "rebelling against and vexing the Holy Spirit"! In Deuteronomy 32:12 we read, "The Lord alone did lead them," yet speaking of the same people, at the same time, Isaiah 63:14 declares "the Spirit of the Lord did lead them." It was Jehovah who bade Isaiah "Go and tell this people, hear ye indeed" (6:8, 9), while the apostle declared, "well spake the Holy Spirit by Isaiah the prophet, saying, Go unto the people and say, Hear ye indeed . . ." (Acts 28:25, 26)! What could more plainly establish the identity of Jehovah and the Holy Spirit? Note that the Holy Spirit is called "the Lord" in II Thessalonians 3:5.

3. The *perfections of God* are all found in the Spirit. By what is the nature of any being determined, but by its properties? He who possesses the properties peculiar to an angel or man, is rightly esteemed one. So He who possesses the attributes or properties which belong alone to God, must be considered and worshipped as God. The Scriptures very clearly and abundantly affirm that the Holy Spirit is possessed of the attributes peculiar to God. They ascribe to Him absolute *holiness.* As God is called "Holy," "the Holy One" being therein described by that superlatively excellent property of His nature wherein He is "glorious in holiness" (Exod. 15:11); so is the third Person of the Trinity designated "the Spirit of Holiness" (Rom. 1:4) to denote the holiness of His nature and the Deity of His person. The Spirit is *eternal* (Heb.

9:14). He is *omnipresent*: "Whither shall I flee from thy Spirit?" (Ps. 139:7). He is *omniscient* (see I Cor. 2:10, 11). He is *omnipotent*: being termed "the Power of the Highest" (Luke 1:35; see also Micah 2:8, and compare Isa. 40:28).

4. The *absolute sovereignty and supremacy* of the Spirit manifest His Godhead. In Matthew 4:1 we are told, "Then was Jesus led up of the Spirit into the wilderness": who but a Divine person had the right to direct the Mediator? and to whom but God would the Redeemer have submitted! In John 3:8 the Lord Jesus drew an analogy between the wind which "bloweth where it listeth" (not being at the disposal or direction of any creature), and the imperial operations of the Spirit. In I Corinthians 12:11 it is expressly affirmed that the Holy Spirit has the distribution of all spiritual gifts, having nothing but His own pleasure for His rule. He *must*, then, be "God over all, blessed forever." In Acts 13:2-4 we find the Holy Spirit calling men unto the work of the ministry, which is solely a Divine prerogative, though wicked men have abrogated it unto themselves. In these verses it will be found that the Spirit appointed their work, commanded them to be set apart by the church, and sent them forth. In Acts 20:28 it is plainly declared that the Holy Spirit set officers over the church.

5. The *works ascribed to the Spirit* clearly demonstrate His Godhead. Creation itself is attributed to Him, no less than to the Father and the Son: "By the Spirit He hath garnished the heavens" (Job 26: 13): "the Spirit of God hath made me" (Job 33:4). He is concerned in the work of providence (Isa. 40:13-15; Acts 16:6, 7). All Scripture is given by inspiration of God (II Tim. 3:16), the source of which is the Spirit Himself (II Peter 1:21). The humanity of Christ was miraculously formed by the Spirit (Matt. 1:20). Christ was anointed for His work by the Spirit (Isa. 61:1; John 3:34). His miracles were performed by the Spirit's power (Matt. 12:38). He was raised from the dead by the Spirit (Rom. 8:11). Who but a Divine person could have wrought such works as these!

Reader, do you have a personal and inward proof that the Holy Spirit is none other than God? Has He wrought in you that which no finite power could? Has He brought you from death unto life, made you a new creature in Christ, imparted to you a living faith, filled you with holy longings after God? Does He breathe into you the spirit of prayer, take of the things of Christ and show them unto you, apply to your heart both the precepts and promises of God? If so, then, these are so many witnesses in your own bosom of the deity of the Blessed Spirit.

4

The Titles of the Holy Spirit

RIGHT views of the Divine character lie at the foundation of all genuine and vital godliness. It should, then, be one of our chief quests to seek after the knowledge of God. Without the true knowledge of God, in His nature and attributes, we can neither worship Him acceptably nor serve Him aright. Now the three Persons in the Godhead have graciously revealed Themselves through a variety of names and titles. The Nature of God we are utterly incapable of comprehending, but His person and character may be known. Each name or title that God has appropriated unto Himself is that whereby He reveals Himself unto us, and whereby He would have us know and own Him. Therefore whatever any name of God expresses Him to be, *that* He *is,* for He will not deceive us by giving Himself a wrong or false name. On this account He requires us to trust in His Name, because He will assuredly be found unto us all that His Name imports.

The names of God, then, are for the purpose of expressing Him unto us; they set forth His perfections and make known the different relations which He sustains unto the children of men and unto His own favored people. Names are given for this intent, that they might declare what the thing is, to which the name belongs. Thus, when God created Adam and gave him dominion over this visible world, He caused the beasts of the field and the fowls of the air to pass before him, that they might receive names from him (Gen. 2:19). In like manner, we may learn of what God is through the names and titles He has taken. By means of them, God spells out Himself to us, sometimes by one of His perfections, sometimes by another. A very wide field of study is here introduced to us, yet we can now say no more than that the prayerful and diligent searcher will find it a highly profitable one to investigate.

What has been said above serves to indicate the importance of the present aspect of our subject. What the Holy Spirit is in His Divine person and ineffable character is made known unto us by means of the many names and varied titles which are accorded to Him in Holy Writ. A whole volume, rather than a brief article, might well be devoted to their contemplation. May we be Divinely guided in using the limited space which is now at our disposal in writing that which will both magnify the Third Person in the blessed Trinity, and serve as a stimulus unto our readers to give more careful study and holy meditation to those titles of His which we cannot here consider. Possibly, we can help our friends most by devoting our attention to those which are more difficult to apprehend.

16

The Holy Spirit is designated by a great many names and titles in Scripture which clearly evince both His personality and Deity. Some of these are peculiar to Himself, others He has in common with the Father and the Son, in the undivided essence of the Divine nature. While in the wondrous scheme of redemption the Father, the Son, and the Holy Spirit, are revealed unto us under *distinct* characters, by which we are taught to ascribe certain operations to one more immediately than to another, yet the agency of each is not to be considered as so detached but that They *co-operate and concur*. For this reason the Third Person of the Trinity is called the Spirit of the Father (John 14:26) and the Spirit of the Son (Gal. 4:6), because, acting in conjunction with the Father and the Son, the operations of the one are in effect the operations of the others, and altogether result from the indivisible essence of the Godhead.

First, He is designated "The Spirit," which expresses two things. First, His Divine nature, for "God is Spirit" (John 4:24); as the Thirty-Nine Articles of the Episcopal Church well express it, "without body, parts, or passions." He is essentially pure, incorporeal Spirit, as distinct from any material or visible substance. Second, it expresses His mode of operation on the hearts of the people of God, which is compared in Scripture to a "breath," or the movement of the "wind" — both of which adumbrate Him in this lower world; suitably so, inasmuch as they are invisible, and yet vitalizing elements. "Come from the four winds, O Breath, and breathe upon these slain, that they may live" (Ezek. 37:9). Therefore was it that in His public descent on the day of Pentecost "suddenly there came a sound from heaven of a rushing, mighty wind, and it filled all the house where they were sitting" (Acts 2:2).

Second, He is called by way of eminency "The Holy Spirit" which is His most usual appelation in the New Testament. Two things are included. First, respect is had unto His nature. As Jehovah is distinguished from all false gods thus, "Who is like unto thee, O Lord, among the gods; who is like thee, glorious in holiness" (Exod. 15:11); so is the Spirit called Holy to denote the holiness of His nature. This appears plainly in Mark 3:29, 30, "He that shall blaspheme against the Holy Spirit hath never forgiveness; because they said, he hath an unclean spirit" — thus opposition is made between His immaculate nature and that of the unclean or unholy spirit. Observe too, how this verse also furnishes clear proof of His personality, for the "unclean spirit" is a person, and if the Spirit were not a person, no comparative opposition could be made between them. So also we see here His absolute Deity, for only *God* could be "blasphemed"! Second, this title views His *operations* and that in respect of *all* His works, for every work of God is holy — in hardening and blinding, equally as in regenerating and sanctifying.

Third, He is called God's "good Spirit" (Neh. 9:20); "Thy Spirit is good" (Ps. 143:10). He is so designated principally from His nature, which is essentially good for "there is none good but one, that is God" (Matt. 19:17); so also from His operations, for "the fruit of the Spirit is in all goodness, and righteousness, and truth" (Eph. 5:9). Fourth,

He is called the "free Spirit" (Ps. 51:12), so designated because He is a most munificent Giver, bestowing His favors severally as He pleases, literally, and upbraiding not; also because it is His special work to deliver God's elect from the bondage of sin and Satan, and bring them into the glorious liberty of God's children. Fifth, He is called "the Spirit of Christ" (Rom. 8:9) because sent by Him (Acts 2:33), and as furthering His cause on earth (John 16:14). Sixth, He is called "the Spirit of the Lord" (Acts 8:29) because He possesses Divine authority and requires unhesitating submission from us.

Seventh, He is called, "the *Eternal* Spirit" (Heb. 9:14). "Among the names and titles by which the Holy Spirit is known in Scripture, that of 'the eternal Spirit' is His *peculiar* appellation — a name, which in the very first face of things, accurately defines His nature, and carries with it the most convincing proof of Godhead. None but 'the High and Holy One, inhabiteth eternity,' can be called *eternal*. Of other beings, who possess a derivative immortality, it may be said that as they are created for eternity, they may enjoy, through the benignity of their Creator, a future eternal duration. But this differs as widely as the east is from the west, when applied to Him of whom we are speaking: He alone, who possesses an underived, independent, and necessary self-existence, 'who was, and is, and is to come,' can be said, in exclusion of all other beings, to be eternal" (Robert Hawker).

Eighth, He is called "the Paraclete" or "the Comforter" (John 14:16) than which no better translation can be given, providing the English meaning of the word be kept in mind. Comforter means more than Consoler. It is derived from two Latin words, *com* "along side of" and *fortis* "strength." Thus a "comforter" is one who stands alongside of one in need, to strengthen. When Christ said He would ask the Father to give His people "another Comforter," He signified that the Spirit would fill His own place, doing for the disciples, what He had done for them while He was with them on earth. The Spirit strengthens in a variety of ways; consoling when cast down, giving grace when weak or timid, guiding when perplexed.

We close this article with a few words from the pen of the late J. C. Philpot (1863), "Nor let anyone think that this doctrine of the distinct Personality of the Holy Spirit is a mere strife of words, or unimportant matter, or an unprofitable discussion, which we may take or leave, believe or deny, without any injury to our faith or hope. On the contrary, let this be firmly impressed on your mind, that if you deny or disbelieve the Personality of the blessed Spirit, you deny and disbelieve with it the grand foundation truth of the Trinity. If your doctrine be unsound, your experience must be a delusion, and your practice an imposition.

5

The Covenant-Offices of the Holy Spirit

THE ground which we are now to tread, will, we fear, be new and
strange to most of our readers. In the January and February 1930
issues of *Studies in the Scriptures,* we wrote two rather lengthy articles
upon "The Everlasting Covenant." There we dwelt principally upon it
in connection with the Father and the Son; here we shall contemplate
the relation of the Holy Spirit unto the same. His covenant-offices are
intimately connected with and indeed flow from His Deity and Personality for if He had not been a Divine Person in the Godhead, He would
not and could not have taken a part in the Covenant of Grace. Before
proceeding further, let us define our terms:

By the "Covenant of Grace," we refer to that holy and solemn compact entered into between the august Persons of the Trinity on behalf
of the elect, before the foundation of the world. By the word "offices"
we understand the whole of that part of this sacred compact which
the Holy Spirit undertook to perform. Lest some should suppose that the
application of such a term to the third Person of the Godhead be
derogatory to His ineffable majesty, let us point out that it by no
means implies subordination or inferiority. It signifies literally a particular charge, trust, duty, or employment, conferred for some public or
beneficial end. Hence we read of "the priest's office" (Exod. 28:1; Luke
1:8), the apostolic "office" (Rom. 11:13), etc.

There is then no impropriety in using the word "office" to express
the several parts which the Son and the blessed Spirit undertook in the
Covenant of Grace. As Persons in the Trinity they were equal; as
covenanting Parties they were equal; and as They in infinite condescension, undertook to communicate to the church unutterable favors and
blessings, Their kind offices, so graciously and voluntarily entered into,
neither destroy nor diminish that original equality in which They from
all eternity subsisted in the perfection and glory of the Divine Essence.
As Christ's susception of the "office" of "Servant" in nowise tarnished or
cancelled His equality as the Son, so the Spirit's free undertaking the
office of *applying* the benefits of the Everlasting Covenant to its bene-
ficiaries in nowise detracts from His essential and personal honor and
glory.

The word "office," then, as applied to the covenant-work of the Holy
Spirit, denotes that which He graciously undertook to perform by way
of stipulated engagement and sets forth, under one comprehensive term,
the whole of His blessed pledgings and performances on behalf of the

election of grace. To an enlightened understanding and a believing heart, there is in the Covenant itself — in the fact of it, and the provisions of it — something singularly marvellous and precious. That there should have been a Covenant at all; that the three Persons in the Godhead should have deigned to enter into a solemn compact on behalf of a section of the fallen, ruined, and guilty race of mankind, should fill our minds with holy wonderment and adoration. But how firm a foundation was thus laid for the salvation of the church. No room was allowed for contingencies, no place left for uncertainties; her being and well-being was forever secured by unalterable compact and eternal decree.

Now the "office-work" of the Holy Spirit in connection with this "everlasting Covenant, ordered in all things and sure" (II Sam. 23:5), may be summed up in a single word, *sanctification*. The third Person of the Holy Trinity agreed to sanctify the objects of the Father's eternal choice, and of the Son's redemptive satisfaction. The Spirit's work of sanctification was just as needful, yea, as indispensable for the church's salvation, as was the obedience and blood-shedding of Christ. Adam's fall plunged the church into immeasurable depths of woe and wretchedness. The image of God in which her members had been created, was defaced. Sin, like a loathsome leprosy, infected them to the very heart's core. Satan tyrannizing over her, dragging her without help or hope towards the brink of the bottomless pit. Spiritual death spreading itself with fatal effect over her every faculty. But the gracious Holy Spirit pledged Himself to sanctify such wretches, and frame and fit them to be partakers of holiness, and live forever in God's spotless presence.

Without the Spirit's sanctification the redemption of Christ would avail no man. True, a perfect atonement was made by Him and a perfect righteousness brought in, and so the persons of the elect are legally reconciled to God. But Jehovah is holy as well as just, and the employments and enjoyment of His dwellingplace are holy too. Holy angels there minister, whose unceasing cry is "Holy, holy, holy is the Lord of hosts" (Isa. 6:3). How then could unholy, unregenerated, unsanctified sinners dwell in that ineffable place into which "there shall in nowise enter anything that defileth, neither whatsoever worketh abomination, or maketh a lie" (Rev. 21:27)? But O the wonder of covenant grace and covenant love! The vilest of sinners, the worst of wretches, the basest of mortals, can and will enter through the gates into the Holy City: "And such *were* some of you, but ye are washed, but ye are sanctified, but ye are justified in the name of the Lord Jesus and *by the Spirit of our God*" (I Cor. 6:11).

From what has been said in the last paragraph it should be clear that sanctification is as indispensable as justification. Now there are many phases presented in Scripture of this important truth of Sanctification, into which we cannot here enter. Suffice it to say that aspect of it which is now before us is the blessed work of the Spirit upon the soul, whereby He internally makes the saints meet for their inheritance in the light (Col. 1:12): without this miracle of grace none can enter

Heaven. "That which is born of the flesh is flesh" (I John 3:6): no matter how it be educated and refined, no matter how disguised by religious ornamentation, it remains still flesh. It is like everything else which earth produces: no manipulation of art can change the original nature of the raw material.

No process of manufacture can transmute cotton into wool, or flax into silk: draw, twist, spin or weave, bleach and surface all we may, its nature remains the same. So men-made preachers and the whole corps of creature religionists may toil night and day, to change flesh into spirit, they may work from the cradle to the grave to fit people for Heaven, but after all their labors to wash the Ethiopian white and to rub the spots out of the leopard, flesh is flesh still and cannot by any possibility enter the kingdom of God. Nothing but the supernatural operations of the Holy Spirit will avail. Not only is man polluted to the very core by sin original and actual, but there is in him an absolute incapability to understand, embrace or enjoy spiritual things (I Cor. 2:14).

The imperative necessity, then, of the Spirit's work of sanctification lies not only in the sinfulness of man, but in the state of spiritual death whereby he is as unable to live, breathe, and act Godward as the corpse in the graveyard is unable to leave the silent tomb and move among the busy haunts of men. We indeed know little of the Word of God and little of our own hearts if we need proof of a fact which meets us at every turn; the vileness of our nature, the thorough deathliness of our carnal heart are so daily and hourly forced upon us that they are as much a matter of painful consciousness to the Christian, as if we should see the sickening sight of a slaughter-house, or smell the death taint of a corpse.

Suppose a man is born blind: he has a natural incapacity of sight. No arguments, biddings, threatenings, or promises can make him see. But let the miracle be wrought: let the Lord touch the eyes with His Divine hand; he sees at once. Though he cannot explain how or why, he can say to all objectors "One thing I know, that whereas I was blind, now I see" (John 9:25). And thus it is in the Spirit's work of sanctification, begun at regeneration, when a new life is given, a new capacity imparted, a new desire awakened. It is carried forward in his daily renewing (II Cor. 4:16); and is completed at glorification. What we would specially emphasize is that whether the Spirit be convicting us, working repentance in us, breathing upon us the spirit of prayer, or taking of the things of Christ and showing them unto our joyful hearts, He is discharging His covenant-offices. May we render unto Him the praise and worship which is His due.

For most of the above we are indebted to some articles by the late J. C. Philpot.

6

The Holy Spirit During the Old Testament Ages

Much ignorance prevails today concerning this aspect of our subject. The crudest ideas are now entertained as to the relation between the Third Person of the Godhead and the Old Testament saints. Yet this is scarcely to be wondered at in view of the fearful confusion which obtains respecting their salvation, many supposing that they were saved in an entirely different way from what we are now. Nor need we be surprised at that, for this, in turn, is only another of the evil effects produced by the misguided efforts of those who have been so eager to draw as many contrasts as possible between the present dispensation and those which preceded it, to the disparaging of the earlier members of God's family. The Old Testament saints had far more in common with the New Testament saints than is generally supposed.

A verse which has been grossly perverted by many of our moderns is John 7:39, "The Holy Spirit was not yet given, because that Jesus was not yet glorified." It seems passing strange that with the Old Testament in their hands, some men should place the construction which they do upon those words. The words "was not yet given" can no more be understood absolutely than "Enoch was not" (Gen. 5:24); they simply mean that the Spirit had not yet been given in His full administrative authority. He was not yet publicly manifested here on earth. All believers, in every age, had been sanctified and comforted by Him, but the "ministration of the Spirit" (II Cor. 3:8) was not at that time fully introduced; the outpouring of the Spirit, in the plentitude of His miraculous gifts, had not then taken place.

Let us first consider, though very briefly, the work of the Spirit in connection with the old or material creation. Before the worlds were framed by the Word of God, and things which are seen were made out of things which do not appear (Heb. 11:3), when the whole mass of inanimate matter lay in one undistinguished chaos, "without form and void," we are told that, "the Spirit of God moved upon the face of the waters" (Gen. 1:2). There are other passages which ascribe the work of creation (in common with the Father and the Son) to His immediate agency. For example, we are told, "by his Spirit he hath garnished the heavens" (Job 26:13). Job was moved to confess, "The Spirit of God hath made me, and the breath of the Almighty hath given me life" (33:4). "Thou sendest forth Thy Spirit, they are created: and Thou renewest the face of the earth" (Ps. 104:30).

Let us next contemplate the Holy Spirit in relation to Adam. As so much darkness now surrounds this particular, we must enter into it more largely. "Three things were required to render man fit unto that life to God for which he was made. First, an ability to discern the mind and will of God, with respect unto all the duty and obedience that God requires of him; as also for to know the nature and properties of God, as to believe Him the only proper object of all acts and duties of religious obedience, and an all-sufficient satisfaction and reward in this world, and to eternity. Secondly, a free, uncontrolled, unentangled, disposition to every duty of the law of his creation, for living unto God. Thirdly, an ability of mind and will, with a readiness of compliance in his affections, for a regular performance of all duties and abstinence from all sin. These things belonged unto the integrity of his nature, with the uprightness of the state and condition wherein he was made. And all these things were the peculiar effects of the immediate operation of the Holy Spirit.

"Thus Adam may be said to have had the Spirit of God in his innocency. He had Him in these peculiar effects of His power and goodness, and he had Him according to the tenor of that covenant, whereby it was possible that he should utterly lose Him, as accordingly it came to pass. He had Him not by especial inhabitation, for the whole world was then the temple of God. In the covenant of grace, founded in the person and on the mediation of Christ, it is otherwise. On whomsoever the Spirit of God is bestowed for the renovation of the image of God in him, He abides with him forever" (J. Owen, 1680).

The three things mentioned above by that eminent Puritan constituted the principal part of that "image of God" wherein man was created by the Spirit. Proof of this is seen in the fact that at regeneration the Holy Spirit restores those abilities in the souls of God's elect: "And hath put on the new man, which is *renewed* in knowledge, after the image of him that created him" (Col. 3:10): that is, the spiritual knowledge which man lost at the Fall is, potentially, restored at the new birth; but it could not be restored or "renewed" if man had never possessed it!

The "knowledge" with which the Holy Spirit endowed Adam was great indeed. Clear exemplification of this is seen in Genesis 2:19. Still, more conclusive evidence is found in Genesis 2:21-23: God put Adam into a deep sleep, took a rib out of his side, formed it into a woman, and then set her before him. On sight of her Adam said, "This is now bone of my bones, and flesh of my flesh." He knew *who* she was and her *origin*, and forthwith gave her a suitable name; and he could only have known all this by the Spirit of revelation and understanding.

That Adam was, originally, made a partaker of the Holy Spirit is quite evident to the writer from Genesis 2:7, "The Lord God formed man of the dust of the ground, and *breathed* into his nostrils the breath of *life*. If those words were interpreted in the light of the Analogy of Faith, they can mean nothing less than that the Triune God imparted the Holy Spirit unto the first man. In Ezekiel 37 we have a vivid parabolic picture of the regenerating of spiritual Israel.

There we are told "Prophesy unto the Wind, prophesy, son of man, and say to the Wind, Thus saith the Lord God, Come from the four winds, O Breath, and *breathe* upon these slain, that they may *live*. So I prophesied as He commanded me, and the Breath came unto them, and they lived" (vv. 9, 10). Again, we find the Saviour, after His resurrection, "Breathed on them [the apostles], and saith unto them, Receive ye the Holy Spirit" (John 20:22): that was the counterpart of Genesis 2:7: the one the original gift, the other the restoration of what was lost.

Rightly has it been said that "The doctrine that man was originally, though mutably, replenished with the Spirit, may be termed the deep fundamental thought of the Scripture doctrine of man. If the first and second Adam are so related that the first man was the analogue or figure of the second, as all admit on the authority of Scripture (Rom. 5:12-14), it is clear that, unless the first man possessed the Spirit, the last man, the Healer or Restorer of the forfeited inheritance, would not have been the medium of giving the Spirit, who was withdrawn on account of sin, and who could be restored only on account of the everlasting righteousness which Christ (Rom. 8:10) brought in" (G. Smeaton, 1880).

Let us next observe the relation of the Holy Spirit unto the nation of Israel. A very striking and comprehensive statement was made by Nehemiah, when he reviewed the Lord's dealings with His people of old: "Thou gavest also Thy good Spirit to instruct them" (Neh. 8:20). He was, until quenched, upon the members of the Sanhedrin (Num. 11: 16, 17). He came upon the judges (Judg. 3:10; 6:34; 11:29; 15:14), upon the kings (I Sam. 11:6; 16:13), and the prophets. But note it is a great mistake to say, as many have done, that the Holy Spirit was never in any believer before Pentecost: Numbers 27:18, Nehemiah 9: 30, I Peter 1:11 clearly prove otherwise. But alas, Israel "rebelled and vexed his Holy Spirit" (Isa. 63:10), as Stephen declared, "Ye do always resist the Holy Spirit: as your fathers did, so do ye" (Acts 7:51).

That the Holy Spirit indwelt saints under the Legal economy is clear from many considerations: how otherwise could they have been regenerated, had faith, been enabled to perform works acceptable to God? The Spirit prompted true prayer, inspired spiritual worship, produced His fruit in the lives of believers then (see Zech. 4:6) as much as He does now. We have "the *same* Spirit of faith" (II Cor. 4:13) as they had. All the spiritual good which has ever been wrought in and through men must be ascribed unto the Holy Spirit. The Spirit was given to the Old Testament saints *prospectively*, as pardon of sin was given — in view of the satisfaction which Christ was to render unto God."

7

The Holy Spirit and Christ

WE are afraid that our treatment of the particular aspect of this man-sided theme which is now before us, is rather too abstruse for some of our readers to follow, yet we trust they will kindly bear with us as we endeavor to write for those who are anxious for help on the deeper things of God. As stated before, we are seeking to minister unto widely different classes, unto those with differing capacities, and therefore we wish to provide a varied spiritual menu. He who is hungry will not leave the table in disgust because one dish thereon appeals not to him. We ask their forebearance while we seek to give something like completeness to our exposition of the subject as a whole.

"As the humanity of Christ was assumed into the hypostatic union, we may fitly say, on the one hand, that *the Person of Christ* was anointed, so far as *the call to office* was concerned; while we bear in mind, on the other hand, that it is *the humanity* that is anointed in as far as we contemplate the actual supplies of God's gifts and graces, aids and endowments, necessary to the execution of His office. But that we may not be engulfed in one-sidedness, it must be also added that the Holy Spirit, according to the order of the Trinity, interposes His power only to execute the will of the Son . . . as to the unction of the Lord Jesus by the Spirit, it was different according to the *three grades* successively imparted. The first grade was at the incarnation; the second coincided with His baptism, the third and highest grade was at the ascension, when He sat down on His mediatorial throne, and received from the Father the gift of the Spirit to bestow upon His Church in abundant measure" (G. Smeaton).

We have already contemplated the *first* anointing of the Lord Jesus when, in His mother's womb, His humanity was endowed with all spiritual graces, and when through childhood and up to the age of thirty He was illuminated, guided, and preserved by the immediate operations of the third person in the Godhead. We come now to briefly consider His *second* anointing, when He was formally consecrated unto His public mission and Divinely endowed for His official work. This took place at the River Jordan, when He was baptized by His forerunner. Then it was, while emerging from the waters, that the heavens were opened, the Holy Spirit descended upon Him in the form of a dove, and the voice of the Father was heard testifying unto His infinite pleasure in His incarnate Son (Matt. 3:16, 17). All the references to that unique transaction call for close examination and prayerful study.

The first thing that is recorded after this is, "And Jesus being full of

25

the Holy Spirit, returned from Jordan, and was led by the Spirit into the wilderness" (Luke 4:14). The reason why we are told this seems to be for the purpose of showing us that Christ's humanity was confirmed by the Spirit and made victorious over the devil by His power; hence it is we read that, right after the temptation, "And Jesus returned in the power of the Spirit into Galilee" (Luke 4:14). Next we are told that He entered the synagogue at Nazareth and read from Isaiah 61, "The Spirit of the Lord is upon me, because he hath anointed me to preach the gospel to the poor; he hath sent me to heal the brokenhearted, to preach deliverance to the captives, and recovering of sight to the blind, to set at liberty them that are bruised; to preach the acceptable year of the Lord," and declared, "This day is this scripture fulfilled in your ears" (Luke 4:18, 19, 21).

Here, then, is to be seen the leading distinction between the first and second "grades" of Christ's "unction" from the Spirit. The first was for the forming of His human nature and the enduing it with perfect wisdom and faultless holiness. The second was to endow Him with supernatural powers for His great work. Thus the former was personal and private, the latter official and public; the one was bestowing upon Him of spiritual graces, the other imparting to Him ministerial gifts. His *need* for this double "anointing" lay in the creature nature He had assumed and the servant-place which He had taken; and also as a public attestation from the Father of His acceptance of Christ's person and His induction into His mediatorial office. Thus was fulfilled that ancient oracle, "The Spirit of the Lord shall rest upon him, the Spirit of wisdom and understanding, the Spirit of counsel and might, the Spirit of knowledge and of the fear of the Lord; and shall make him of quick understanding" (Isa. 11:2, 3).

"For he whom God hath sent speaketh the words of God; for God giveth not the Spirit by measure unto him" (John 3:34). This at once brings out the pre-eminence of Christ, for *He* receiveth the Spirit as no mere man could. Observe the contrast pointed out by Ephesians 4:7, "But unto every one of us is given grace *according to the measure* of the gift of Christ." In none but the Mediator did "all the fulness of the Godhead" dwell "bodily" (Col. 2:9). The uniqueness of the Spirit's relation to our Lord comes out again in Romans 8:2, "For the law of the Spirit of life *in Christ Jesus* hath made me free from the law of sin and death." Note carefully the words we have italicised: not only does this statement reveal to us the source of all Christ's actions, but it intimates that more habitual grace dwell in Him than in all created beings.

The third degree of Christ's unction was reserved for His exaltation, and is thus described, "Therefore being by the right hand of God exalted, and having received of the Father the promise of the Holy Spirit, he hath shed forth this, which ye now see and hear" (Acts 2:33). This highest grade of unction, when Christ was anointed with the oil of gladness *above* his fellows" (Ps. 45:7) and which became apparent at Pentecost, was an ascension-gift. The declaration which

Peter gave of it was but a paraphrase of Psalm 68:18, "Thou hast ascended on high, thou hast led captivity captive: thou hast received gifts for men; yea, for the rebellious also, that the Lord might dwell among them." That bountiful supply of the Spirit was designed for the erecting and equipping of the New Testament church, and it was fitly bestowed after the ascension upon those for whom the Spirit was purchased.

As Mediator the Lord Jesus was anointed with the Holy Spirit for the execution of all His offices, and for the performance of all His mediatorial work. His right to send the Spirit into the hearts of fallen men was acquired by His atonement. It was the well-earned *reward* of all His toil and sufferings. One of the chief results of the perfect satisfaction which Christ offered to God on behalf of His people, was His right now to bestow the Spirit upon them. Of old it was promised Him, "By his knowledge shall my righteous Servant justify many, for he shall bear their iniquities: therefore will I divide him a portion with the great, and he shall divide the spoil with the strong; because he hath poured out his soul unto death" (Isa. 53:11, 12). So too, His forerunner had announced, "He shall baptize you with the Holy Spirit and fire" (Matt. 3:11).

What has just been said above is further borne out by Galatians 3:13, 14. "Christ hath redeemed us from the curse of the law, being made a curse for us . . . that the blessing of Abraham might come on the Gentiles through Jesus Christ, that we might receive the promise of the Spirit through faith." The promised Spirit followed the great work of cancelling the curse as the effect follows the cause. To give the *Holy* Spirit to men, clearly implied that their sins had been put away; see Leviticus 14:14, 17 for the type of this — the "oil" (emblem of the Spirit) placed *upon* the "blood"! Not only does Christ's right to bestow the Holy Spirit upon His redeemed intimate the cancellation of their sins, but it also clearly argues His *Divine* dignity, for no mere *Servant*, however exalted his station, could act thus or confer such a Gift!

From the varied quotations which have been made from Scripture in reference to Christ's unction for all His offices, it sometimes appears as if He were in the subordinate position of needing direction, aid, and miraculous power for the purposes of His mission (Isa. 11:1-3; 61:1, 2, e.g.); at other times He is said to *have* the Spirit (Rev. 3:1), to *give* the Spirit (Acts 2:33), to *send* the Spirit (John 15:26) as if the Spirit's operations were subordinated to the Son. But all difficulty is removed when we perceive, from the whole tenor of Scripture, that there was a *conjoined* mission in which the Son and the Spirit act together for the salvation of God's elect. The Son effected redemption; the Spirit reveals and applies it to all for whom it was purchased.

In writing on the Holy Spirit and Christ, it is to be understood that we are not now contemplating our Lord as the second person of the Trinity, but rather as the God-man *Mediator,* and the Holy Spirit not in His Godhead abstractedly considered, but in His *official* discharge of the work assigned Him in the everlasting covenant. This is undoubtedly the most difficult aspect of our subject, yet it is very important that we should prayerfully strive after clear scriptural views thereof. To apprehend aright, even according to our present limited capacity, the relation between the Holy Spirit and the Redeemer, throws much light on some difficult problems, supplies the key to a number of perplexing passages in Holy Writ, and better enables us to understand the work of the Spirit in the saint. May we be mercifully preserved from all error as we endeavor to give our best attention to the present theme, and be guided to write that which will glorify our Triune God and edify His dear people.

"Come ye near unto me, hear ye this; I have not spoken in secret from the beginning: from the time that it was, there am I: and now the Lord God and his Spirit hath sent me" (Isa. 48:16). This remarkable verse presents to us the Lord Jesus speaking of old by the spirit of prophecy. He declares that He had always addressed the Nation in the most open manner, from the time when He appeared unto Moses at the burning bush and called Himself, "I am that I am" (Exod. 3); and He was constantly present with Israel as their Lord and Deliverer. And now the Father and the Spirit had sent Him to effect the promised spiritual deliverance of His people; sent Him in the likeness of sin's flesh, to preach the gospel, fulfil the law, and make a perfect satisfaction unto Divine justice for His church. Here, then, is a glorious testimony unto a Trinity of Persons in the Godhead: the Son of God is sent in human nature and as Mediator; Jehovah the Father *and the Spirit* are the Senders, and so is a proof of Christ's mission, commission, and authority, who came not of Himself, but was sent of God (John 8:42).

"The Lord hath created a new thing in the earth: A woman shall compass a man" (Jer. 31:22). Here we have one of the prophetic announcements of the wonder of the Divine incarnation, the eternal Word becoming flesh, a human body and soul being prepared for Him by the miraculous intervention of the Holy Spirit. Here the prophet intimates that the creating power of God was to be put forth under which a woman was to compass a Man. The virgin Mary, under the overshadowing power of the Highest (Luke 1:35) was to conceive and bring forth a Child, without the help or cooperation of man. This transcendent wonder Isaiah calls a "sign" (7:14). Jeremiah "a new thing in the earth"; the New Testament record of which is, "When as his mother Mary was espoused to Joseph, before they came together, she was found with child of the Holy Spirit" (Matt. 1:18).

"And the Child grew, and waxed strong in spirit, filled with wisdom, and the grace of God was upon him. And Jesus increased in wisdom and stature, and in favor with God and man" (Luke 2:40, 52). Not only was the humanity of Christ supernaturally begotten by the Holy Spirit, but it was "anointed" by Him (cf. Lev. 2:1 for the type), endued with all spiritual graces. All the progress in the Holy Child's mental and spiritual development, all His advancement in knowledge and holiness must be ascribed unto the Spirit. "Progress," in the human nature which He deigned to assume, side by side with His own Divine perfection, is quite compatible, as Hebrews 2:14, 17 plainly intimate. As George Smeaton has so helpfully pointed out in his book, the Spirit's operations "formed the link between Christ's deity and humanity, perpetually imparting the full consciousness of His personality, and making Him inwardly aware of His Divine Sonship at all times."

Thus the Spirit, at the incarnation, became the great guiding principle of all Christ's earthly history, and that, according to the order of operation that ever belongs to the Holy Trinity: all proceeds *from* the Father, *through* the Son, and is *by* the Holy Spirit. It was the Spirit who formed Christ's human nature, and directed the whole tenor of His earthly life. Nothing was undertaken but by the Spirit's directing, nothing was spoken but by His guidance, nothing executed but by His power. Unless this be steadfastly maintained, we are in grave danger of confounding the two natures of Christ, absorbing the one in the other, instead of keeping them separate and distinct in our thoughts. Had His Diety been absorbed by His humanity, then grief, fear, and compassion had been impossible. The right use of the faculties of His soul owed their exercise to the Holy Spirit who fully controlled Him.

"From birth to baptism the Spirit directed His mental and moral development, and strengthened and kept Him through all the years of preparation and toil. He was in the Carpenter as truly as in the Messiah, and the work at the bench was as perfect as the sacrifice on the cross" (S. Chadwick). At first sight, such a statement may seem to derogate from the *personal* honor of the Lord Jesus, but if we perceive that, according to the *order* of the Trinity, the Spirit exercises His power only to execute the will of the Father and the Son, then the seeming difficulty disappears. So far is the interposition of the Spirit's operations from interfering with the glory of the Son, it rather reveals Him the more conspicuously: that in the work of redemption the activities of the Spirit are next in order to those of the Son. To this we may add another excerpt from G. Smeaton:

"The two natures of our Lord *actively concurred* in every mediatorial act. If He assumed human nature in the true and proper sense of the term into union with His Divine person, that position must be maintained. The Socinian objection that there could be no further need for the Spirit's agency, and, in fact, no room for it — if the Divine nature was *active* in the whole range of Christ's mediation — is meant to perplex the question, because these men deny the existence of any Divine nature in Christ's person. That style of reasoning is futile, for the question simply is, What do the Scriptures teach? Do they affirm that *Christ was anointed by the Spirit* (Acts 10:38)? that He was led out into the wilderness by the Spirit? that He returned in the power of the Spirit to begin His public ministry? that He performed His miracles by the Spirit? and that, previously to His ascension, He gave commandments by the Spirit to His disciples whom He had chosen (Acts 1:2)?

"No warrant exists for anything akin to the *Kenotic* or depotentiation theory, which denudes Him of the essential attributes of His Godhead, and puts His humanity on a mere level with that of other men. And as little warrant exists for denying the Spirit's work on Christ's humanity in every mediatorial act which He performed on earth or performs in Heaven. The unction of the Spirit must be traced in all His personal and official gifts. In Christ the Person and office coincide. In His Divine Person He was the substance of all the offices to which He was appointed, and these He was fitted by the Spirit to discharge. The offices would be nothing apart from Himself, and could have neither coherence nor validity without the underlying Person."

If the above still appears to derogate from the glory of our Lord's Person, most probably the difficulty is created by the objector's failing to realize the *reality* of the Son's humanity. The mystery is indeed great, and our only safeguard is to adhere strictly unto the several statements of Scripture thereon. Three things are to be kept steadily in view. First, in *all* things (sin excepted) the eternal Word was "made like unto his brethren" (Heb. 2:17): all His human faculties developed normally as He passed through infancy, childhood and youth. Second, His Divine nature underwent no change or modification when He became incarnate, yet it was not merged into His humanity, but preserved its own distinctness. Third, He *was* "anointed with the Spirit" (Acts 10:38), nay, He was the absolute receiver of the Spirit, poured on Him in such a plentitude, that it was *not* by measure (John 3:34).

3

The Advent of the Spirit

It is highly important we should closely observe *how* that each of the Eternal Three has been at marked pains to provide for the honor of the other Divine Persons, and we must be as particular to give it to Them accordingly. How careful was the Father to duly guard the ineffable glory of the Darling of His bosom when He laid aside the visible insignia of His Deity and took upon Him the form of a servant: His voice was then heard more than once proclaiming, "This is my beloved Son." How constantly did the incarnate Son divert attention from Himself and direct it unto the One who had sent Him. In like manner, the Holy Spirit is not here to glorify Himself, but rather Him whose Vicar and Advocate He is (John 16:14). Blessed is it then to mark how jealous both the Father and the Son have been to safeguard the glory and provide for the honor of the Holy Spirit.

" 'If I go not away, the Comforter will not come' (John 16:7); He will not do these works while I am here, and I have committed all to Him. As My Father hath visibly 'committed all judgment unto the Son: that all men should honor the Son, even as they honor the Father' (John 5:22, 23), so I and my Father will send him having committed all these things to him, that all men might honor the Holy Spirit, even as they honor the Father and the Son. Thus wary and careful are every one of the Persons to provide for the honor of each other in our hearts" (T. Goodwin, 1670).

The public advent of the Spirit, for the purpose of ushering in and administering the new covenant, was second in importance only unto the incarnation of our Lord, which was in order to the winding up of the old economy and laying the foundations of the new. When God designed the salvation of His elect, He appointed two great means: the gift of His Son for them, and the gift of His Spirit to them; thereby each of the Persons in the Trinity being glorified. Hence, from the first entrance of sin, there were two great heads to the promises which God gave His people: the sending of His Son to obey and die, the sending of His Spirit to make effectual the fruits of the former. Each of these Divine gifts was bestowed in a manner suited both to the august Giver Himself and the eminent nature of the gifts. Many and marked are the parallels of correspondence between the advent of Christ and the advent of the Spirit.

1. God appointed that there should be a signal coming accorded unto the descent of Each from Heaven to earth for the performance of the work assigned Them. Just as the Son was present with the redeemed Is-

31

raelites long before His incarnation (Acts 7:37, 38; I Cor. 10:4), yet God decreed for Him a visible and more formal advent, which all of His people knew of; so though the Holy Spirit was given to work regeneration in men all through the Old Testament era (Neh. 9:20, etc.), and moved the prophets to deliver their messages (II Peter 1:21), nevertheless God ordained that He should have a coming in state, in a solemn manner, accompanied by visible tokens and glorious effects.

2. Both the advents of Christ and of the Spirit were the subjects of Old Testament prediction. During the past century much has been written upon the Messianic prophecies, but the promises which God gave concerning the coming of the Holy Spirit constitute a theme which is generally neglected. The following are among the principal pledges which God made that the Spirit should be given unto and poured out upon His saints: Psalm 68:18; Proverbs 1:23; Isaiah 32:15; Ezekiel 36:26, 39:29; Joel 2:28; Haggai 2:9: in them the descent of the Holy Spirit was as definitely announced as was the incarnation of the Saviour in Isaiah 7: 14. 3. Just as Christ had John the Baptist to announce His incarnation and to prepare His way, so the Holy Spirit had Christ Himself to foretell His coming, and to make ready the hearts of His own for His advent.

4. Just as it was not until "the fulness of time had come" that God sent forth His Son (Gal. 4:4), so it was not until "the day of Pentecost was fully come" that God sent forth His Spirit (Acts 2:1). 5. As the Son became incarnate in the holy land, Palestine, so the Spirit descended in Jerusalem. 6. Just as the coming of the Son of God into this world was auspiciously signalized by mighty wonders and signs, so the descent of God the Spirit was attended and attested by stirring displays of Divine power. The advent of Each was marked by supernatural phenomena: the angel choir (Luke 2:13) found its counterpart in the "sound from Heaven" (Acts 2:1), and the Shekinah "glory" (Luke 2:9) in the "tongues of fire" (Acts 2:3). 7. As an extraordinary star marked the "house" where the Christ-child was (Matt. 2:9), so a Divine shaking marked the "house" to which the Spirit had come (Acts 2:2).

8. In connection with the advent of Christ there was both a private and a public aspect to it: in like manner too was it in the giving of the Spirit. The birth of the Saviour was made known unto a few, but when He was to "be made manifest to Israel" (John 1:31), He was publicly identified, for at His baptism the heavens were opened, the Spirit descended upon Him in the form of a dove, and the voice of the Father audibly owned Him as His Son. Correspondingly, the Spirit was communicated to the apostles privately, when the risen Saviour "breathed on, and said unto them, Receive ye the Holy Spirit" (John 20:22); and later He came publicly on the day of Pentecost when all the great throng then in Jerusalem were made aware of His descent (Acts 2:32-36).

9. The advent of the Son was in order to His becoming incarnate, when the eternal Word was made flesh (John 1:14); so too the advent of the Spirit was in order to His becoming incarnate in Christ's redeemed: as the Saviour had declared to them, the Spirit of truth

THE ADVENT OF THE SPIRIT

"shall be *in* you" (John 14:17). This is a truly marvelous parallel. As the Son of God became man, dwelling in a *human* "temple" (John 2:19), so the third person of the Trinity took up His abode *in men*, to whom it is said, "Know ye not that ye are the temple of God, and that the Spirit of God dwelleth in you?" (I Cor. 3:16). As the Lord Jesus said to the Father, "A body hast thou prepared me" (Heb. 10:5), so the Spirit could say to Christ, "A body hast thou prepared me" (see Eph. 2:22).

10. When Christ was born into this world, we are told that Herod "was *troubled*" "and all Jerusalem with him" (Matt. 2:3); in like manner, when the Holy Spirit was given we read, "And there were dwelling at Jerusalem Jews, devout men out of every nation under heaven. Now when this was noised abroad, the multitude came together, and were *troubled* in mind" (Acts 2:5, 6). 11. It had been predicted that when Christ should appear He would be unrecognized and unappreciated (Isa. 53), and so it came to pass; in like manner, the Lord Jesus declared, "The Spirit of truth, whom the world cannot receive, because it seeth him not, neither knoweth him" (John 14:17). 12. As the Messianic claims of Christ were called into question, so the advent of the Spirit was at once challenged: "They were all amazed and *were in doubt*, saying one to another, What meaneth this?" (Acts 2:12). 13. The analogy is yet closer: as Christ was termed "a winebibber" (Matt. 11: 19), so of those filled with the Spirit it was said, "These men are full of new wine" (Acts 2:13)!

14. As the public advent of Christ was heralded by John the Baptist (John 1:29), so the meaning of the public descent of the Spirit was interpreted by Peter (Acts 2:15-36). 15. God appointed unto Christ the executing of a stupendous work, even that of purchasing the redemption of His people; even so to the Spirit has been assigned the momentous task of effectually applying to His elect the virtues and benefits of the atonement. 16. As in the discharge of His work the Son honored the Father (John 14:10), so in the fulfilment of His mission the Spirit glorifies the Son (John 16:13, 14). 17. As the Father paid holy deference unto the Son by bidding the disciples, "hear ye him" (Matt. 17:5), in like manner the Son shows respect for His Paraclete by saying, "He that hath an ear, let him hear *what the Spirit saith* unto the churches" (Rev. 2:7). 18. As Christ committed His saints into the safe-keeping of the Holy Spirit (John 16:7; 14:16), so the Spirit will yet deliver up those saints unto Christ, as the word "receive" in John 14:3 plainly implies. We trust that the reader will find the same spiritual delight in perusing this article as the writer had in preparing it.

At Pentecost the Holy Spirit came as He had never come before. Something then transpired which inaugurated a new era for the world, a new power for righteousness, a new basis for fellowship. On that day the fearing Peter was transformed into the intrepid evangelist. On that day the new wine of Christianity burst the old bottles of Judaism, and the Word went forth in a multiplicity of Gentile tongues. On that day more souls seem to have been truly regenerated, than during all the three and one half years of Christ's public ministry. What had happened? It is not enough to say that the Spirit of God was given, for He had been given long before, both to individuals and the nation of Israel (Neh. 9:20; Hag. 2:5); no, the pressing question is, *In what sense* was He then given? This leads us to carefully consider *the meaning of* the Spirit's advent.

1. *It was the fulfilment of the Divine promise.* First, of the Father Himself. During the Old Testament dispensation, He declared, again and again, that He would pour out the Spirit upon His people (see Prov. 1: 23; Isa. 32:15; Joel 2:28, etc.); and now these gracious declarations were accomplished. Second, of John the Baptist. When he was stirring the hearts of multitudes by his call to repentance and his demand of baptism, many thought he must be the long-expected Messiah, but he declared unto them, "I indeed baptize you with water, but one mightier than I cometh, the latchet of whose shoes I am not worthy to unloose: *he* shall baptize you *with the Holy Spirit and with fire*" (Luke 3:15, 16). Accordingly He did so on the day of Pentecost, as Acts 2:32, 33 plainly shows.

Third, of Christ. Seven times over the Lord Jesus avowed that He would give or send the Holy Spirit: Luke 24:49; John 7:37-39; 14:16-19; 14:26; 15:26; 16:7; Acts 1:5, 8. From these we may particularly notice, "When the Comforter is come, whom *I will send* unto you from the Father . . . he shall testify of me" (John 15:26): "It is expedient for you that I go away; for if I go not away, the Comforter will not come unto you; but if I depart, *I will send him* unto you" (John 16: 7). That which took place in John 20:22 and in Acts 2 was the fulfilment of those promises. In them we behold the faith of the Mediator: He had appropriated the promise which the Father had given Him, "Therefore being by the right hand of God exalted, and having received of the Father the promise of the Holy Spirit, *he* hath shed forth this, which ye now see and hear" (Acts 2:33) — it was by faith's anticipation the Lord Jesus spoke as He did in the above passage.

"The Holy Spirit was God's ascension gift to Christ, that He might be bestowed by Christ, as His ascension gift to the church. Hence Christ had said, 'Behold, I send the promise of my Father upon you.' This was the promised gift of the Father to the Son, and the Saviour's promised gift to His believing people. How easy now to reconcile the apparent contradiction of Christ's earlier and later words: 'I will pray the Father and *he shall give you* another Comforter'; and then, afterward, 'If I depart *I will send him* unto you.' The Spirit was the Father's answer to the prayer of the Son; and so the gift was transferred by Him to the mystical body of which He is the head" (A. T. Pierson in *The Acts of the Holy Spirit*).

2. *It was the fulfilment of an important Old Testament type.* It is this which explains to us why the Spirit was given on the day of "Pentecost," which was one of the principal religious feasts of Israel. Just as there was a profound significance to Christ's dying on Passover Day (giving us the antitype of Exod. 12), so there was in the coming of

the Spirit on the fiftieth after Christ's resurrection. The type is recorded in Leviticus 23, to which we can here make only the briefest allusion. In Leviticus 23:4 we read, "These are the feasts of the Lord." The first of them is the passover (v. 5) and the second "unleavened bread" (v. 6, etc.). The two together speaking of the sinless Christ offering Himself as a sacrifice for the sins of His people. The third is the "wave sheaf" (v. 10, etc.) which was the "firstfruits of the harvest (v. 10), presented to God "on the morrow after the (Jewish) Sabbath" (v. 11), a figure of Christ's resurrection (I Cor. 15:23).

The fourth is the feast of "weeks" (see Exod. 34:22; Deut. 16:10, 16) so-called because of the seven complete weeks of Leviticus 23:15; also known as "Pentecost" (which means "Fiftieth") because of the "fifty days" of Leviticus 23:16. It was then the balance of the harvest *began* to be gathered in. On that day Israel was required to present unto God "two wave loaves," which were also designated "the *first-fruits* unto the Lord" (Lev. 23:17). The antitype of which was the saving of the three thousand on the day of Pentecost: the "firstfruits" of Christ's atonement, compare James 1:18. The first loaf represented those redeemed from among the Jews, the second loaf *was anticipatory* and pointed to the gathering in of God's elect from among the Gentiles, begun in Acts 10.

3. *It was the beginning of a new dispensation.* This was plainly intimated in the type of Leviticus 23, for on the day of Pentecost Israel was definitely required to offer a *"new* meal offering unto the Lord" (v. 16). Still more clearly was it foreannounced in a yet more important and significant type, namely, that of the beginning of the Mosaic economy, which took place only when the nation of Israel formally entered into covenant relationship with Jehovah at Sinai. Now it is exceedingly striking to observe that just *fifty days* elapsed from the time when the Hebrews emerged from the house of bondage till they received the law from the mouth of Moses. They left Egypt on the fifteenth of the first month (Num. 33:3), and arrived at Sinai the first of the third month (Exod. 19:1, note "the same day"), which would be the forty-sixth. The next day Moses went up into the mount, and three days later the law was delivered (Exod. 19:11)! And just as there was a period of fifty days from Israel's deliverance from Egypt until the beginning of the Mosaic economy, so the same length of time followed the resurrection of Christ (when His people were delivered from Hell) to the beginning of the Christian economy!

That a new dispensation commenced at Pentecost further appears from the "tongues like as *of fire"* (Acts 2:1). When John the Baptist announced that Christ would baptize "with the Holy Spirit and with fire" the last words might have suggested material burning to any people except Jews, but in their minds far other thoughts would be awakened. To them it would recall the scene when their great progenitor asked God, who promised he should inherit that land wherein he was a stranger, "Lord, *whereby shall I know* that I shall inherit it?" The answer was "Behold a smoking furnace and a burning lamp . . ." (Gen. 15:17). It would recall the fire which Moses saw in the burning bush. It would recall the "pillar of fire" which guided by night, and the Shekinah which descended and filled the tabernacle. Thus, in the promise of baptism by fire, they would at once recognize the approach of *a new manifestation of the presence and power of God!*

Again: when we read that "there appeared unto them cloven tongues like as of fire, and it sat upon each of them" (Acts 2:2), further evidence is found that a new dispensation had now commenced. "The word 'sat' in Scripture marks *an ending and a beginning.* The process of preparation is ended and the established order has begun. It marks the end of creation and the beginning of normal forces. 'In six days the Lord made heaven and earth, the sea, and all that in them is, and rested the seventh day.' There is no weariness in God. He did not rest from fatigue: what it means is that all creative work was accomplished. The same figure is used of the Redeemer. Of Him it is said 'when he had made purification for sins [He] *sat down* on the right hand of the Majesty on high.' No other priesthood had sat down. The priests of the Temple ministered standing because their ministry was provisional and preparatory, a parable and prophecy. Christ's own ministry was part of the preparation for the coming of the Spirit. Until He 'sat down' in glory, there could be no dispensation of the Spirit . . . When the work of redemption was complete, the Spirit was given, and when He came he '*sat.*' He reigns in the Church as Christ reigns in the Heavens" (S. Chadwick in *The Way to Pentecost*).

"There are few incidents more illuminating than that recorded in 'the last day of the feast' in John 7:37-39. The feast was that of Tabernacles. The feast proper lasted seven days, during which all Israel dwelt in booths. Special sacrifices were offered and special rites observed. Every morning one of the priests brought water from the pool of Siloam, and amidst the sounding of trumpets and other demonstrations of joy, the water was poured upon the altar. The rite was a celebration and a prophecy. It commemorated the miraculous supply of water in the wilderness, and it bore witness to the expectation of the coming of the Spirit. On the seventh day the ceremony of the poured water ceased, but the eighth was a day of holy convocation, the greatest day of all.

"On that day there was no water poured upon the altar, and it was on the waterless day that Jesus stood on the spot and cried, saying: 'If any man thirst, let him come unto me and drink.' Then He added those words: 'He that believeth on me, as the scripture has said, from within him shall flow rivers of living water.' The apostle adds the interpretative comment: 'But this spake he of the Spirit, which they that believe on him were to receive: for the Spirit was not given because Jesus was not yet glorified.' 'As the scripture hath said.' There is no such passage in the Scripture as that quoted, but the prophetic part of the water ceremony was based upon certain Old Testament symbols and prophecies in which water flowed forth from Zion to cleanse, renew, and fructify the world. A study of Joel 3:18 and Ezekiel 47 will supply the key to the meaning both of the rite and our Lord's promise.

THE ADVENT OF THE SPIRIT

The Holy Spirit was 'not yet given,' but He was promised, and His
coming should be from the place of blood, the altar of sacrifice. Calvary opened the fountain from which poured forth the blessing of
Pentecost" (S. Chadwick).

We have considered *the meaning* of the Spirit's descent, and pointed
out that it was the fulfilment of Divine promise, the accomplishment of
Old Testament types, and the beginning of a new dispensation. It was
also *the Grace of God flowing unto the Gentiles.* But first let us
observe and admire the marvellous grace of God extended unto the
Jews themselves. In His charge to the apostles, the Lord Jesus gave
orders that "repentance and remission of sins should be preached in his
name among all nations, *beginning at Jerusalem"* (Luke 24:47), not
because the Jews had any longer a covenant standing before God —
for the Nation was abandoned by Him before the crucifixion — see
Matthew 28:38 — but in order to display His matchless mercy and
sovereign benignity. Accordingly, in the Acts we see His love shining
forth in the midst of the rebellious city. In the very place where the
Lord Jesus had been slain the full Gospel was now preached, and three
thousand were quickened by the Holy Spirit.

But the gospel was to be restricted to the Jews no longer. Though
the apostles were to commence their testimony in Jerusalem, yet Christ's
glorious and all-efficacious Name was to be proclaimed "among all nations." The earnest of this was given when "devout men out of every
nation under heaven" (Acts 2:5) exclaimed, "How hear we every man
in his own tongue?" (v. 8). It was an entirely new thing. Until this
time, God had used Hebrew, or a modification of it. Thus Bullinger's
view that a new "Jewish" dispensation (the "Pentecostal") was then
inaugurated is Divinely set aside. What occurred in Acts 2 was a part
reversal and in blessed contrast from what is recorded in Genesis 11.
There we find "the tongues were divided to destroy an *evil* unity, and
to show God's holy hatred of Babel's iniquity. In Acts 2 we have
grace at Jerusalem, and a new and precious unity, suggestive of another
building (Matt. 16:18), with living *stones* — contrast the 'bricks' of
Genesis 11:3 and its tower" (P. W. Heward). In Genesis 11 the dividing
of tongues was *in judgment;* in Acts 2 the cloven tongues was *in grace;*
and in Revelation 7:9, 10 we see men of all tongues *in glory.*

We next consider *the purpose* of the Spirit's descent. 1. *To witness
unto Christ's exaltation.* Pentecost was God's seal upon the Messiahship
of Jesus. In proof of His pleasure in and acceptance of the sacrificial
work of His Son, God raised Him from the dead, exalted Him to His
own right hand, and gave Him the Spirit to bestow upon His Church
(Acts 2:33). It has been beautifully pointed out by another that, on
the hem of the ephod worn by the high priest of Israel were golden
bells and pomegranates (Exod. 28:33, 34). The sound of the bells
(and that which gave them sound was their *tongues*) furnished evidence that he was alive while serving in the sanctuary. The high priest
was a type of Christ (Heb. 8:1); the holy place was a figure of Heaven
(Heb. 9:24); the "sound from heaven" and the speaking "in tongues"

(Acts 2:2, 4) were a witness that our Lord was alive in heaven, ministering there as the High Priest of His people.

2. *To take Christ's place.* This is clear from His own words to the apostles, "And I will pray the Father, and he shall give you another Comforter, that he may abide with you forever" (John 14:16). Until then, Christ had been their "Comforter," but He was soon to return to Heaven; nevertheless, as He went on to assure them, "I will not leave you orphans, I will come to you" (marginal rendering of John 14:18); He did "come" to them corporately after His resurrection, but He "came" to them spiritually and abidingly in the person of His Deputy on the day of Pentecost. The Spirit, then, fills the place on earth of our absent Lord in Heaven, with this additional advantage, that, during the days of His flesh the Saviour's body confined Him unto one location, whereas the Holy Spirit — not having assumed a body as the mode of His incarnation — is equally and everywhere resident in and abiding with every believer.

3. *To further Christ's Cause.* This is plain from His declaration concerning the Comforter: "He shall glorify me" (John 16:14). The word "Paraclete" (translated "Comforter" all through the gospel) is also rendered "Advocate" in I John 2:1, and an "advocate" is one who appears as *the representative* of another. The Holy Spirit is here to interpret and vindicate Christ, to administer for Christ in His Church and Kingdom. He is here to accomplish His redeeming purpose in the world. He fills the mystical Body of Christ, directing its movements, controlling its members, inspiring its wisdom, supplying its strength. The Holy Spirit becomes to the believer individually and the church collectively all that Christ would have been had He remained on earth. Moreover, He seeks out each one of those for whom Christ died, quickens them into newness of life, convicts them of sin, gives them faith to lay hold of Christ, and causes them to grow in grace and become fruitful.

It is important to see that the mission of the Spirit is for the purpose of continuing and completing that of Christ's. The Lord Jesus declared, "I am come to send fire on the earth: and what will I, if it be already kindled? But I have a baptism to be baptised with; and how am I straitened till it be accomplished!" (Luke 12:49, 50). The preaching of the gospel was to be like "fire on the earth," giving light and warmth to human hearts; it was "kindled" then, but would spread much more rapidly later. Until His death Christ was "straitened": it did not consist with God's purpose for the gospel to be preached more openly and extensively; but after Christ's resurrection, it went forth unto all nations. Following the ascension, Christ was no longer "straitened" and the Spirit was poured forth in the plenitude of His power.

4. *To endue Christ's servants.* "Tarry ye in Jerusalem until ye be endued with power from on high" (Luke 24:49) had been the word of Christ to His apostles. Sufficient for the disciple to be as his Master. *He* had waited, waited till He was thirty, ere He was "anointed to preach good tidings" (Isa. 61:1). The servant is not above his Lord: if He was indebted to the Spirit for the power of His ministry, the

apostles must not attempt their work without the Spirit's unction. Accordingly they waited, and the Spirit came upon them. All was changed: boldness supplanted fear, strength came instead of weakness, ignorance gave place to wisdom, and mighty wonders were wrought through them.

Unto the apostles whom He had chosen, the risen Saviour "commanded them that they should not depart from Jerusalem, but wait for the promise of the Father," assuring them that "Ye shall receive power after that the Holy Spirit is come unto you; and ye shall be witnesses unto me both in Jerusalem, and in all Samaria, and unto the uttermost part of the earth" (Acts 1:2, 4, 8). Accordingly we read that, "And when the day of Pentecost was fully come, they were all with one accord in one place" (Acts 2:1): their unity of mind evidently looked back to the Lord's command and promise, and their trustful expectancy of the fulfilment thereof. The Jewish "day" was from sunset unto the following sunset, and as what took place here in Acts 2 occurred during the early hours of the morning — probably soon after sunrise — we are told that the day of Pentecost was "fully come."

The outward marks of the Spirit's advent were three in number: the "sound from heaven as of a rushing mighty wind," the "cloven tongues as of fire," and the speaking "with other tongues as the Spirit gave them utterance." Concerning the precise signification of these phenomena, and the practical bearing of them on us today, there has been wide difference of opinion, especially during the past thirty years. Inasmuch as God Himself has not seen fit to furnish us with a full and detailed explanation of them, it behoves all interpreters to speak with reserve and reverence. According to our own measure of light, we shall endeavor briefly to point out some of those things which appear to be most obvious.

First, the "rushing mighty wind" which filled all the house was the *collective* sign, in which, apparently, all the hundred and twenty of Acts 1:15 shared. This was an emblem of the invincible energy with which the third Person of the Trinity works upon the hearts of men, bearing down all opposition before Him, in a manner which cannot be explained (John 3:8), but which is at once apparent by the effects produced. Just as the course of a hurricane may be clearly traced after it has passed, so the transforming work of the Spirit in regeneration is made unmistakably manifest unto all who have eyes to see spiritual things.

Second, "there appeared unto them cloven tongues like as of fire, and it sat upon each of them" (Acts 2:3), that is, upon the Twelve, and upon them alone. The proof of this is conclusive. First, it was to the apostles only that the Lord spoke in Luke 24:49. Second, to them only did He, by the Spirit, give commandments after His resurrection (Acts 1:2). Third, to them only did He give the promise of Acts 1:8. Fourth, at the end of Acts 1 we read, "he [Matthias] was numbered with *the eleven* apostles." Acts 2 opens with "And" connecting it with 1:26 and says, "they [the twelve] were all with one accord in one place" and on *them* the Spirit now "sat" (Acts 2:3). Fifth, when the astonished multitude came together they exclaimed, "Are not *all* these which speak *Galileans?*" (Acts 2:7), namely, the "men (Greek, "males") *of Galilee*" of 1:11! Sixth, in Acts 2:14, 15, we read, "But Peter standing up *with the eleven* lifted up his voice and said unto them, 'Ye men of Galilee and all ye that dwell in Judea, be this known unto you and hearken unto my words: For *these* are not drunk" — the word "these" can only refer to the "eleven" standing up with Peter!

These "cloven tongues like as of fire" which descended upon the apostles was the *individual* sign, the Divine credential that they were the authorized ambassadors of the enthroned Lamb. The baptism of the Holy Spirit was a baptism of *fire.* " 'Our God is a consuming fire.' The elect sign of His presence is the fire unkindled of earth, and the chosen symbol of His approval is the sacred flame: covenant and sacrifice, sanctuary and dispensation were sanctified and approved by the descent of fire. 'The God that answereth by fire, he is the God' (I Kings 18:24). That is the final and universal test of Deity. Jesus Christ came to bring fire on the earth. The symbol of Christianity is not a Cross, but a Tongue of Fire." (Samuel Chadwick).

Third, the apostles "speaking with other tongues" was the *public* sign. I Corinthians 14:22 declares "tongues are for a sign, not to them that believe, but to them that believe not," and as the previous verse (where Isa. 28:11 is quoted) so plainly shows, they were a sign unto *unbelieving Israel.* A striking illustration and proof of this is found in Acts 11, where Peter sought to convince his sceptical brethren in Jerusalem that God's grace was now flowing forth unto the Gentiles: it was his description of the Holy Spirit's falling upon Cornelius and his household (Acts 11:15-18 and cf. 10:45, 46) which convinced them. It is highly significant that the Pentecostal type of Leviticus 23:22 divided the harvest into three degrees and stages: the "reaping" or *main* part, corresponding to Acts 2 at Jerusalem; the "corners of the field" corresponding to Acts 10 at "Caesarea Philippi," which was in the corner of Palestine; and the "gleaning" for "the stranger" corresponding to Acts 19 at Gentile Ephesus! These were the only three occasions of "tongues" recorded in Acts.

It is well known to some of our readers that during the last generation many earnest souls have been deeply exercised by what is known as "the Pentecostal movement," and the question is frequently raised as to whether or not the strange power displayed in their meetings, issuing in unintelligible sounds called "tongues," is the genuine gift of the Spirit. Those who have joined the movement — some of them godly souls, we believe — insist that not only is the gift genuine, but it is the duty of all Christians to seek the same. But surely such seem to overlook the fact that it was not any *"unknown* tongue" which was spoken by the apostles: foreigners who heard them had no difficulty in understanding what was said (Acts 2:8).

If what has just been said be not sufficient, then let our appeal be unto II Timothy 3:16, 17. God has now *fully* revealed His mind to us: all that we need to *"thoroughly* furnish" us "unto *all* good works" is

THE ADVENT OF THE SPIRIT

already in our hands! Personally the writer would not take the trouble
to walk into the next room to hear any person deliver a message which
he claimed was inspired by the Holy Spirit; with the *completed* Scriptures in our possession, nothing more is required except for the Spirit to
interpret and apply them. Let it also be duly observed that there is not
a single exhortation in all the Epistles of the New Testament that the
saints should seek "a fresh Pentecost," no, not even to the carnal Corinthians or the legal Galatians.

As a sample of what was believed by the early "fathers" we quote
the following: "Augustine saith, 'Miracles were once necessary to make
the world believe the Gospel, but he who now seeks a sign that he may
believe is a wonder, yea a monster.' Chrysostom concludeth upon the
same grounds that, 'There is now in the Church no necessity of working
miracles,' and calls him 'a false prophet' who now takes in hand to work
them" (From W. Perkins, 1604).

In Acts 2:16 we find Peter was moved by God to give a general
explanation of the great wonders which had just taken place. Jerusalem was, at this time of the feast, filled with a great concourse of
people. The sudden sound from Heaven "as of a rushing mighty wind,"
filling the house where the apostles were gathered together, soon drew
thither a multitude of people; and as they, in wonderment, heard the
apostles speak in their own varied languages, they asked, "What meaneth
this?" (Acts 2:12). Peter then declared, *"This* is that which was spoken
of by the prophet Joel." The prophecy given by Joel (2:28-32) now
began to receive its fulfilment, the latter part of which we believe is to
be understood symbolically.

And what is the bearing of all this upon us to-day? We will reply
in a single sentence: the advent of the Spirit *followed the exaltation of
Christ*: if then we desire to enjoy more of the Spirit's power and blessing, we must give Christ the throne of our hearts and crown Him the
Lord of our lives.

Having dwelt upon the doctrinal and dispensational aspects of our
subject, next we hope to take the "practical" and "experimental" bear-
ings of it.

9

The Work of the Spirit

It is a great mistake to suppose that the works of the Spirit are all of one kind, or that His operations preserve an equality as to degree. To insist that they are and do, would be ascribing less freedom to the Third Person of the Godhead than is enjoyed and exercised by men. There is variety in the activities of all voluntary agents: even human beings are not confined to one sort of works, nor to the production of the same kind of effects; and where they design so to do, they moderate them as to degrees according to their power and pleasure. Much more so is it with the Holy Spirit. The nature and kind of His works are regulated by His own will and purpose. Some He executes by the touch of His finger (so to speak), in others He puts forth His hand, while in yet others (as on the day of Pentecost) He lays bare His arm. He works by no necessity of His nature, but solely according to the pleasure of His will (I Cor. 12:11).

Many of the works of the Spirit, though perfect in kind and fully accomplishing their design, are wrought by Him upon and within men who, nevertheless, are not saved. "The Holy Spirit is present with many as to powerful operations, with whom He is not present as to gracious inhabitation. Or, many are made partakers of Him in His spiritual gifts, who are not made partakers of Him in His saving grace: Matt. 7:22, 23" (John Owen on Heb. 6:4). The light which God furnishes different souls varies considerably, both in kind and degree. Nor should we be surprised at this in view of the adumbration in the natural world: how wide is the difference between the glimmering of the stars from the radiance of the full moon, and that again from the shining of the midday sun. Equally wide is the gulf which separates the savage with his faint illumination of conscience from one who has been educated under a Christian ministry, and greater still is the difference between the spiritual understanding of the wisest unregenerate professor and the feeblest babe in Christ; yet each has been a subject of the Spirit's operations.

"The Holy Spirit works in two ways. In some men's hearts He works with restraining grace only, and the restraining grace, though it will not save them, is enough to keep them from breaking out into the open and corrupt vices in which some men indulge who are totally left by the restraints of the Spirit. . . . God the Holy Spirit may work in men some good desires and feelings, and yet have no design of saving them. But mark, none of these feelings are things that accompany salvation, for if so, they would be continued. But He does not work Omnipotently to save, except in the persons of His own elect, whom He assuredly bringeth unto Himself. I believe, then, that the trembling of Felix is to be accounted for by the restraining grace of the Spirit quickening his conscience and making him tremble" (C. H. Spurgeon on Acts 24: 25).

The Holy Spirit has been robbed of much of His distinctive glory through Christians failing to perceive His varied workings. In concluding that the operations of the blessed Spirit are confined unto God's elect, they have been hindered from offering to Him that praise which is His due, for keeping this wicked world a fit place for them to live in. Few today realize how much the children of God owe to the third Person of the Trinity for holding in leash the children of the Devil, and preventing them from utterly consuming Christ's church on earth. It is true there are comparatively few texts which specifically refer to the distinctive person of the Spirit as reigning over the wicked, but once it is seen that in the Divine economy all is from God the Father, all is through God the Son, and all is *by* God the Spirit, each is given his proper and separate place in our hearts and thoughts. Let us, then, now point out a few of the Spirit's *general and inferior* operations in the non-elect, as distinguished from His *special and superior* works in the redeemed.

1. *In restraining evil.* If God should leave men absolutely to their own natural corruptions and to the power of Satan (as they fully deserve to be, as He will in Hell, and as He would now but for the sake of His elect), all show of goodness and morality would be entirely banished from the earth: men would grow past feeling in sin, and wickedness would swiftly and entirely swallow up the whole world. This is abundantly clear from Genesis 6:3, 4, 5, 12. But He who restrained the fiery furnace of Babylon *without* quenching it, He who prevented the waters of the Red Sea from flowing *without* changing their nature, now hinders the working of natural corruption *without* mortifying it. Vile as the world is, we have abundant cause to adore and praise the Holy Spirit that it is not a thousand times worse.

The world *hates* the people of God (John 15:19): why, then, does it not devour them? What is it that holds back the enmity of the wicked against the righteous? Nothing but the restraining power of the Holy Spirit. In Psalm 14:1-3 we find a fearful picture of the utter depravity of the human race. Then in verse 4 the Psalmist asks, "Have all the workers of iniquity no knowledge? who eat up my people as they eat bread, and call not upon the Lord." To which answer is made, "There were they in great fear: *for* God is in the generation of the righteous" (v. 5). It is the Holy Spirit who places that "great fear" within them, to keep them back from many outrages against God's people. He curbs their malice. So completely are the reprobate shackled by His almighty hand, that Christ could say to Pilate, "thou couldest have *no* power against me, *except* it were given thee from above" (John 19:11)!

2. *In inciting to good actions.* All the obedience of children to parents, all the true love between husbands and wives, is to be attributed

unto the Holy Spirit. Whatever morality and honesty, unselfishness and kindness, submission to the powers that be and respect for law and order, which is still to be found in the world, must be traced back to the gracious operations of the Spirit. A striking illustration of His benign influence is found in I Samuel 10:26, "Saul also went home to Gibeah: and there went with him a band of men, whose hearts *God* [the Spirit] had touched." Men's hearts are naturally inclined to rebellion, are impatient against being ruled over, especially by one raised out of a mean condition among them. The Lord the Spirit inclined the hearts of those men to be subject unto Saul, gave them a disposition to obey him. So too, later, the Spirit touched the heart of Saul to spare the life of David, melting him to such an extent that he wept (I Sam. 24:16). In like manner, it was the Holy Spirit who gave the Hebrews favor in the eyes of the Egyptians — who hitherto had bitterly hated them — so as to give earrings to them (Exod. 12:35, 36).

3. *In convicting of sin.* Few seem to understand that conscience in the natural man is inoperative unless stirred up by the Spirit. As a fallen creature, thoroughly in love with sin (John 3:19), man resists and disputes against any conviction of sin. "My Spirit shall not always strive with man, *for* that he also *is flesh*" (Gen. 6:3): man, being "flesh," would never have the least distaste of any iniquity unless the Spirit excited those remnants of natural light which still remain in the soul. Being "flesh," fallen man is perverse against the convictions of the Spirit (Acts 7:51), and remains so forever unless quickened and made "spirit" (John 3:6).

4. *In illuminating.* Concerning Divine things, fallen man is not only devoid of light, but *is* "darkness" itself (Eph. 5:8). He had no more apprehension of spiritual things than the beasts of the field. This is very evident from the state of the heathen. How, then, shall we explain the intelligence which *is* found in thousands in Christendom, who yet give no evidence that they are new creatures in Christ Jesus? They have been enlightened by the Holy Spirit (Heb. 6:4). Many are constrained to enquire into those scriptural subjects which make no demand on the conscience and life; yea, many take great delight in them. Just as the multitudes took pleasure in beholding the miracles of Christ, who could not endure His searching demands, so the *light* of the Spirit is pleasant to many to whom His *convictions* are grievous.

We have dwelt upon some of the general and inferior operations which the Holy Spirit performs upon the non-elect, who are never brought unto a saving knowledge of the truth. Now we shall consider His special and saving work in the people of God, dwelling mainly upon the absolute necessity for the same. It should make it easier for the Christian reader to perceive the absoluteness of this necessity when we say that the whole work of the Spirit within the elect is to plant in the heart a hatred for and a loathing of *sin* as sin, and a love for and longing after *holiness* as holiness. This is something which no human power can bring about. It is something which the most faithful preaching as such cannot produce. It is something which the mere circulating and reading of the Scripture does not impart. It is a miracle of grace, a Divine wonder, which none but God can or does perform.

Of course if men are only partly depraved (which is *really* the belief today of the vast majority of preachers and their hearers, never having been experimentally taught by God *their own* depravity), if deep down in their hearts all men really love God, if they are so good-natured as to be easily persuaded to become Christians, then there is no need for the Holy Spirit to put forth His Almighty power and do for them what they are altogether incapable of doing for themselves. And again: if "being saved" consists merely in believing I am a lost sinner and on my way to Hell, and by simply believing that God loves me, that Christ died for me, and that He will save me now on the one condition that I "accept Him as my personal Saviour" and "rest upon His finished work," then no supernatural operations of the Holy Spirit are required to induce and enable me to fulfil *that* condition — self-interest moves me to, and a decision of my will is all that is required.

But if, on the other hand, all men *hate* God (John 15:23, 25), and have minds which are "enmity against Him" (Rom. 8:7), so that "there is *none* that seeketh after God" (Rom. 3:11), preferring and determining to follow their own inclinations and pleasures; if instead of being disposed unto that which is good, "the heart of the sons of men is *fully* set in them to do evil" (Eccles. 8:11); and if when the overtures of God's mercy are made known to them and they are freely invited to avail themselves of the same, they "*all* with one consent begin to make excuse" (Luke 14:18) — then it is very evident that the invincible power and transforming operations of the Spirit are indispensably required if the heart of a sinner is thoroughly changed, so that rebellion gives place to submission and hatred to love. This is why Christ said, "No man can come to me, *except* the Father (by the Spirit) which hath sent me *draw* him" (John 6:44).

Again; if the Lord Jesus Christ came here to uphold and enforce the high claims of God, rather than to lower or set them aside; if He declared that "strait is the gate and narrow is the way that leadeth unto Life, and few there be that find it," rather than pointing to a smooth and broad road which any one would find it easy to tread; if the salvation which He has provided is a deliverance from sin and self-pleasing, from worldliness and indulging the lusts of the flesh, and the bestowing of a nature which desires and determines to live for *God's* glory and please Him in *all* the details of our present lives — then it is clear beyond dispute that none but the Spirit of God can impart a *genuine* desire for *such* a salvation. And if instead of "accepting Christ" and "resting upon His finished work" be the sole condition of salvation, He demands that the sinner throw down the weapons of his defiance, abandon every idol, unreservedly surrender himself and his life, and receive Him as His only Lord and Master, then naught but a miracle of grace can enable any captive of Satan's to meet *such* requirements.

Against what has been said above it may be objected that no such hatred of God as we have affirmed exists in the hearts of the great majority of our fellow-creatures: that while there may be a few degenerates, who have sold themselves to the Devil and are thoroughly hardened in sin, yet the remainder of mankind *are* friendly disposed to God, as is evident by the countless millions who have some form or other of religion. To such an objector we reply, The fact is, dear friend, that those to whom you refer are almost entirely ignorant of *the God of Scripture*: they have heard that He loves everybody, is benevolently inclined toward all His creatures, and is so easy-going that in return for their religious performances will wink at their sins. Of course, they have no hatred for such a "god" as this! But tell them something of the character of the true God: that *He hates* "all the workers of iniquity" (Ps. 5:5), that He is inexorably just and ineffably holy, that He is an uncontrollable Sovereign, who "hath mercy on whom he will have mercy, and whom he will he hardeneth" (Rom. 9:18), and their enmity against *Him* will soon be manifested — an enmity which none but the Holy Spirit can overcome.

It may be objected again that so far from the gloomy picture which we have sketched above being accurate, the great majority of people *do* desire to be saved, and make more or less endeavor after their salvation. This is readily granted. There is in every human heart a desire for deliverance from misery and a longing after happiness and security, and those who come under the sound of God's Word are *naturally* disposed to be delivered from the wrath to come and wish to be assured that Heaven will be their eternal dwelling-place — who *wants* to endure the everlasting burnings? But that desire and disposition is quite compatible and consistent with the greatest love to sin and most entire opposition of heart to that holiness without which no man shall see the Lord (Heb. 12:14). But what the objector here refers to is a vastly different thing from desiring Heaven upon *God's* terms, and being willing to tread the *only* path which leads there!

The instinct of self-preservation is sufficiently strong to move multitudes to undertake many performances and penances in the hope that thereby they shall escape Hell. The stronger men's belief of the truth of Divine revelation, the more firmly they become convinced that there is a Day of Judgment, when they must appear before their Maker, and render an account of all their desires, thoughts, words and deeds, the most serious and sober will be their minds. Let conscience convict them of their mis-spent lives, and they are ready to turn over a new leaf; let them be persuaded that Christ stands ready as a Fire-escape and is willing to rescue them, though the world still claims their *hearts*, and thousands are ready to "believe in Him." Yes, this *is* done by multitudes who still hate the true character of the Saviour, and reject with all their hearts the salvation which *He* has. Far, far different is this from an unregenerate person longing for deliverance *from self and sin*, and the impartation of that *holiness* which Christ purchased for His peoples.

All around us are those willing to receive Christ as their Saviour, who are altogether unwilling to surrender to Him as their Lord. They would like His peace, but they refuse His "yoke," without which *His* peace cannot be found (Matt. 11:29). They admire His promises, but have no heart for His precepts. They will rest upon His priestly work, but will not be subject to His kingly scepter. They will believe in a "Christ" who is suited to their own corrupt tastes or sentimental dreams, but they despise and reject the Christ of God. Like the multitudes of old, they want His loaves and fishes, but for His heart-searching, flesh-withering, sin-condemning teaching, they have no appetite. They approve of Him as the Healer of their bodies, but as the Healer of their depraved souls they desire Him not. And nothing but the miracle-working power of the Holy Spirit, can change this bias and bent in any soul.

It is just because modern Christendom has such an inadequate estimate of the fearful and universal effects which the Fall has wrought, that the imperative need for the supernatural power of the Holy Spirit is now so little realized. It is because such false conceptions of human depravity so widely prevail that, in most places, it is supposed all which is needed to save half of the community is to hire some popular evangelist and attractive singer. And the reason why so few *are* aware of the awful depths of human depravity, the terrible enmity of the carnal mind against God and the heart's inbred and inveterate hatred of Him, is because *His* character is now so rarely declared from the pulpit. If the preachers would deliver the same type of messages as did Jeremiah in his degenerate age, or even as John the Baptist did, they would soon discover how their hearers were *really* affected toward God; and then they would perceive that unless the power of the Spirit attended their preaching they might as well be silent.

10

The Holy Spirit Regenerating

THE absolute necessity for the regenerating operation of the Holy Spirit in order for a sinner's being converted to God, lies in his being totally depraved. Fallen man is without the least degree of right disposition or principles from which holy exercises may proceed; yea, he is completely under a contrary disposition: there is no right exercise of heart in him, but *every* motion of his will is corrupt and sinful. If this were not the case, there would be no need for him to be born again and made "a new creature." If the sinner were not wholly corrupt he would submit to Christ without any supernatural operation of the Spirit; but fallen man is so completely sunk in corruption that he has not the faintest real desire for God, but is filled with enmity against Him (Rom. 8:7). Therefore does Scripture affirm him to be "*dead* in trespasses and sins" (Eph. 2:1).

"But as many as received him, to them gave he power to become the sons of God, to them which believe on his name: Which were born, not of blood, nor of the will of the flesh, nor of the will of man, but of God" (John 1:12, 13). The latter verse expounds the former. There an explanation is given as to why any fallen descendant of Adam ever spiritually receives Christ as His Lord and Master, and savingly believes on His name.

First, it is not because grace runs in the blood — as the Jews supposed. Holiness is not transmitted from father to son. The child of the most pious parents is by nature equally as corrupt and is as far from God as is the offspring of infidels. Second, it is not because of any natural willingness — as Arminians contend: "nor of the will of the flesh" refers to man in his natural and corrupt state. He is not regenerated by any instinct, choice, or exertion of his own; he does not by any personal endeavor contribute anything towards being born again; nor does he cooperate in the least degree with the efficient cause: instead, every inclination of his heart, every exercise of his will, is in direct opposition thereto.

Third, the new birth is not brought about by the power and influence of others. No sinner is ever born again as the result of the persuasions and endeavors of preachers or Christian workers. However pious and wise they are, and however earnestly and strenuously they exert themselves to bring others to holiness, they do in no degree produce the effect. "If all the angels and saints in heaven and all the godly on earth should join their wills and endeavors and unitedly exert all their powers to regenerate one sinner, they could not effect it; yea, they could do nothing toward it. It is an effect *infinitely* beyond the reach of finite wisdom and power: I Cor. 3:6, 7" (S. Hopkins).

"You may listen to the preacher
God's own truth be clearly shown,
But you need a greater teacher
From the everlasting throne;
Application is the work of God alone."

In regeneration one of God's elect is the subject, and the Spirit of God is the sole agent. The subject of the new birth is wholly passive: he does not act, but is acted upon. The sovereign work of the Spirit in the soul precedes *all* holy exercises of heart — such as sorrow for sin, faith in Christ, love toward God. This great change is wrought in spite of all the opposition of the natural heart against God: "So then it is not of him that willeth, nor of him that runneth, but of God that showeth mercy" (Rom. 9:16). This great change is not a gradual and protracted process, but is *instantaneous*: in an instant of time the favored subject of it passes from death unto life.

In regeneration the Spirit imparts a real, new, and immortal life; a life not such as that which was inherited from the first Adam, who was "a living soul," but such as is derived from the last Adam, who is "a quickening Spirit" (I Cor. 15:45). This new creation, though as real as the first, is widely different from it; that was an original or primary creation in the dust of the earth becoming man by the word of God's power; this is the regeneration of an actual and existing man — fallen and depraved, yet rational and accountable — into an heir of God and joint-heir with Christ. The outcome is a "new man," yet it is the same person, only "renewed."

"Regeneration consists in a new, spiritual, supernatural, vital principle, or habit of grace infused into the soul, the mind, the will, and affections, by the power of the Holy Spirit, disposing and enabling them in whom it is, unto spiritual, supernatural, vital actings and spiritual obedience" (John Owen). No new faculties are created, but instead, the powers of the soul are spiritualized and made alive unto God, fitted to enjoy God and hold communion with Him. Regeneration consists in a radical change of heart, for there is implanted a new disposition as the foundation of all holy exercises; the mind being renovated, the affections elevated, and the will emancipated from the bondage of sin. The effect of this is that the one who is born again loved spiritual things *as spiritual*, and values spiritual blessings on account of their being purely spiritual.

In view of a certain school of teaching upon "the two *natures* in the believer," some readers may experience difficulty over our statement above that at regeneration no new faculties are created, the soul remaining, substantially, the same as it was before. No, not even in the glorified state will any addition be made to the human constitution, though its faculties will then be completely unfettered and further enlarged and elevated. Perhaps this thought will be the more easily grasped if we illustrate it by a striking case recorded in II Kings 6:17, "Elisha prayed, and said, Lord, I pray Thee, open his eyes, that he may see. And the Lord opened the eyes of the young man, and he saw; and, behold, the mountain was full of horses and chariots of fire round about Elisha."

No new faculties were communicated unto Elisha's servant, but the powers of his visive organ were so enlarged that he was now able to discern objects which before were invisible to him. So it is with our understandings at regeneration: the mind (abstractly considered) is the same in the unregenerate as in the regenerate, but in the case of the latter, the Spirit has so quickened it that it is now able to take in spiritual objects and act toward them. This new spiritual visive power with which the understanding is endowed at the new birth is a *quality*, superadded to the original faculties. As this is a point of importance, yet one which some find it difficult to grasp, we will proceed to dwell upon it a moment longer.

The bodily eye of the saint after resurrection will be elevated to see angels (which are now invisible), and therefore may be rightly termed a *new* eye, yea, a spiritual eye — even as the whole body will be a "spiritual body" (I Cor. 15:44) — yet that change will be but the superinduction of new spiritual qualities for the eye (and the whole body) unto spiritual objects. In like manner, the entire being of one who is born again is so spiritualized or endued with "spirit" (John 3:6) as to be styled a "new man," a "spiritual" man; nevertheless, it is but the original man "renewed," and not the creating of a new being.

After regeneration things appear in an altogether new light, and the heart exercises itself after quite a new manner. God is now seen as the sum of all excellency. The reasonableness and spirituality of His law is so perceived that the heart approves of it. The infinite evil of sin is discerned. The one born again, judges, condemns, and loathes himself, and wonders that he was not long ago cast into Hell. He marvels at the grace of God in giving Christ to die for such a wretch. Constrained by the love of Christ, he now renounces the ways of sin and gives himself up to serve God. Hereby we may discover *what it is* which persons are to inquire after in order to determine whether they have been born again, namely, by the exercises of their hearts, and the influence and effects these have upon their conduct.

We have pointed out that at regeneration the faculties of the soul are *spiritually enlivened*, grace putting into them a new ability so that they are capable of performing spiritual acts. At the new birth the Holy Spirit communicates principles of spiritual life, whereby the soul is qualified to act as a supernatural agent and produce supernatural works. The need-be for this should be evident; God and Christ, as they are revealed in the gospel, are supernatural objects to the natural faculties or powers of the soul, and there is no proportion between them — not only such a disproportion as the bat's eye hath unto the sun, but as a blind man's eye to the sun. Thus there is a greater necessity for the soul to be given new principles and abilities to act holily and spiritually than at the first creation to act naturally.

Holiness in the heart is the main and ultimate birth brought forth in regeneration, for to make us partakers of God's holiness is the sum and scope of His gracious purpose toward us, both of His election (Eph. 1: 4), and of all His dealings afterward (Heb. 12:10), without which "no man shall see the Lord" (Heb. 12:14). Not that finite creatures can ever be partakers of the essential holiness that is in God, either by imputation, or much less by real transubstantiation. We can be no otherwise partakers of it than in the *image* thereof — "which after God [as pattern or prototype] is created in righteousness and true holiness" (Eph. 4:24); "after the image of Him that created him" (Col. 3:10).

Regeneration is the first discovery and manifestation of election and redemption to the persons for whom they were intended: "But after the kindness and love of God our Saviour toward man *appeared*" (Titus 3:4); and *how* and *when* did it appear? "According to His mercy He saved us *by* the washing of regeneration and renewing of the Holy Spirit" (v. 5). "God's eternal love, like a mighty river, had from everlasting run, as it were underground; and when Christ came, it took its course through His heart, hiddenly ran through it, He bearing when on the cross the names of them whom God had given Him; but was yet still hidden here as to us, and our knowledge of it. But the first breaking of it forth, and particular appearing of it in and to the persons, is when we are converted, and is as the first opening of a fountain" (T. Goodwin).

There is a great display of God's *power* apparent in our regeneration; yea, an "exceeding greatness" thereof, no less than that which raised up Christ from the dead (Eph. 1:19, 20). Because the work of regeneration is often repeated, and ,accomplished in a trice, as seen in the dying thief and Paul, and often accomplished (apparently) by a few words from one frail mortal falling on the ears of another, we are apt to lose sight of the omnipotent working of the Holy Spirit in the performing thereof. Indeed the Spirit so graciously hides the exceeding greatness of His power working in sinners' hearts, by using such sweet persuasive motives and gentle inducements — drawing with "the cords of a man" (Hos. 11:4) — that *His* might is inadequately recognized, owned, and adored by us.

The marvel of regeneration is the bringing of a soul out of spiritual death into spiritual life. It is a new creation, which is a bringing of something out of nothing. Moreover the new creation is a far greater wonder than is the old: in the first creation there was nothing to oppose, but in the new all the powers of sin and Satan are set against it. Regeneration is not like the changing of water into wine, but of contrary into contrary — of hearts of stone into flesh (Ezek. 36:26), of wolves into lambs (Isa. 11:6). This is greater than any miracle Christ showed, and therefore did He tell His apostles that, under the mighty enduement of the Holy Spirit, they should work "greater works" than He did (John 14:12).

Not only is there a wondrous exhibition of His power when the Spirit regenerates a soul, but there is also a blessed manifestation of His *love*. In the exercise of His gracious office towards God's elect and in His work in them, the Holy Spirit proves to a demonstration that His love toward the heirs of glory is ineffable and incomprehensible. As the principal work of the Spirit consists in making our souls alive to God, in giving us to apprehend the transactions of the Father and the Son in the everlasting covenant, and in imparting to them spiritual principles wl.ereby they are fitted to enjoy and commune with God, it is *internal;* hence it is that, His work being *within* us, we are more apt to overlook *Him*, and are prone to neglect the giving to Him the glory which is distinctly His due, and most sadly do we fail to praise and adore Him for His gracious work in us.

Thus it is with all believers: they find themselves more disposed to think on the love of Christ, or on the Father's love in the gift of Him than in exercising their minds spiritually in soul-inflaming and heart-warming meditations on the love and mercy of the Holy Spirit towards them, and His delight in them; though all that they really know and enjoy of the Father's love by faith in the finished work of the Son, is entirely from the inward teaching and supernatural influences of the eternal Spirit. This is too plainly evident in our neglect to ascribe distinctive glory to Him as a Divine person in the Godhead as God and Lord.

"For God hath not appointed us to wrath, but to obtain salvation by our Lord Jesus Christ. Who died for us, that, whether we wake or sleep, we should live together with Him" (I Thess. 5:9, 10): yet, the Father's appointment and the Son's redemption, with all the unspeakable blessings thereof, remained for a season quite unknown to us. In their fallen, sinful, and guilty state, Christians lay "dead in trespasses and sins," without hope. To bring them out of this state, and raise them from a death of sin into a life of righteousness, is the great and grand work reserved for the Holy Spirit, in order to display and make manifest thereby His love for them.

The Holy Spirit is fully acquainted with the present and everlasting virtue and efficacy of the person and work of Immanuel, and what His heart was set upon when He made His soul an offering for sin, and how infinitely and eternally well pleased was Jehovah the Father with it, who hath it in perpetual remembrance. The Father and the Son having committed the revelation and application of this great salvation unto the persons of all the elect *to the Holy Spirit*, He is pleased therefore, out of the riches of His own free and sovereign grace, to work in due season in all the heirs of glory. And as Christ died but once — His death being all-sufficient to answer every design to be effected by it — so the Holy Spirit *by one act* works effectually in the soul, producing a spiritual birth and changing the state of its partaker once for all, so that the regenerated are brought out of and delivered from the power of death and translated into the kingdom of God's dear Son. Without this spiritual birth we cannot see spiritual objects and heavenly blessings in their true worth and excellency.

The effect of the new birth is that the man born again loves spiritual things *as spiritual* and values spiritual blessings on account of their being purely spiritual. The spring of life from Christ enters into him, and is the spring of all his spiritual life, the root of all his graces, the perpetual source of every Divine principle within him. So says Christ: "But whosoever drinketh of the water that I shall give him shall never thirst; but the water that I shall give him shall be in him a well of water springing up into everlasting life" (John 4:14). This regeneration introduces the elect into a capacity for the enjoyments which are peculiar to the spiritual world, and makes the one alteration in their state before God which lasts forever. *All* our meetness for the heavenly state is wrought at our regeneration (Col. 1:12, 13). Regeneration is one and the same in all saints. It admits of no increase or diminution. All grace and holiness are then imparted by the Spirit: His subsequent work is but to draw it forth into exercise and act.

11

The Spirit Quickening

WE shall now confine ourselves to *the initial* operation of the Spirit within the elect of God. Different writers have employed the term "regeneration" with varying latitude: some restricting it unto a single act, others including the whole process by which one becomes a conscious child of God. This has hindered close accuracy of thought, and has introduced considerable confusion through the confounding of things which, though intimately related, are quite distinct. Not only has confusion of thought resulted from a loose use of terms, but serious divisions among professing saints have issued therefrom. We believe that much, if not all, of this would have been avoided had theologians discriminated more sharply and clearly between the principle of grace (spiritual life) which the Spirit first imparts unto the soul, and His consequent stirrings of that principle into exercise.

In earlier years we did not ourselves perceive the distinction which is pointed by John 6:63 and I Peter 1:23: the former referring unto the initial act of the Spirit in "quickening" the spiritually-dead soul, the latter having in view the consequent "birth" of the same. While it is freely allowed that *the origin* of the "new creature" is shrouded in impenetrable mystery, yet of this we may be certain, that *life precedes birth.* There is a strict analogy between the natural birth and the spiritual: necessarily so, for God is the Author of them both, and He ordained that the former should adumbrate the latter. Birth is neither the cause nor the beginning of life itself: rather is it the *manifestation* of a life already existent: there had been a Divine "quickening" before the child could issue from the womb. In like manner, the Holy Spirit "quickens" the soul, or imparts spiritual life to it, *before* its possessor is "brought forth" (as James 1:18 is rightly rendered in the R.V.) and "born again" by the Word of God (I Peter 1:23).

James 1:18, I Peter 1:23, and parallel passages, *refer not* to the original communication of spiritual life to the soul, but rather to our being enabled to act from that life and induced to love and obey God by means of the Word of Truth; which presupposes a principle of grace already planted in the heart. In His work of illumination, conviction, conversion, and sanctification, the Spirit uses the Word as the means thereto, but in His initial work of "quickening" He employs no means, operating immediately or directly upon the soul. First there is a "new creation" (II Cor. 5:17; Eph. 2:10), and then the "new creature" is stirred into exercise. Faith and all other graces *are* wrought in us by the Spirit through the instrumentality of the Word, but *not so* with the principle of life and grace from which these graces proceed.

In His work of "quickening," by which we mean the impartation of spiritual life to the soul, the Spirit acts immediately from within, and not by applying something from without. Quickening is a *direct* operation of the Spirit without the use of any instrument: the Word is used by Him afterwards to call into exercise the life then communicated. "Regeneration is a direct operation of the Holy Spirit upon the human spirit. It is the action of Spirit upon spirit, of a Divine Person upon a human person, whereby spiritual life is imparted. Nothing, therefore, of the nature of means or instruments can come between the Holy Spirit and the soul that is made alive. God did not employ an instrument or means when He infused physical life into the body of Adam. There were only two factors: the dust of the ground and the creative power of God which vivified that dust. The Divine omnipotence and dead matter were brought into direct contact, with nothing interposing. The dust was not a means or instrument by which God originated life. So in regeneration there are only two factors: the human soul destitute of spiritual life, and the Holy Spirit who quickens it.

"The word and truth of God, the most important of all the means of grace, is not a means of regeneration, *as distinct from* conviction, conversion and sanctification. This is evident when we remember that it is the office of a means or instrument, to excite or stimulate an *already existing* principle of life. Physical food is a means of physical growth, but it supposes physical vitality. If the body is dead, bread cannot be a means or instrument. Intellectual truth is a means of intellectual growth, but it supposes intellectual vitality. If the mind be idiotic, secular knowledge cannot be a means or instrument. Spiritual truth is a means of spiritual growth, in case there be spiritual vitality. But if the mind be dead to righteousness, spiritual truth cannot be a means or instrument.

"The unenlightened understanding is unable to apprehend, and the unregenerate will is unable to believe. Vital force is lacking in these two principal factors. What is needed at this point is life and force itself. Consequently, the Author of spiritual life Himself must operate directly, without the use of means or instruments; and outright give spiritual life and power from the dead: that is, ex nihilo. The new life is not imparted because man perceives the truth, but he perceives the truth because the new life is imparted. A man is not regenerated because he has first believed in Christ, but he believes in Christ because he has been regenerated" (W. T. Shedd, *Presbyterian,* 1889).

Under the guise of honoring the written word, many have (no doubt unwittingly) dishonored the Holy Spirit. The idea which seems to prevail in "orthodox" circles today is, that all which is needed for the salvation of souls is to give out the Word in its purity, God being pledged to bless the same. How often we have heard it said, "The Word will do its own work." Many suppose that the Scriptures are quite sufficient of themselves to communicate light to those in darkness and life to those who are dead in sins. But the record which we have of Christ's life ought at once to correct such a view: who preached the Word as faithfully as He, yet how very few were saved during His three and a half years' ministry!

The parable of the Sower exposes the fallacy of the theory now so widely prevailing. The "seed" sown is the Word. It was scattered upon various kinds of ground, yet notwithstanding the purity and vitality of the seed, where the soil was unfavorable, no increase issued therefrom. Until the ground was made good, the seed yielded no increase. That seed might be watered by copious showers and warmed by a genial sum, but while the soil was bad there could be no harvest. *The ground must be changed* before it could be fertile. Nor is it the seed which *changes the soil*: what farmer would ever think of saying, The seed will change the soil! Make no mistake upon this point: the Holy Spirit must first quicken the dead soul into newness of life *before* the Word obtains any entrance.

To say that life is communicated to the soul by the Spirit's application of the Word, and then to affirm that it is the principle of life which gives efficacy to the Word, is but to reason in a circle. The Word cannot profit any soul spiritually until it be "mixed with faith" (Heb. 4:2), and faith cannot be put forth unless it proceeds from a principle of life and grace; and therefore that principle of life is not produced by it. "We might as well suppose that the presenting of a picture to a man who is blind can enable him to see, as we can suppose that the presenting of the Word in an objective way is the instrument whereby God produces the internal principle by which we are enabled to embrace it" (Thos. Ridgley, *Presbyterian*, 1730 — quoted by us to show we are not here inculcating some *new* doctrine.)

Yet notwithstanding what has been pointed out above, many are still likely to insist upon the quickening power which inheres in the Word itself, reminding us that *its* voice is that of the Almighty. This we freely and fully acknowledge, but do not all the unregenerate resist, and refuse to heed that Voice? How, then, is that opposition to be *removed?* Take an illustration. Suppose the window of my room is darkened by an iron wall before it. The sun's beams beat upon it, but still the wall remains. Were it of ice, it would melt away, but the nature of iron is to harden and not soften under the influence of heat. How, then, is the sun to enter my room? Only by removing that wall: a direct power must be put forth for its destruction. In like manner, the deadly enmity of the sinner must be removed by the immediate operation of the Spirit, communicating life, before the Word enters and affects him.

"The light of the body is the eye: if therefore thine eye be single, thy whole body shall be full of light. But if thine eye be evil, thy whole body shall be full of darkness" (Matt. 7:22, 23). By the "eye" is not here meant the mind only, but the disposition of the heart (cf. Mark 7:22). Here Christ tells us *in what* man's blindness consists, namely, *the evil disposition of his heart,* and that the only way to remove the darkness, and let in the light, is *to change the heart*. An "evil eye" is not cured or its darkness removed merely by casting light upon it, any more than the rays of the sun communicate sight unto one whose visive faculty is dead. The eye must be cured, made "single," and then it is capable of receiving the light.

"It is said the Lord opened the heart of Lydia, *that* she attended unto the things that were spoken by Paul (Acts 16:14). It would be a contradiction, and very absurd, to say, that God's Word spoken by Paul was that by which her heart was opened; for she knew not what he did speak, until her heart was opened to attend to his words and understand them. Her heart was first opened *in order for* his words to have any effect or give any light to her. And this must be done by an *immediate* operation of the Spirit of God on her heart. This was the regeneration now under consideration, by which her heart was renewed, and formed *unto* true discerning like the single eye" (Sam. Hopkins, 1792).

The soul, then, is quickened into newness of life by the direct and supernatural operation of the Spirit, without any medium or means whatever. It is not accomplished by the light of the Word, for it is His very imparting of life which fits the heart to receive the light. This initial work of the Spirit is absolutely indispensable *in order to* have spiritual illumination. It is depravity or corruption of heart which holds the mind in darkness, and it is in *this* that unregeneracy consists. It is just as absurd to speak of illumination being conveyed by the Word *in order to* have a change of heart, or the giving of a relish for spiritual things, as it would be to speak of giving the capacity to a man to taste the sweetness of honey while he was devoid of a palate.

No, men are not "quickened" *by* the Word, they must be quickened in order to receive and understand the Word. "And I will give them a heart *to* know me, that I am the Lord; and they shall be my people, and I will be their God" (Jer. 24:7): that statement would be quite meaningless if a saving knowledge of or experimental acquaintance with God were obtained through the Word *previous to* the "new heart" or spiritual life being given, and was the *means of* our being quickened. "The fear of the Lord is the beginning of knowledge" (Prov. 1:7); the "fear of the Lord" or Divine grace communicated to the heart (spiritual life imparted) alone lays the foundation for spiritual knowledge and activities.

"For as the Father raiseth up the dead, and quickeneth, even so the Son quickeneth whom He will" (John 5:21); "It is the Spirit that quickeneth: the flesh profiteth nothing" (John 6:63). All the Divine operations in the economy of salvation proceed from the Father, are through the Son, and are executed by the Spirit. Quickening is His *initial* work in the elect. It is that supernatural act by which He brings them out of the grave of spiritual death on to resurrection ground. By it He imparts a principle of grace and habit of holiness; it is the communication of the life of God to the soul. It is an act of creation (II Cor. 5:17). It is a Divine "workmanship" (Eph. 2:10). All of these terms denote an act of Omnipotency. The origination of life is utterly impossible to the creature. He can receive life; he can nourish life; he can use and exert it; but he cannot create life.

In this work the Spirit acts as *sovereign*. "The wind bloweth *where it listeth* [or "pleaseth"] . . . so is every one that is born of the Spirit" (John 3:8). This does not mean that He acts capriciously, or without reason and motive, but that He is above any obligation to the creature, and is quite uninfluenced by us in what He does. The Spirit might justly have left every one of us in the hardness of our hearts to perish forever. In quickening one and not another, in bringing a few from death unto life and leaving the mass still dead in trespasses and sins, the Spirit has mercy "on whom He will have mercy." He is absolutely free to work in whom He pleases, for none of the fallen sons of Adam have the slightest claim upon Him.

The quickening of the spiritually dead into newness of life is therefore an act of *amazing grace*: it is an unsought and unmerited favor. The sinner, who is the chosen subject of this Divine operation and object of this inestimable blessing, is infinitely ill-deserving in himself, being thoroughly disposed to go on in wickedness till this change is wrought in him. He is rebellious, and will not hearken to the Divine command; he is obstinate and refuses to repent and embrace the gospel. However terrified he may be with the fears of threatened doom, however earnest may be his desire to escape misery and be happy forever, no matter how many prayers he may make and things he may do, he has not the least inclination to repent and submit to God. His heart is defiant, full of enmity against God, and daily does he add iniquity unto iniquity. For the Spirit to give a new heart unto *such an one* is indeed an act of amazing and sovereign grace.

This quickening by the Spirit is *instantaneous*: it is a Divine act, and not a process; it is wrought at once, and not gradually. In a moment of time the soul passes from death unto life. The soul which before was dead toward God, is now alive to Him. The soul which was completely under the domination of sin, is now set free; though the sinful nature itself is not removed nor rendered inoperative, yet the heart is no longer en rapport (in sympathy) with it. The Spirit of God finds the heart wholly corrupt and desperately wicked, but by a miracle of grace He changes its bent, and this by implanting within it the imperishable seed of holiness. There is no medium between a carnal and a spiritual state: the one is what we were by nature, the other is what we become by grace, by the instantaneous and invincible operation of the Almighty Spirit.

This initial work of quickening is entirely *unperceived* by us, for it lies outside the realm and the range of human consciousness. Those who are *dead* possess no perception, and though the work of bringing them on to resurrection ground is indeed a great and powerful one, in the very nature of the case its subjects can know nothing whatever about it until *after* it has been accomplished. When Adam was created, he was conscious of nothing but that he now existed and was free to act:

the Divine operation which was the cause of his existence was over and finished before he began to be conscious of anything. This initial operation of the Spirit by which the elect become new creatures can only be known by its effects and consequences. "The wind bloweth where it listeth," that is first; then *"thou hearest the sound thereof"* (John 3:8): it is now made known, in a variety of ways, to the conscience and understanding.

Under this work of quickening *we* are entirely *passive*, by which is meant that there is no co-operation whatever between the will of the sinner and the act of the Holy Spirit. As we have said, this initial work of the Spirit is effected by free and sovereign *grace*, consisting of the infusion of a principle of spiritual life into the soul, by which all its faculties are supernaturally renovated. This being the case, the sinner must be entirely passive, like clay in the hands of a potter, for until Divine grace is exerted upon him he is utterly incapable of any spiritual acts, being *dead* in trespasses and sins. Lazarus co-operated not in his resurrection: he knew not that the Saviour had come to his sepulchre to deliver him from death. Such is the case with each of God's elect when the Spirit commences to deal with them. They must first be quickened into newness of life before they can have the slightest desire or motion of the will toward spiritual things; hence, for them to contribute the smallest iota unto their quickening is utterly impossible.

The life which the Spirit imparts when He quickens is *uniform* in all its favored subjects. "As seed virtually contains in it all that afterwards proceeds from it, the blade, stalk, ear, and full corn in the ear, so the first principle of grace implanted in the heart seminally contains all the grace which afterwards appears in all the fruits, effects, acts, and exercises of it" (John Gill). Each quickened person experiences the same radical change, by which the image of God is stamped upon the soul: *"that which is born of the Spirit is spirit"* (John 3:6), never anything less, and never anything more. Each quickened person is made a new creature in Christ, and possesses all the constituent parts of "the new man." Later, some may be more lively and vigorous at their birth, as God gives stronger faith unto one than to another; yet there is no difference in their original: all partake of the same life.

While there is great variety in our perception and understanding of the work of the Spirit within us, there is no difference in the initial work itself. While there is much difference in the carrying on of this work unto perfection in the *growth* of the "new creature" — some making speedy progress, others thriving slowly and bringing forth little fruit — yet the new creation itself is the same in all. Each alike enters the kingdom of God, becomes a vital member of Christ's mystical body, is given a place in the living family of God. Later, one may appear more beautiful than another, by having the image of his heavenly Father more evidently imprinted upon him, yet not more truly so. There are degrees in sanctification, but none in vivification. There has never been but one kind of spiritual quickening in this world, being in its essential nature specifically the same in all.

Let it be pointed out in conclusion that the Spirit's quickening is only *the beginning* of God's work of grace in the soul. This does not wholly renew the heart at once: no indeed, the inner man needs to be "renewed day by day" (II Cor. 4:16). But from that small beginning, the work continues — God watering it "every moment" (Isa. 27:3) — and goes on to perfection; that is, till the heart is made perfectly clean and holy, which is not accomplished till death. God continues to work in His elect, "both to will and to do of His good pleasure," they being as completely dependent upon the Spirit's influence for every right exercise of the will after, as for the first. "Being confident of this very thing, that He which hath begun a good work within you *will finish it* until the day of Jesus Christ" (Phil. 1:6).

12

The Spirit Enlightening

By nature fallen man is in a state of darkness with respect unto God. Be he ever so wise, learned, and skillful in natural things, unto spiritual things he is blind. Not until we are renewed in the spirit of our minds by the Holy Spirit can we see things in God's light. But this is something which the world cannot endure to hear of, and when it be insisted upon, they will hotly deny the same. So did the Pharisees of Christ's day angrily ask, with pride and scorn, "Are we blind also?" (John 9:40), to which our Lord replied by affirming that their presumption of spiritual light and knowledge only aggravated their sin and condemnation (v. 41); unhesitatingly, He told the blind leaders of religion, that, notwithstanding all their boasting, they had never heard the Father's voice "at any time" (John 5:37).

There is a twofold spiritual darkness, outward and inward. The former, is the case with those who are without the gospel, until God sends the external means of grace to them: "The people which sat in darkness saw a great light" (Matt. 4:16). The latter, is the case with all, until God the Spirit performs a miracle of grace within the soul and quickens the dead into newness of life: "And the light shineth in darkness, and the darkness *comprehended it not*" (John 1:5). No matter how well we be acquainted with the letter of Scripture, no matter how sound and faithful be the preaching we sit under and the books we read, until the soul be Divinely quickened it has *no* spiritual discernment or experimental perception of Divine things. Until a man be born again, he *cannot* "see" the kingdom of God (John 3:3).

This inward darkness which fills the soul of the natural man is something far more dreadful than a mere intellectual ignorance of spiritual things. Ignorance is a negative thing, but this spiritual "darkness" is a positive thing — an energetic principle which is opposed to God. The "darkness" which rests upon the human soul gives the heart a bias toward evil, prejudicing it against holiness, fettering the will so that it never moves Godwards. Hence we read of "*the power of* darkness" (Col. 1:13): so great is its power, that all under it *love* darkness "rather than light" (John 3:19). Why is it that men have little difficulty in learning a business and are quick to discover how to make money and gratify their lusts, but are stupid and unteachable in the things of God? Why is it that men are so prone and ready to believe religious lies, and so averse to the Truth? None but the Spirit can deliver from this terrible darkness. Unless the Sun of righteousness arises upon us (Mal. 4:2), we are shut up in "the blackness of darkness forever" (Jude 13).

Because of the darkness which rests upon and reigns within his entire soul, the natural man can neither know, admire, love, adore, or serve the true God in a spiritual way. How can God appear infinitely lovely to one whose every bias of his heart prompts unto hatred of the Divine perfections? How can a corrupt soul be charmed with a Character which is the absolute opposite of its own? What fellowship can there be between darkness and Light; what concord can there be between sin and Holiness; what agreement between a carnal mind and Him against whom it is enmity? *False* notions of God may charm even an unregenerate heart, but none save a Divinely-quickened soul can spiritually know and love God. The true God can never appear as an infinitely amiable and lovely Being to one who is dead in trespasses and sins and completely under the dominion of the Devil.

"It is true that many a carnal man is ravished to think that God loves him, and will save him; but in this case, it is not the true character of God which charms the heart: it is not *God* that is loved. Strictly speaking, he can only love himself, and self-love is the source of all his affections. Or, if we call it 'love' to God, it is of no other kind than sinners feel to one another: 'for sinners also love those that love them' (Luke 6:32). The carnal Israelites gave the fullest proof of their disaffection to the Divine character (in the wilderness), as exhibited by God himself before their eyes, yet were once full of this same kind of 'love' at the side of the Red Sea" (Joseph Bellamy).

My reader, the mere fact that your heart is thrilled with a belief *that God loves you,* is no proof whatever that God's *true* character would suit your taste had you right notions of it. The Galatians loved Paul while they considered him as the instrument of their conversion; but on further acquaintance with him, they turned his enemies, for his character, rightly understood, was not at all congenial to them. If God is "of purer eyes than to behold evil" and cannot but look upon sin with infinite detestation (Hab. 1:13); if all those imaginations, affections, and actions which are so sweet to the taste of a carnal heart, are so infinitely odious in the eyes of God as to appear to Him worthy of the eternal pains of Hell, then it is utterly impossible for a carnal heart to see any beauty in the Divine character until it perceives its *own* character to be infinitely odious.

There is no spiritual love for the true God until self be hated. The one necessarily implies the other. I cannot look upon God as a lovely Being, without looking upon myself as infinitely vile and hateful. When Christ said to the Pharisees "Ye serpents, ye generation of vipers, how can ye escape the damnation of hell?" (Matt. 23:33). Those words determined *His* character in their eyes, and it implies a contradiction to suppose that Christ's character might appear lovely to them, *without* their own appearing odious, answerable to the import of His words. There was nothing in a Pharisee's heart to look upon his *own* character in such a detestable light, and therefore all the Saviour's words and works could only exasperate them. The more they knew of Christ, the more they hated Him; as it was natural to approve of their own character, so it was natural to condemn His.

The Pharisees were completely under the power of "darkness," and so is every human being till the Spirit quickens him into newness of life. If the fault was not in the Pharisees, it must have been in Christ; and for them to own it was *not* in Christ, was to acknowledge they *were* "vipers" and worthy of eternal destruction. They could not look upon Him as *lovely,* until they looked upon themselves as *infinitely odious;* but *that* was diametrically opposite to every bias of their hearts. Their old heart, therefore, *must* be taken away, and a new heart be given them, or they would never view things in a true light. "Except a man be born again, he *cannot see* the kingdom of God" (John 3:3).

"Darkness was upon the face of the deep" (Gen. 1:2) — fallen man's state by nature. "And the Spirit of God moved upon the face of the waters" (Gen. 1:2) — adumbrating His initial work of quickening. "And God said, Let there be light, and there was light" (Gen. 1:3). Natural light was the first thing produced in the making of the world, and spiritual light is the first thing given at the new creation: "But God, who commanded the light to shine out of darkness, hath shined in our hearts, to give the light of the knowledge of the glory of God in the face of Jesus Christ" (II Cor. 4:6). This Divine light shining into the mind, occasions *new apprehensions* of what is presented before it. Hitherto the favored subject of it had heard much about Christ: "by the hearing of the ear," but *now* his eye *seeth* Him (Job 42:5): he clearly apprehends a transcendent excellency in Him, an extreme necessity of Him, a complete sufficiency in Him.

"In thy light shall we see light" (Ps. 36:9). This is of what spiritual illumination consists. It is not a mere informing of the mind, or communication of intellectual knowledge, but an experimental and efficacious consciousness of the reality and nature of Divine and spiritual things. It is capacitating the mind to see sin in its real hideousness and heinousness, and to perceive "the *beauty* of holiness" (Ps. 96:9) so as to fall heartily in love with it. It is a spiritual light superadded to all the innate conceptions of the human mind, which is so pure and elevated that it is entirely beyond the power of the natural man to reach unto. It is something which the natural heart cannot even conceive of, but the knowledge of which is communicated by the Spirit's enlightenment (I Cor. 2:9, 10).

A dead man can neither see nor hear: true alike naturally and spiritually. There must be *life* before there can be perception: the Spirit must quicken the soul before it be capable of discerning and being affected by Divine things in a spiritual way. We say "in a *spiritual* way," because even a blind man may obtain an accurate idea of objects which his eye has never beheld; even so the unregenerate may acquire a natural knowledge of Divine things. But there is a far greater difference between an unregenerate man's knowledge of Divine things — no matter how orthodox and Scriptural be his views — and the knowledge possessed by the regenerate, than there is between a blind man's conception of a gorgeous sunset and what it would appear to him were sight communicated and he was permitted to gaze upon one for himself. It is not merely that the once-blind man would have a more correct conception of the Creator's handiwork, but *the effect produced upon him* would be such as words could not describe.

The Spirit's quickening of the dead soul into newness of life lays the foundation for all His consequent operations. Once the soul is made the recipient of spiritual life, all its faculties are capacitated unto spiritual exercises: the understanding to perceive spiritually, the conscience to feel spiritually, the affections to move spiritually, and the will to act spiritually. Originally, God formed man's body out of the dust of the ground, and it then existed as a complete organism, being endowed with a full set of organs and members; but it was not until God "breathed into" him the "breath of *life*" (Gen. 2:7) that Adam was able to move and act. In like manner, the soul of the natural man is vested with all these faculties which distinguish him from the beasts, but it is not until the Spirit *quickens* him that he is capable of discerning and being affected by Divine things in a spiritual way.

Once the Spirit has brought one of God's dead elect on to resurrection ground, He proceeds to illumine him. The light of God now shines upon him, and the previously-blind soul, having been Divinely empowered to see, is able to *receive* that light. The Spirit's enlightenment commences immediately after quickening, continues throughout the Christian's life, and is consummated in glory: "The path of the just is as the shining light, that shineth *more and more* unto the perfect day" (Prov. 4:18). As we stated in a previous article, this spiritual enlightenment is not a mere informing of the mind or communication of spiritual knowledge, but is an experimental and efficacious consciousness of the Truth. It is that which is spoken of in I John 2:20, 27, "But ye have *an unction* from the Holy One, and ye *know* all things. . . . But *the anointing* which ye have received of Him abideth in you, and ye need not that any man teach you."

By this "anointing" or enlightenment the quickened soul is enabled to perceive the true nature of sin — opposition against God, expressed in self-pleasing. By it he discerns the plague of his own heart, and finds that he is a moral leper, totally depraved, corrupt at the very center of his being. By it he detects the deceptions of Satan, which formerly made him believe that bitter was sweet, and sweet bitter. By it he apprehends the claims of God: that He is absolutely worthy of and infinitely entitled to be loved with *all* the heart, soul, and strength. By it he learns God's *way of* salvation: that the path of practical holiness is the only one which leads to Heaven. By it he beholds the perfect suitability and sufficiency of Christ: that He is the only One who could meet all God's claims upon him. By it he feels his own impotency unto all that is good, and presents himself as an empty vessel to be filled out of Christ's fulness.

A Divine light now shines into the quickened soul. Before, he was "darkness," but now is he "light in the Lord" (Eph. 5:8). He now perceives that those things in which he once found pleasure, are loathsome and damnable. His former conceits of the world and its enjoyments, he now sees to be erroneous and ensnaring, and apprehends that no real happiness or contentment is to be found in any of them. That holiness of heart and strictness of life which before he criticized as needless preciseness or puritanic extremeness, is now looked upon not only as absolutely necessary, but as most beautiful and blessed. Those moral and religious performances he once prided himself in and which he supposed merited the approval of God, he now regards as filthy rags. Those whom he once envied, he now pities. The company he once delighted in, now sickens and saddens him. His whole outlook is completely changed.

Divine illumination, then, is the Holy Spirit imparting to the quickened soul accurate and spiritual views of Divine things. To hear and *understand* is peculiar to the "good-ground" hearer (Matt. 13:23). None but the *real* "disciple" *knows* the Truth (John 8:31, 32). Even the gospel is "hid" from the lost (II Cor. 4:4). But when a quickened soul is enlightened by the Spirit, he has a feeling realization of the excellency of the Divine character, the spirituality of God's law, the exceeding sinfulness of sin in general and of his own vileness in particular. It is a Divine work which capacitates the soul to have real communion with God, to receive or take in spiritual objects, enjoy them, and live upon them. It is in this way that Christ is "formed *in* us" (Gal. 4:19). Thus, at times, the Christian is able to say:

"Thy shining grace can cheer
This dungeon where I dwell.
'Tis paradise when Thou art here,
If Thou depart, 'tis hell."

In closing, let us seek to define a little more definitely some of the characteristics of this Divine enlightenment. First, it is one which gives *certainty* to the soul. It enables its favored possessor to say "One thing I *know*, that, whereas I was blind, now I see" (John 9:25); and again, "I *know* whom I have believed, and am persuaded that He is able to keep that which I have committed unto Him against that day" (II Tim. 1:12). Later, Satan may be permitted to inject unbelieving and atheistical thoughts into his mind, but it is utterly impossible for him to *persuade* any quickened and enlightened soul that God has no existence, that Christ is a myth, that the Scriptures are a human invention. God in Christ has become a living reality to him, and the more He appears to the soul the sum of all excellency, the more is He loved.

Second, this Divine enlightenment is *transforming*. Herein it differs radically from a natural knowledge of Divine things, such as the unregenerate may acquire intellectually, but which produces no real and lasting impression upon the soul. A spiritual apprehension of Divine things is an efficacious one, stamping the image thereof upon the heart, and molding it into their likeness: "But we all, with open face beholding as in a glass the glory of the Lord, are *changed into the same image from glory to glory, by the Spirit of the Lord*" (II Cor. 3:18). Thus this spiritual illumination is vastly different from a mere notional and inoperative knowledge of Divine things. The Spirit's enlightenment enables the Christian to "*show forth* the praises of him who hath called him out of darkness into his marvellous light" (I Peter 2:9).

Third, this Divine enlightenment is a spiritual *preservative*. This is evident from I John 2:20, though to make it fully clear unto the reader an exposition of that verse in the light of its context is required. In I John 2:18 the apostle had mentioned the "many antichrists" (to be headed up in *the* antichrist), which were to characterize this final dispensation: seducers from the Faith were numerous even before the close of the first century A.D. In I John 2:19 reference is made to those who had fallen under the spell of these deceivers, and who had in consequence, apostatised from Christianity. In sharp contrast therefrom, the apostle affirms, "*But ye* have an unction from the Holy One, and ye know all things" (v. 20). Here was the Divine preservative: the Spirit's enlightenment ensured the saints from being captured by Satan's emissaries. Apostates had never been anointed by the Spirit; renewed souls are, and this safeguards them. The voice of a stranger "will they not follow" (John 10:5). It is not possible to fatally "decieve" one of God's elect (Matt. 24:24). The same precious truth is found again in I John 2:27: the Spirit indwells the Christian "forever" (John 14:16), hence the "anointing" he has received "*abideth* in him" and thus guarantees that he shall "abide in Christ."

13

The Spirit Convicting

THOUGH man in his natural estate is spiritually dead, that is, entirely destitute of any spark of *true holiness*, yet is he still a rational being and has a conscience by which he is capable of perceiving the difference between good and evil, and of discerning and feeling the force of moral obligation (Rom. 1:32; 2:15). By having his sins clearly brought to his mind and conscience, he can be made to realize what his true condition is as a transgressor of the holy law of God. This sight and sense of sin, when aroused from moral stupor, under the common operations of the Holy Spirit, is usually termed "conviction of sin"; and there can be no doubt that the views and feelings of men may be very clear and strong even while they are in an unregenerate state. Indeed, they do not differ in *kind* (though they do in degree), from what men will experience in the Day of Judgment, when their own consciences shall condemn them, and they shall stand guilty before God (Rom. 3:19).

But there is nothing whatever in the kind of conviction of sin mentioned above which has any tendency to *change the heart* or make it better. No matter how clear or how strong such convictions be, there is nothing in them which approximates to those that the Spirit produces in them whom He quickens. Such convictions may be accompanied by the most alarming apprehensions of danger, the imagination may be filled with the most frightful images of terror, and Hell may seem almost uncovered to their terrified view. Very often, under the sound of the faithful preaching of Eternal Punishment, some are aroused from their lethargy and feelings of the utmost terror are awakened in their souls, while there is no real *spiritual* conviction of the exceeding sinfulness of sin. On the other hand, there may be deep and permanent spiritual convictions where the passions and the imagination are very little excited.

Solemn is it to realize that there are now in Hell multitudes of men and women who on earth were visited with deep conviction of sin, whose awakened conscience made them conscious of their rebellion against their Maker, who were made to feel something of the reality of the everlasting burnings, and the *justice* of God meting out such punishment to those who spurn His authority and trample His laws beneath their feet. How solemn to realize that many of those who experienced such convictions were aroused to flee from the wrath to come, and became very zealous and diligent in seeking to escape the torments of Hell, and who under the instinct of self-preservation, took up with "religion"

as offering the desired means of escape. And how unspeakably solemn
to realize that many of those poor souls fell victims to men who spoke
"smooth things," assuring them that they were the objects of God's love,
and that nothing more was needed than to "receive Christ as your
personal Saviour." How unspeakably solemn, we say, that such souls
look to Christ merely as a *fire-escape*, who never — from a supernatural
work of the Spirit in their hearts — surrendered to Christ as *Lord*.

Does the reader say, Such statements as the above are most un-
settling, and if dwelt upon would destroy my peace. We answer, O
that it *may* please God to use these pages to disturb some who have
long enjoyed a *false* peace. Better far, dear reader, to be upset, yea,
searched and terrified *now*, than die in the *false* comfort produced by
Satan, and weep and wail for all eternity. If you are unwilling to be
tested and searched that is clear proof that you *lack* an "honest heart."
An "honest" heart desires to know the truth. An "honest" heart hates
pretense. An "honest" heart is fearful of being deceived. An "honest"
heart welcomes the most searching diagnosis of its condition. An "honest" heart is humble and tractable, not proud, presumptuous, and self-
confident. O how very few there are who *really* possess an "honest
heart."

The "honest" heart will say, If it is possible for an *un*-regenerate soul
to experience the convictions of sin you have depicted above, if one who
is dead in trespasses and sins may, nevertheless, have a vivid and frightful anticipation of the wrath to come, and engage in such sincere and
earnest endeavors to escape from the same, then how am I to ascertain
whether *my* convictions have been of a different kind from theirs? A
very pertinent and a most important question, dear friend. In answering
the same, let us first point out that, *soul terrors of Hell* are not, in themselves any proof of a supernatural work of God having been wrought
in the heart: it is not horrifying alarms of the everlasting burnings felt
in the heart which distinguishes the experience of quickened souls from
that of the unquickened; though such alarms *are* felt (in varying degrees) by both classes.

In His particular saving work of Conviction the Holy Spirit occupies
the soul more with *sin itself*, than with punishment. This is an exercise
of the mind to which fallen men are exceedingly averse: they had rather
meditate on almost anything than upon their own wickedness: neither
argument, entreaty, nor warning, will induce them so to do; nor will
Satan suffer one of his captives — till a mightier One comes and frees
him — to dwell upon sin, its nature, and vileness. No, he constantly
employs all his subtle arts to keep his victim from such occupation, and
his temptations and delusions are mixed with the natural darkness and
vanity of men's hearts so as to fortify them against convictions; so that
he may keep "his goods *in peace*" (Luke 11:21).

It is by the exceeding greatness of His power that the Holy Spirit
fixes the mind of a quickened and enlightened soul upon the due consideration of sin. Then it is that the subject of this experience cries,
"my sin is ever before me" (Ps. 51:3), for God now reproves him and

"sets his sins in order" before his eyes (Ps. 50:21). Now he is forced to behold them, no matter which way he turns himself. Feign would he cast them out of his thoughts, but he cannot: "the arrows" of God stick in his heart (Job 6:4), and he cannot get rid of them. He now realizes that his sins are more in number than the hairs of his head (Ps. 40:12). Now it is that "the grass withereth, the flower fadeth; *because the Spirit of the Lord bloweth upon it*" (Isa. 40:7).

The Spirit occupies the quickened and enlightened soul with the exceeding *sinfulness of sin*. He unmasks its evil character, and shows that all our self-pleasing and self-gratification was but a species of continued insubjection to God, of enmity against Him — against His person, His attributes, His government. The Spirit makes the convicted soul feel how grievously he has turned his back upon God (Jer. 32:33), lifted up his heel against Him and trampled His laws underfoot. The Spirit causes him to see and *feel* that he has forsaken the pure Fountain for the foul stream, preferred the filthy creature above the ineffable Creator, a base lust to the Lord of glory.

The Spirit convicts the quickened soul of the *multitude of his sins*. He realizes now that all his thoughts, desires and imaginations, are corrupt and perverse; conscience now accuses him of a thousand things which hitherto never occasioned him a pang. Under the Spirit's illumination the soul discovers that his very righteousnesses are as "filthy rags," for the motive which prompted even his best performances were unacceptable to Him who "weigheth the spirits." He now sees that his very prayers are polluted, through lack of pure affections prompting them. In short, he sees that "from the sole of the foot even unto the head there is no soundness in him; but wounds, and bruises, and putrifying sores" (Isa. 1:6).

The Spirit brings before the heart of the convicted one the *character and claims of God*. Sin is now viewed in the light of the Divine countenance, and he is made to feel what an evil and bitter thing it is to sin against God. The pure light of God, shining in the conscience over against vile darkness, horrifies the soul. The convicted one both sees and feels that God is holy and that he is completely unholy; that God is good and he is vile; that there is a most awful disparity between Him and us. He is made to feelingly cry, "How can such a corrupt wretch like me ever stand before such a holy God, whose majesty I have so often slighted?" Now it is that the soul is made to realize how it has treated God with the basest ingratitude, abusing His goodness, perverting His mercies, scorning his best Friend. Reader, has this been your experience?

In the last chapter we sought to point out something of the real and radical difference which exists between that conviction of sin which many of the unregenerate experience under the common operations of the Spirit, and that conviction of sin which follows His work of quickening and enlightening the hearts of God's elect. We pointed out that in the case of the latter, the conscience is occupied more with sin itself, than with its punishment; with the real *nature* of sin, as rebellion against

God; with its exceeding sinfulness, as enmity against God; with the multitude of sins, every action being polluted; with the character and claims of God, as showing the awful disparity there is between Him and us. Where the soul has not only been made to perceive, but also to *feel* — to have a heart-horror and anguish over the same — there is good reason to believe that the work of Divine grace has been begun in the soul.

Many other contrasts may be given between that conviction which issues from the common operations of the Spirit in the unregenerate and His special work in the regenerate. The convictions of the former are generally light and uncertain, and of short duration, they are sudden frights which soon subside; whereas those of the latter are deep, pungent and lasting, being *repeated* more or less frequently throughout life. The former work is more upon the emotions; the latter upon the judgment. The former diminishes in its clarity and efficacy, the latter grows in its intensity and power. The former arises from a consideration of God's justice; the latter are more intense when the heart is occupied with God's goodness. The former springs from a horrified sense of God's power; the latter issues from a reverent view of His holiness.

Unregenerate souls regard eternal punishment as the greatest evil, but the regenerate look upon *sin* as the worst thing there is. The former groan under conscience's presages of damnation; the latter mourn from a sense of their lack of holiness. The greatest longing of the one is to be assured of escape from the wrath to come; the supreme desire of the other is to be delivered from the burden of sin and conformed to the image of Christ. The former, while he may be convicted of many sins, still cherishes the conceit that he has some good points; the latter is painfully conscious that in his flesh there "dwelleth *no* good thing," and that his best performances are defiled. The former greedily snatches at comfort, for assurance and peace are now regarded as the highest good; the latter fears that he has sinned beyond the hope of forgiveness, and is slow to believe the glad tidings of God's grace. The convictions of the former harden, those of the latter melt and lead to submission. (The above two paragraphs are condensed from the *Puritan,* Charnock.)

The great instrument which the Holy Spirit uses in this special work of conviction is *the law,* for that is the one rule which God has given whereby we are to judge of the moral good or evil of actions, and conviction is nothing more or less than the formal impression of sin by the law upon the conscience. Clear proof of this is found in the passages that follow. "By the law is the knowledge of sin" (Rom. 3:20): it is the design of all laws to impress the understanding with what is to be done, and consequently with man's deviation from them, and so absolutely necessary is the law for this discernment, the apostle Paul declared, "I had not known sin but by the law" (Rom. 7:7) — its real nature, as opposition to God; its inveterate enmity against Him; its unsuspected lustings within. "The law entered that sin might abound" (Rom. 5:20): by deepening and widening the conviction of sin upon the conscience.

Now it is that God holds court in the human conscience and a reckoning is required of the sinner. God will no longer be trifled with, and sin can no longer be scoffed at. Thus a solemn trial begins: the law condemns, and the conscience is obliged to acknowledge its guilt. God appears as holy and just and good, but as awfully insulted, and with a dark frown upon His brow. The sinner is made to feel how dreadfully he has sinned against both the justice and goodness of God, and that his evil ways will no longer be tolerated. If the sinner was never solemn before, he is solemn now: fear and dismay fills his soul, death and destruction seem his inevitable and certain doom. When the Lord Almighty Himself appears in the court of conscience to vindicate His honor, the poor criminal trembles, sighs for mercy, but fears that pardoning mercy cannot justly be granted such a wretch.

Now it is that the Holy Spirit brings to light the hidden things of darkness. The whole past life is made to pass in review before the convicted soul. Now it is that he is made to experimentally realize that "the Word of God is quick and powerful, and sharper than any twoedged sword, piercing even to the dividing asunder of soul and spirit, and of the joints and marrow, and is a discerner of the thoughts and intents of the heart" (Heb. 4:12). Secret things are uncovered, forgotten deeds are recalled; sins of the eyes and sins of the lips, sins against God and sins against man, sins of commission and sins of omission, sins of ignorance and sins against light, are brought before the startled gaze of the enlightened understanding. Sin is now seen in all its excuselessness, filthiness, heinousness, and the soul is overwhelmed with horror and terror.

Whatever step the sinner now takes, all things appear to be against him; his guilt abounds, and his soul tremblingly sinks under it; until he feels obliged, in the presence of a heart-searching God, to sign his own death-warrant, or in other words, freely acknowledge that his condemnation is just. This is one of "the solemnities of Zion" (Isa. 32:20). As to whether this conviction is experienced at the beginning of the Christian life (which is often though not always the case), or at a later stage; as to how long the sinner remains under the spirit of bondage (Rom. 8:15); as to what extent he feels his wretchedness and ruin, or how deeply he sinks into the mire of despair, varies in different cases. God is absolute sovereign, and here too He acts as He sees good. But to this point every quickened soul is brought: to see the spirituality of God's law, to hear its condemning sentence, to feel his case is hopeless so far as all self-help is concerned.

Here is the fulfillment of Deuteronomy 30:6, "The Lord thy God will circumcise thine heart." The blessed Spirit uses the sharp knife of the Law, pierces the conscience, and convicts of the exceeding sinfulness of sin. By this Divine operation the hardness of the heart is removed, and the iniquity of it laid open, the plague and corruption of it discovered, and all is made naked to the soul's view. The sinner is now exceedingly pained over his rebellions against God, is broken down before Him, and is filled with shame, and loathes and abhors himself. "Ask

72 THE HOLY SPIRIT

ye now, and see whether a man doth travail with child: wherefore do I see every man with his hands on his loins, as a woman in travail, and all faces are turned into paleness? Alas! for that day is great, so that none is like it: it is even the time of Jacob's trouble; but he shall be saved out of it" (Jer. 30:6, 7) — such is, sooner or later, the experience of all God's quickened people.

Of ourselves we could never be truly convicted of our wretched state, for "the heart is deceitful above all things," and God alone can search it (Jer. 17:9). O the amazing grace of the Holy Spirit that *He* should rake into such foul and filthy hearts, amid the dunghill of putrid lusts, of enmity against God, of wickedness unspeakable! What a loathsome work it must be for the *Holy* Spirit to perform! If God the Son humbled Himself to enter the virgin's womb and be born in Bethlehem's manger, does not God the Spirit humble Himself to enter our depraved hearts and stir up their vile contents in order that we may be made conscious thereof! And if praise is due unto the One for the immeasurable humiliation which He endured on our behalf, is not distinctive praise equally due unto the Other for His amazing condescension in undertaking to convict us of *sin!* Thanksgiving, honor and glory for ever be ascribed unto Him who operates as "the Spirit of judgment" and "the Spirit of burning" (Isa. 4:4).

14

The Spirit Comforting

THE saving work of the Spirit in the heart of God's elect is a gradual and progressive one, conducting the soul step by step in the due method and order of the gospel to Christ. Where there is no self-condemnation and humiliation there can be no saving faith in the Lord Jesus: "Ye repented not afterward, *that ye might believe* Him" (Matt. 21:32) was His own express affirmation. It is the burdensome sense of sin which prepares the soul for the Saviour: "Come unto me all ye that labor and are *heavy laden*" (Matt. 11:28). Without conviction there can be no contrition and compunction: he that sees not his wickedness and guilt never mourns for it; he that feels not his filthiness and wretchedness never bewails it.

Never was there one tear of true repentance seen to drop from the eye of an unconvicted sinner. Equally true is it that without illumination there can be no conviction, for what is conviction but the application to the heart and conscience of the light which the Spirit has communicated to the mind and understanding: Acts 2:37. So, likewise, there can be no effectual illumination until there has been a Divine quickening, for a dead soul can neither see nor feel in a spiritual manner. In this order, then, the Spirit draws souls to Christ: He brings them from death unto life, shines into their minds, applies the light to their consciences by effectual conviction, wounds and breaks their hearts for sin in compunction, and then moves the will to embrace Christ in the way of faith for salvation.

These several steps are more distinctly discerned in some Christians than in others. They are more clearly to be traced in the *adult* convert, than in those who are brought to Christ in their youth. So, too, they are more easily perceived in such as are drawn to Him out of a state of *profaneness* than those who had the advantages of a pious education. Yet in them, too, after conversion, the exercises of their hearts — following a period of declension and backsliding — correspond thereto. But *in this order* the work of the Spirit is carried on, ordinarily, in all, however it may differ in point of clearness in the one and in the other. God is a God of order both in nature and in grace, though He be tied down to no hard and fast rules.

By His mighty work of illumination and conviction, with the humiliation which is wrought in the soul, the Spirit effectually weans the heart forever from the comfort, pleasure, satisfaction or joy that is to be found in sin, or in any creature, so that his soul can never be quiet and contented, happy or satisfied, till it finds the comfort of God in Christ.

Once the soul is made to feel that sin is the greatest of all evils, it sours for him the things of the world, he has lost his deep relish for them forever, and nothing is now so desirable unto him as the favor of God. All creature comforts have been everlastingly marred and spoiled, and unless he finds comfort in the Lord there is none for him anywhere.

"Therefore, behold, I will allure her, and bring her into the wilderness, and speak comfortably unto her" (Hos. 2:14). When God would win His church's heart to Him, what does He do? He brings her into *"the wilderness,"* that is, into a place which is barren or devoid of all comforts and delights; and then and there He "speaks comfort to her." Thus, too, He deals with the individual. A man who has been effectually convicted by the Spirit, is like a man condemned to die: what pleasure would be derived from the beautiful flowers as a murderer was led through a lovely garden to the place of execution! Nor can any Spirit-convicted sinner find contentment in anything till he be assured of the favor of Him whom he has so grievously offended. And none but *God* can "speak comfortably" to one so stricken.

Though God acts as a sovereign, and does not always shine in the same conspicuous way into the hearts of all His children, nevertheless, He brings them all to *see light* in His light: to know and feel that there can be no salvation for them but in the Lord alone. By the Spirit's powerful illuminating and convicting operations the sinner is made to realize the awful disparity there is between God and himself, so that he feebly cries "How can a poor wretch like me ever stand before such a holy God, whose righteous law I have broken in so many ways, and whose ineffable majesty I have so often insulted?" By that light the convicted soul, eventually, is made to feel its utter inability to help itself, or take one step toward the obtainment of holiness and happiness. By that light the quickened soul both sees and feels there can be no access to God, no acceptance with Him, save through the person and blood of Christ; but how to get at Christ the stricken soul knows not.

"And I will give her vineyards *from thence,* and the valley of Achor for a door of hope" (Hos. 2:15): such is the comforting promise of God to the one whom He proposes to "allure" or win unto Himself. First, He hedges up the sinner's way with "thorns" (Hos. 2:6), piercing his conscience with the sharp arrows of conviction. Second, He effectually battles all his attempts to drown his sorrows and find satisfaction again in his former lovers (v. 7). Third, He discovers his spiritual nakedness, and makes all his mirth to cease (vv. 10, 11). Fourth, He brings him into "the wilderness" (v. 14), making him feel his case is desperate indeed. And then, when all hope is gone, when the poor sinner feels there is no salvation for him, "a door *of hope*" is opened for him even in "the valley of Achor" or "trouble," and what is that "door of hope" but the *mercy* of God!

It is by putting into his mind thoughts of God's mercy that the Spirit supports the fainting heart of the convicted sinner from sinking beneath abject despair. Now it is that the blessed Spirit helps his infirmities with "groanings that cannot be uttered," and in the midst of a thousand fears he is moved to cry, "God be merciful *to me* a sinner." But "we must through *much* tribulation enter into the kingdom of God" (Acts 14:22) — true alike of the initial entrance into the kingdom of grace and the ultimate entrance into the kingdom of glory. The Lord heard the "groaning" of the poor Hebrews in Egypt, and "had respect unto them" (Exod. 2:23-25), nevertheless, He saw it was good for them to pass through yet sorer trials before He delivered them. The deliverer was presented to them and hope was kindled in their hearts (Exod. 4:29-31), yet the time appointed for their exodus from the house of bondage had not yet arrived.

And *why was* the deliverance of the Hebrews delayed after Moses had been made manifest before them? Why were they caused to experience yet more sorely the enmity of Pharaoh? Ah, the Lord would make them to feel their *impotency* as well as their wretchedness, and would exhibit more fully *His* power over the enemy. So it is very often (if not always) in the experience of the quickened soul. Satan is now permitted to rage against him with increased violence and fury (Zech. 3:1). The Devil accuses him of his innumerable iniquities, intensifies his remorse, seeks to persuade him that he has committed the unpardonable sin, assures him he has transgressed beyond all possibility of Divine mercy, and tells him his case is hopeless. And, my reader, were the poor sinner left to himself, the Devil would surely succeed in making him do as Judas did!

But, blessed be His name, the Holy Spirit does not desert the convicted soul, even in its darkest hour: He secretly upholds it and grants at least temporary respites, as the Lord did the Hebrews in Egypt. The poor Satan-harassed soul is enabled "*against* hope" to "believe *in* hope" (Rom. 4:18) and to cry, "Let the sighing of the prisoner come before Thee: according to the greatness of Thy power, preserve Thou those that are appointed to destruction" (Ps. 79:11). Yet before deliverance is actually experienced, before that peace which passeth all understanding is communicated to his heart, before the redemption "which is in Christ Jesus" becomes his conscious portion, the soul is made to feel its complete impotency to advance one step toward the same, that it is entirely dependent upon the Spirit for that faith which will enable him to "lay hold of Christ."

One would naturally suppose that the good news of a free Saviour and a full salvation would readily be embraced by a convicted sinner. One would think that, as soon as he heard the glad tidings, he could not forbear exclaiming, in a transport of joy, "This is the Saviour I want! *His* salvation is every way suited to my wretchedness. What can I desire more? Here will I rest." But as a matter of fact this is not always the case, yea, it is rarely so. Instead, the stricken sinner, like the Hebrews in Egypt after Moses had been made manifest before them, is left to groan under the lash of his merciless taskmasters. Yet this arises from no defect in God's gracious provision, nor because of any inadequacy in the salvation which the gospel presents, nor because of any distress in the sinner which the gospel is incapable of relieving; but because the workings of self-righteousness hinder the sinner from seeing the fullness and glory of Divine grace.

Strange as it may sound to those who have but a superficial and non-experimental acquaintance with God's truth, awakened souls are exceedingly backward from receiving comfort in the glorious gospel of Christ. They think they are utterly unworthy and unfit to come to Christ just as they are, in all their vileness and filthiness. They imagine some meetness must be wrought in them before they are qualified to believe the gospel, that there must be certain holy dispositions in their hearts before they are entitled to conclude that Christ will receive them. They fear that they are not sufficiently humbled under a sense of sin, that they have not a suitable abhorrence of it, that their repentance is not deep enough; that they must have fervent breathings after Christ and pantings after holiness, before they can be warranted to seek salvation with a well-grounded hope of success. All of which is the same thing as hugging the miseries of unbelief in order to obtain permission *to* believe.

Burdened with guilt and filled with terrifying apprehensions of eternal destruction, the convicted sinner, yet experimentally ignorant of the perfect righteousness which the gospel reveals for the justification of the ungodly, strives to obtain acceptance with God by his own labors, tears, and prayers. But as he becomes better acquainted with the high demands of the Law, the holiness of God, and the corruptions of his own heart, he reaches the point where he utterly despairs of being justified by his own strivings. "What *must* I do to be saved?" is now his agonized cry. Diligently searching God's Word for light and help, he discovers that "faith" is the all-important thing needed, but exactly what faith is, and how it is to be obtained, he is completely at a loss to ascertain. Well-meaning people, with more zeal than knowledge, urge him *to* "believe," which is the one thing above all others he desires to do, but finds himself utterly *unable* to perform.

If saving faith was nothing more than a mere mental assent to the contents of John 3:16, then any man could make himself a true believer whenever he pleased — the supernatural enablement of the Holy Spirit would be quite unnecessary. But *saving* faith is very much more than a mental assenting to the contents of any verse of Scripture; and when a soul has been *Divinely* quickened and awakened to its awful state by nature, it is made to realize that no creature-act of faith, no resting on the bare letter of a text by a "decision" of his own will, can bring pardon and peace. He is now made to realize that "faith" is *a Divine gift* (Eph. 2:8, 9), and not a creature work; that it is wrought by "the *operation of God*" (Col. 2:12), and not by the sinner himself. He is now made conscious of the fact that if ever he is to be saved, the same God who invites him to believe (Isa. 45:22), yea, who commands him to believe (I John 3:23), must also *impart* faith to him (Eph. 6:23).

Cannot you see, dear reader, that if a saving belief in Christ was the *easy* matter which the vast majority of preachers and evangelists of today *say* it is, that the work of the Spirit would be *quite unnecessary!* Ah, is there any wonder that the mighty power of the Spirit of God is now so rarely witnessed in Christendom? — He has been grieved, insulted, quenched, not only by the skepticism and worldliness of "Modernists," but equally so by the creature-exalting freewillism and self-ability of man to "receive Christ as his personal Saviour" of the "Fundamentalists"! ! Oh, how very few today *really* believe those clear and emphatic words of Christ, "No man *can* come to me, *except* the Father which hath sent me [by His Spirit] *draw* him" (John 6:44).

Ah, my reader, when GOD truly takes a soul in hand, He brings him to *the end of himself*. He not only convicts him of the worthlessness of his own *works*, but He convinces him of the impotency of his will. He not only strips him of the filthy rags of his own self-righteousness, but He empties him of all self-sufficiency. He not only enables him to perceive that there is "no good thing" in him (Rom. 7:18), but he also makes him feel he is "*without* strength" (Rom. 5:6). Instead of concluding that *he* is the man whom God will save, he now fears that he is the man who *must* be lost forever. He is now brought down into the very dust and made to feel that he is no more able to savingly believe in Christ than he can climb up to Heaven.

We are well aware that what has been said above differs radically from the current preaching of this decadent age; but we will appeal to the experience of the Christian reader. Suppose you had just suffered a heavy financial reverse and were at your wits' end to know how to make ends meet: bills are owing, your bank has closed, you look in vain for employment, and are filled with fears over future prospects. A preacher calls and rebukes your unbelief, bidding you lay hold of the promises of God. *That* is the very thing which you *desire* to do, but *can* you by an act of your own will? Or, a loved one is suddenly snatched from you: your heart is crushed, grief overwhelms you. A friend kindly bids you to "sorrow not even as others who have no hope." Are you able by a "personal decision" to throw off your anguish and rejoice in the Lord? Ah, my reader, if a mature Christian can only "cast all his care" upon the Lord *by the Holy Spirit's gracious enablement,* do you suppose that a poor sinner who is yet "in the gall of bitterness and the bond of iniquity" can lay hold of Christ by a mere act of his own will?

Just as to trust in the Lord with all his heart, to be anxious for nothing, to let the morrow take care of its own concerns, is the *desire* of every Christian, but "*how* to *perform* that which is good" he "finds *not*" (Rom. 7:18), until the Holy Spirit is pleased to graciously grant the needed enablement; so the one supreme yearning of the awakened and convicted sinner *is* to lay hold of Christ, but until the Spirit draws him *to* Christ, he finds he has no power to go out of himself, no ability to embrace what is proffered him in the gospel. The fact is, my reader, that the heart of a sinner is as naturally indisposed for loving and appropriating the things of God, as the wood which Elijah laid on the altar was to ignite, when he had poured so much water upon it, as not only to saturate the wood, but also to fill the trench round about it (I Kings 18:33): a *miracle* is required for the one as much as it was for the other.

The fact is that if souls were left to themselves — to their own "free will" — after they had been truly convicted of sin, *none* would ever savingly come to Christ! A further and distinct operation of the Spirit is still needed to actually "draw" the heart to close with Christ Himself. Were the sinner left to himself, he would sink in abject despair; he would fall victim to the malice of Satan. The Devil is far more powerful than we are, and never is his rage more stirred than when he fears he is about to lose one of his captives: *see* Mark 9:20. But blessed be His name, the Spirit does not desert the soul when His work is only half done: He who is "the Spirit of life" (Rom. 8:2) to quicken the dead, He who is "the Spirit of truth" (John 16:13) to instruct the ignorant, is also "the Spirit *of faith*" (II Cor. 4:13) to enable us to savingly believe.

And *how* does the Spirit work faith in the convicted sinner's heart? By effectually testifying to him of the sufficiency of Christ for his every need; by assuring him of the Saviour's readiness to receive the vilest who comes to Him. He effectually teaches him that no good qualifications need to be sought, no righteous acts performed, no penance endured in order to fit us for Christ. He reveals to the soul that conviction of sin, deep repentings, a sense of our utter helplessness, are *not* grounds of acceptance with Christ, but simply a consciousness of our spiritual wretchedness, rendering relief in a way of *grace* truly welcome. Repentance is needful not as inducing Christ to give, but as disposing us to receive. The Spirit moves us to come to Christ in the very character in which alone He receives sinners — as vile, ruined, lost. Thus, from start to finish "Salvation is *of the Lord*" (Jonah 2:9) — of the Father in ordaining it, of the Son in purchasing it, *of the Spirit* in applying it.

15

The Spirit Drawing

THERE seems to be a pressing need for a clear and full exposition of the Spirit's work of grace in the souls of God's people. It is a subject which occupies a place of considerable prominence in the Scriptures — far more so than many are aware — and yet, sad to say, it is grievously neglected by most preachers and writers of to-day; and, in consequence, the saints are to a large extent ignorant upon it.

The supernatural and special work of the Holy Spirit in the soul is that which distinguishes the regenerate from the unregenerate. The religion of the vast majority of people to-day consists merely in an outward show, having a name to live among men, but being spiritually dead toward God. Their religion comprises little more than bare speculative notions, merely knowing the Word in its letter; in an undue attachment to some man or party; in a blazing zeal which is not according to knowledge; or in censoriously contending for a certain order of things, despising all who do not rightly pronounce *their* particular shibboleths. The fear of God is not upon them, the love of God does not fill and rule their hearts, the power of God is not working in their souls — they are strangers to it. They have never been the favored subjects of the Spirit's quickening operation.

"No man can come to me, *except* the Father which hath sent me *draw* him; and I will raise him up at the last day" (John 6:44). This emphatic and man-humbling fact is almost universally ignored in Christendom to-day, and when it *is* pressed upon the notice of the average preacher or "church member," it is hotly denied and scornfully rejected. The cry is at once raised, "If that were true, then man is nothing more than a machine, and all preaching is useless. If people are *unable* to come to Christ by an act of their own will, then evangelistic effort is needless, worthless." No effort is made to understand the meaning of those words of our Lord: they clash with modern thought, they rile the proud flesh, so they are summarily condemned and dismissed. No wonder the Holy Spirit is now "quenched" in so many places, and that *His* saving power is so rarely in evidence.

With others the supernatural agency of the Spirit is effectually shut out by the belief that *Truth will prevail*: that if the Word of God be faithfully preached, souls *will be* truly saved. Far be it from us to undervalue the Truth, or cast the slightest reflection on the living Word of God; yet modern ideas and present conditions demand that we plainly point out that *it is not the truth,* the Scriptures, the gospel, which

79

renews the soul; but instead, the power and operations of *the Holy Spirit.* "You may teach a man the holiest of truths, and yet leave him a wretched man. Many who learn in childhood that 'God is love,' live disregarding, and die blaspheming, God. Thousands who are carefully taught 'Believe on the Lord Jesus Christ, and thou shalt be saved,' neglect so great salvation all their days. Some of the most wicked and miserable beings that walk the earth are men into whose consciences, when yet youthful and unsophisticated, the truth was carefully instilled.

"Unmindful of this, and not considering the danger of diverting faith *from the power to the instrument,* however beautiful and perfect the instrument may be, many good men, by a culpable inadvertence, constantly speak as if the Truth had an inherent ascendancy over man, and would certainly prevail when justly presented. We have heard this done till we have been ready to ask, 'Do they take men for angels, that mere Truth is to captivate them so certainly?' ay, and even to ask 'Have they ever heard whether there be any Holy Spirit?'

"The belief that Truth is mighty, and *by reason of its might* must prevail, is equally fallacious in the abstract, as it is opposed to the facts of human history, and to the Word of God. We should take the maxim, the Truth must prevail, as perfectly sound, did you only give us a community of angels on whom to try the Truth. With every intellect clear and every heart upright, doubtless Truth would soon be discerned, and, when discerned, cordially embraced. But, Truth, in descending among us, does not come among friends. The human heart offers ground whereon it meets Truth at an immeasurable disadvantage. Passions, habits, interests, ay, nature itself, lean to the side of error; and though the judgment may assent to the Truth, which, however, is not always the case, still error may gain a conquest only the more notable because of this impediment. Truth is mighty in pure natures, error in depraved ones.

"Do they who know human nature best, when they have a political object to carry, trust most of all to the power of truth over a constituency, or would they not have far more confidence in corruption and revelry? The whole history of man is a melancholy reproof to those who mouth about the mightiness of Truth. 'But,' they say 'Truth will prevail in the long run.' Yes, blessed be God, It will; but not because of *its own power* over human nature, but because *the Spirit* will be poured out from on high, opening blind eyes and unstopping deaf ears.

"The sacred writings, while ever leaving us to regard the Truth as the one instrument of the sinner's conversion and the believer's sanctification, are very far from proclaiming its power over human nature, merely because it is Truth. On the contrary, they often show us that this very fact will enlist the passions of mankind *against it,* and awaken enmity instead of approbation. We are ever pointed *beyond the Truth* to HIM who is the Source and Giver of Truth; and, though we had apostles to minister the Gospel, are ever lead not to deem it enough that it should be 'in word only, but in *demonstration of the Spirit and in power*'" (Wm. Arthur, 1859).

John the Baptist came preaching "the baptism of repentance for the remission of sins" (Mark 1:4), but by what, or rather *Whose* power was it, that repentance was wrought in the hearts of his hearers? It was that of the Holy Spirit! Of old it was said, "He shall go before Him in the spirit and power of Elijah" (Luke 1:17), Now the "spirit and power of Elijah" was that of *the Holy Spirit,* as is clear from Luke 1:15, "he [the Baptist] shall be filled with the Holy Spirit." Similarly, it should be duly observed that, when Christ commissioned His apostles to preach in His name among all nations (Luke 24:47), that He added, "Behold, I send the promise of my Father upon you: but tarry ye in the city of Jerusalem, *until ye be endued with power from on high*" (v. 49). Why was the latter annexed to the former, and prefaced with a "Behold" but to teach them (and us) that there could be no saving repentance produced by their preaching, except by the mighty operations of the third Person of the Godhead?

None will ever be *drawn to Christ,* savingly, by mere preaching; no, not by the most faithful and Scriptural preaching: there must first be the supernatural operations of the Spirit to open the sinner's heart *to receive* the message! And how can we expect the Spirit to work among us while *He* is so slighted, while our confidence is not in Him, but in our preaching! How can we expect Him to work miracles in our midst, while there is no humble, earnest, and trustful *praying* for His gracious activities! Most of us are in such a ferverish rush to "win souls," to do "personal work," preach, that we have no time for definite, reverent, importunate crying unto the Lord for His Spirit to go before us and prepare the soil for the Seed. Hence it is that the converts we make, are but "*man* made," and their subsequent lives make it only too apparent unto those who have eyes to see, that the *Holy Spirit* does not indwell them, and produce *His* fruits through them. O brethren, join the writer, in contritely owning to God your sinful failure to give the Spirit His proper place.

The renewed heart is moved and melted when it contemplates the holy Saviour having our iniquities imputed to Him and bearing "our sins in His own body on the tree." But how rarely is it considered, that it is little less wonderful for the *Holy Spirit* to exercise Himself with *our sins* and hold them up to the eyes of our understanding. Yet this is precisely what He does: He rakes in our foul hearts and makes us conscious of what a stench they are in the nostrils of an infinitely pure God. He brings to light and to sight the hidden and hideous things of darkness and convicts us of our vile and lost condition. He opens to our view the "horrible pit" in which by nature we lie, and makes us to realize that we are fit for nothing but the everlasting burnings. O how truly marvellous that the Third Person of the Godhead should condescend to stoop to *such* a work as that!

"No man can come to me, except the Father which hath sent me *draw* him" (John 6:44). No sinner ever knocks (Matt. 7:7) at His door for mercy, by earnest and importunate prayer, until Christ has first knocked (Rev. 3:20) at his door by the operations of the Holy Spirit.

As the Christian now loves God "because *he first* loved" him (I John 4:19), so he sought Christ, because Christ first sought him (Luke 19: 10). Before Christ seeks us, we are well content to lie fast asleep in the Devil's arms, and therefore does the Lord say, "I am found of them that *sought me not*" (Isa. 65:1). When the Spirit first applies the Word of Conviction, He finds the souls of all men as the angel found the world in Zechariah 1:11; "all the earth sitteth still, and is at rest." What a strange silence and midnight stillness there is among the unsaved! "There is *none* that seeketh after God" (Rom. 3:11).

It is because of failure to perceive the dreadful condition in which the natural man lies, that any difficulty is experienced in seeing the imperative need for the Spirit's *drawing power* if he is to be brought out of it. The natural man is so completely enslaved by sin and enchained by Satan, that he is unable to take the first step toward Christ. He is so bent on having his own way and so averse to pleasing God, he is so in love with the things of this world and so out of love with holiness, that nothing short of Omnipotence can produce a radical *change of heart* in him, so that he will come to hate the things he naturally loved, and love what he previously hated. The Spirit's "drawing" is the freeing of the mind, the affections, and the will, from the reigning power of depravity; it is His emancipating of the soul from the dominion of sin and Satan.

Prior to that deliverance, when the requirements of God are pressed upon the sinner, he in every case, *rejects* them. It is not that he is averse from being saved from Hell — for none *desire* to go there — but that he is unwilling to *"forsake"* (Prov. 28:13; Isa. 55:7) his idols — the things which hold the first place in his affections and interests. This is clearly brought out in our Lord's parable of "The Great Supper." When the call went forth, "Come for all things are now ready," we are told, "they *all* with one consent began to make excuse" (Luke 14:18). The meaning of that term "excuse" is explained in what immediately follows: they preferred other things; they were unwilling to *deny* themselves; they would not relinquish the competitive objects — the things of time and sense ("a piece of ground," "oxen," "a wife") were their all-absorbing concerns.

Had nothing more been done by "the Servant" — in this parable, the Holy Spirit — all had *continued* to "make excuse" unto the end: that is, all had gone on cherishing their idols, and turning a deaf ear to the holy claims of God. But the Servant was commissioned to "bring in hither" (v. 21), yea, to *"compel* them to come in" (v. 23): it is a holy compulsion and not physical force which is there in view — the melting of the hard heart, the wooing and winning of the soul to Christ, the bestowing of faith, the imparting of a new nature, so that the hitherto despised One is now desired and sought after: "I *drew* them with cords of a man [using means and motives suited to a rational nature] with *bands of love*" (Hos. 11:4). And again, God says of His people "with *loving-kindness have I drawn thee*" (Jer. 31:10).

Even after the elect have been quickened by the Spirit, a further and distinct work of His is needed to *draw* their hearts to actually close with Christ. The work of *faith* is equally His operation, and therefore is it said "we having *received* [not "exercised!"] the *same* Spirit of faith" (II Cor. 4:13) i.e., "the same" as Abraham, David, and the other Old Testament saints received, as the remainder of the verse indicates. Hence, observe the careful linking together in Acts 6:5, where of Stephen we read that, he was "a man full of faith and of the Holy Spirit;" full of "faith," *because* filled with the Spirit. So of Barnabas we are told, "he was a good man, and full of the Holy Spirit and of faith" (Acts 11:24). Seek to realize more definitely, Christian reader, that spiritual faith is the gift of the Spirit, and that *He* is to be thanked and praised for it. Equally true is it that we are now entirely dependent upon Him to call it into exercise and act.

The Divine Drawer is unto God's people "the Spirit of grace and of supplications" (Zech. 12:10): of *grace*, in making to their smitten consciences and exercised hearts a wondrous discovery of the rich grace of God unto penitent rebels; of *supplications*, in moving them to act as a man fleeing for his life, to seek after Divine mercy. Then it is He leads the trembling soul to Calvary, "before whose eyes Jesus Christ" is now "evidently [plainly] set forth crucified" (Gal. 3:1), beholding the Saviour (by faith) bleeding for and making atonement for his sins — more vividly and heart-affectingly than all the angels in heaven could impart; and hence it follows in Zechariah 12:10 "they shall *look upon me* whom they have pierced." Then it is that their eyes are opened to see that which was hitherto hidden from them, namely the "Fountain opened . . . for sin and for uncleanness" (Zech. 13:1), into which they are now moved to plunge for cleansing.

Yes, that precious "Fountain" has to be *opened to us,* or, experimentally, we discern it not. Like poor Hagar, ready to perish from thirst, knowing not that relief was near to hand, we — convicted of our fearful sins, groaning under the anguish of our lost condition — were ready to despair. But as God opened Hagar's eyes *to see* the "well," or "fountain" (Gen. 21:19), so the Spirit of God now opens the understanding of the awakened soul to see Christ, His precious blood, His all-sufficient righteousness. But more; when the soul is brought to see the Fountain or Well, he discovers it is "deep" and that he has "nothing to draw with" (John 4:11). And though he looks in it with a longing eye, he cannot reach unto it, so as to wash in it. He finds himself like the "impotent man" of John 5, desirous of "stepping in," but utterly without strength to do so. Then it is *the Holy Spirit* applies the atonement, "sprinkling the conscience" (Heb. 10:23), effectually granting a realization of its *cleansing* efficacy (see Acts 15:8, 9; I Cor. 6:11 — it is Christ's blood, but the Spirit must apply it.

And when the awakened and convicted soul has been brought to Christ for cleansing and righteousness, *who is it* that brings him to the Father, to be justified by Him? Who is it that bestows freedom of access unto him from whom the sinner had long been absent in the "far country"? Ephesians 2:18 tell us, "for through Him [Christ, the Mediator] we both [regenerated Jews and Gentiles, O.T. and N.T. saints alike] have access *by one Spirit* unto the Father." Ah, dear reader, it was naught but the secret and invincible operations of the blessed Spirit which caused you — a wandering prodigal — to seek out Him, whom before you dreaded as a "consuming fire." Yes, it was none other than the third Person of the Holy Trinity who drew you with the bands of love, and taught you to call God "Father" (Rom. 8:15)!

16

The Spirit Working Faith

THE principal bond of union between Christ and His people is the Holy Spirit; but as the union is mutual, something is necessary on our part to complete it, and this is faith. Hence, Christ is said to dwell in our hearts "by faith" (Eph. 3:17). Yet, let it be said emphatically, the faith which unites to Christ and saves the soul is not merely a natural act of the mind assenting to the gospel, as it assents to any other truth upon reliable testimony, but is a supernatural act, an effect produced by the power of the Spirit of grace, and is such a persuasion of the truth concerning the Saviour as calls forth exercises suited to its Object. The soul being quickened and made alive spiritually, begins to act spiritually, "The soul is the life of the body, faith is the life of the soul, and Christ is the life of faith" (John Flavell).

It is a great mistake to define Scriptural terms according to the narrow scope and meaning which they have in common speech. In ordinary conversation, "faith" signifies credence or the assent of the mind unto some testimony. But in God's word, so far from faith — saving faith, we mean — being merely a natural act of the mind, it includes the concurrence of the will and an action of the affections: it is "with the heart," and not with the head, "that man believeth unto righteousness" (Rom. 10:10). Saving faith is a cordial approbation of Christ, an acceptance of Him in His entire character as Prophet, Priest, and King; it is entering into covenant with Him, receiving Him as Lord and Saviour. When this is understood, it will appear to be a fit instrument for completing our union with Christ, for the union is thus formed by *mutual* consent.

Were people to perceive more clearly the implications and the precise character of saving faith, they would be the more readily convinced that it is "the gift of God," an effect or fruit of the Spirit's operations on the heart. Saving faith is a coming to Christ, and coming to Christ necessarily presupposes a forsaking of all that stands opposed to Him. It has been rightly said that "true faith includes in it the renunciation of the flesh as well as the reception of the Saviour; true faith admires the precepts of holiness as well as the glory of the Saviour" (J. H. Thornwell, 1850). Not until these facts are recognised, enlarged upon, and emphasized by present-day preachers is there any real likelihood of the effectual exposure of the utter inadequacy of that *natural* "faith" which is all that thousands of empty professors possess.

"Now he which *stablisheth* us with you in Christ, and hath anointed us, is God" (II Cor. 1:21). None but God (by His Spirit) can "stablish" the soul in all its parts — the understanding, the conscience, the affections, the will. The ground and reason why the Christian believes the Holy Scriptures to be the Word of God is neither the testimony nor the authority of the church (as Rome erroneously teaches), but rather the testimony and power of the Holy Spirit. Men may present arguments which will so convince the intellect as to cause a consent, but establish the soul and conscience so as to assure the heart of the Divine authorship of the Bible, they cannot. A spiritual faith must be imparted before the Word is made, *in a spiritual way*, its foundation and warrant.

The same blessed Spirit who moved holy men of old to write the Word of God, works in the regenerate a faith which nothing can shatter. That Word *is* the Word of God. The stablishing argument is by the power of God's spirit, who causes the quickened soul to see such a Divine Majesty shining forth in the Scriptures that the heart is established in this first principle. The renewed soul is made to feel that there is such a pungency in that Word that it must be Divine. No born-again soul needs any labored argument to convince him of the Divine inspiration of the Scriptures: he has *proof within himself* of their Heavenly origin. Faith wrought in the heart by the power of the Spirit is that which satisfies its possessor that the Scriptures are none other than the Word of the living God.

Not only does the blessed Spirit work faith in the written Word — establishing the renewed heart in its Divine veracity and authority — but He also produces faith in the personal Word, the Lord Jesus Christ. The imperative necessity for this distinct operation of His was briefly shown in a previous article upon "The Spirit Comforting," but a further word thereon will not here be out of place. When the soul has been Divinely awakened and convicted of sin, it is brought to realize and feel its depravity and vileness, its awful guilt and criminality, its utter unfitness to approach a holy God. It is emptied of self-righteousness and self-esteem, and is brought into the dust of self-abasement and self-condemnation. Dark indeed is the cloud which now hangs over it; hope is completely abandoned, and despair fills the heart. The painful consciousness that Divine goodness has been abused, Divine law trodden under foot, and Divine patience trifled with, excludes the expectation of any mercy.

When the soul has sunk into the mire of despair, no human power is sufficient to lift it out and set it upon the Rock. Now that the renewed sinner perceives that not only are all his past actions transgressions of God's law, but that his very heart is desperately wicked — polluting his very prayers and tears of contrition — he feels that he must inevitably perish. If he hears the gospel, he tells himself that its glad tidings are not for such an abandoned wretch as he; if he reads the Word he is assured that only its fearful denunciations and woes are *his* legitimate portion. If godly friends remind him that Christ came to seek and to save that which was lost, he supposes they are ignorant of the extremities of his case: should they urge him to believe or cast himself on the mercy of God in Christ, they do but mock him in his misery, for he now discovers that he can no more do this of himself than he can grasp the sun in his hands. All self-help, all human aid, is useless.

In those in whom the Spirit works faith, He first blows down the building of human pretensions, demolishes the walls which were built with the untempered mortar of man's own righteousness, and destroys the foundations which were laid in self-flattery and natural sufficiency, so that they are entirely shut up to Christ and God's *free grace*. Once awakened, instead of fondly imagining I am the man whom God will save, I am now convinced that I am the one who must be damned. So far from concluding I have any ability to even help save myself, I now *know* that I am "without strength" and no more able to receive Christ as my Lord and Saviour than I can climb up to heaven. Evident it is, then, that a mighty supernatural power is needed if I am to come to Him who "justifieth the ungodly." None but the all-mighty Spirit can lift a stricken soul out of the gulf of despair and enable him to believe to the saving of his soul.

To God the Holy Spirit be the glory of His sovereign grace in working faith in the heart of the writer and of each Christian reader. Thou hast attained unto peace and joy in believing, but hast thou thanked that peace-bringer — "the Holy Spirit" (Rom. 15:13)? All that "joy unspeakable and full of glory" (I Peter 1:8) and that peace which "passeth all understanding" (Phil. 4:7), to whom is it ascribed? The *Holy Spirit*. It is particularly appropriated to Him: "peace and joy *in the Holy Spirit*" (Rom. 14:17 and cf. I Thess. 1:6). Then render unto Him the praise which is His due.

17

The Spirit Uniting to Christ

ONE of the principal ends or designs of the gospel is the communication to God's elect of those benefits or blessings which are in the Redeemer; but the communication of benefits necessarily implies communion, and all communion as necessarily presupposes union with His person. Can I be rich with another man's money, or advanced by another man's honors? Yes, if that other be my surety, or my husband. Peter could not be justified by the righteousness of Paul, but both could be justified by the righteousness of Christ imputed to them, seeing they are both knit to one common Head. Principal and surety are one in obligation and construction of law. Head and members are one body; branch and stock are one tree, and a slip will live by the sap of another stock when once engrafted into it. We must, then, be *united* to Christ before we can receive any benefits *from* Him.

Now there are two kinds of union between Christ and His people: a judicial and a vital, or a legal and a spiritual. The first is that union which was made by God between the Redeemer and the redeemed when He was appointed their federal Head. It was a union in law, in consequence of which He represented them and was responsible for them, the benefits of His transactions redounding to them. It may be illustrated by the case of suretyship among men: a relation is formed between the surety and that person for whom he engages, by which the two are thus far considered as one — the surety being liable for the debt which the other has contracted, and his payment is held as the payment of the debtor, who is thereby absolved from all obligation to the creditor. A similar connection is established between Christ and those who had been given to Him by the Father.

But something further was necessary in order to actually enjoy the benefits procured by Christ's representation. God, on whose sovereign will the whole economy of grace is founded, had determined not only that His Son should sustain the character of their Surety, but that there should be a vital, as well as legal, relation between them, as the foundation of communion with Him in all the blessings of His purchase. It was His good pleasure that as they were one in law, they should also be one spiritually, that Christ's merit and grace might not only be imputed, but also imparted to them, as the holy oil poured on the head of Aaron descended to the skirt of his garments. It is this latter, this vital and spiritual union, which the Christian has with Christ, that we now purpose to discuss.

88

The preaching of the gospel by the ambassadors of the Lord Jesus is the instrument appointed for the reconciling or bringing home of sinners to God in Christ. This is clear from Romans 10:14 and I Corinthians 1:21, and more particularly from II Corinthians 5:20, "Now then we are ambassadors for Christ, as though God did beseech by us: we pray you in Christ's stead, be ye reconciled to God." But, as we have pointed out in previous papers, the mere preaching of the Word — no matter how faithfully — will never bring a single rebel to the feet of Christ in penitence, confidence, and allegiance. No, for *that* there must be the special and supernatural workings of the Holy Spirit: only thus are any actually drawn to Christ to receive Him as Lord and Saviour: and only as this fact is carefully kept prominently before us does the blessed Spirit have His true place in our hearts and minds.

"Thy people shall be willing in the day of Thy power" (Ps. 110:3). It is by moral suasion — "with cords of a man" (Hos. 11:4) — that the Holy Spirit draws men to Christ. Yet by moral persuasion we must not understand a simple and bare proposal or tender of Christ, leaving it still to the sinner's choice whether he will comply with it or no. For though God does not force the will contrary to its nature, nevertheless He puts forth a real efficacy when He "draws," which consists of an immediate operation of the Spirit upon the heart and will, whereby its native rebellion and reluctance is removed, and from a state of unwillingness the sinner is made willing to come to Christ. This is clear from Ephesians 1:19, 20 which we quote below.

"And what is the exceeding greatness of his power to usward, who believe according to the working of His mighty power which He wrought in Christ when he raised him from the dead, and set him at his own right hand in the heavenlies." Here is much more than a mere proposal made to the will: there is the putting forth of Divine power, great power, yea the exceeding greatness of God's power; and this power hath a sure and certain efficacy ascribed to it: God works upon the hearts and wills of His people "according to the working of his mighty power which he *wrought in Christ* when he raised him from the dead" — both are *miracles* of Divine might. Thus God fulfils "all the good pleasure of his goodness, and the work of faith *with power*" (II Thess. 1:11). Unless the "arm of the Lord" is revealed (Isa. 53:1) none believe His "report."

Spiritual union with Christ, then, is effected both by the *external* preaching of the gospel and the *internal* "drawing" of the Father. Let us now take note of the *bands* by which Christ and the believer are knit together. These bands are two in number, being the Holy Spirit on Christ's part, and faith on our part. The Spirit on Christ's part, is His quickening us with spiritual life, whereby Christ first takes hold of us. Faith on our part, when thus quickened, is that whereby we take hold of Christ. We must first be "apprehended" (laid hold of) by Christ, before we can apprehend Him (Phil. 3:12). No vital act of faith can be exercised till a vital principle be first communicated to us. Thus, Christ is in the believer by His Spirit; the believer is in Christ by faith.

Christ is in the believer by inhabitation; the believer is in Christ by implantation (Rom. 6:3-5). Christ is in the believer as the head is in the body; we are in Christ as the members are in the head. "He that is joined unto the Lord is one spirit" with Him (I Cor. 6:17). The same Spirit which is in the Head is in the members of His mystical body, a vital union being effected between them. Christ is in heaven, we upon earth, but the Spirit being omnipresent is the connecting link. "For by one Spirit are we all baptized into one body, whether we be Jews or Gentiles" (I Cor. 12:13) — what could be plainer than that? "Hereby know we that we dwell in him, and he in us, because he hath given us of his Spirit" (I John 4:13). Thus, Christ is unto His people a Head not only of government, but also of *influence*. Though the ties which connect the Redeemer and the redeemed are spiritual and invisible, yet are they so real and intimate that He lives in them and they live in Him, for "the Spirit of life *which is in Christ Jesus* hath made me free from the law of sin and death" (Rom. 8:2).

"But if the Spirit of him that raised up Jesus from the dead dwell in you, he that raised up Christ from the dead shall also quicken your mortal bodies by his Spirit that dwelleth in you" (Rom. 8:11), and this, because the Spirit is the bond of union between us and Christ. Because there is the same Spirit in the Head and in His members, He will therefore work the same effects in Him and in us. If the Head rise, the members will follow after, for they are appointed to be conformed unto Him (Rom. 8:29) — in obedience and suffering now, in happiness and glory hereafter. Christ was raised by the Spirit of holiness (Rom. 1:4), and so shall we be — the earnest of which we have already received when brought from death unto life.

18

The Spirit Indwelling

"BUT ye are not in the flesh, but in the Spirit, if so be that the Spirit of God dwell in you. Now if any man have not the Spirit of Christ, he is none of his" (Rom. 8:9). The possession of the Holy Spirit is the distinguishing mark of a Christian, for to be without the Spirit is proof positive that we are out of Christ — "none of his": fearful words! And, my reader, if we are not Christ's, whose are we? The answer must be, *The devil's*, for there is no third possessor of men. In the past, all of us were subjects of the kingdom of darkness, the slaves of Satan, the heirs of wrath; and the great questions which each one of us needs to accurately answer are, Have I been taken out of that terrible position? Have I been translated into the kingdom of God's dear Son, made an heir of God, and become indwelt by His Holy Spirit?

Observe that the Spirit and Christ go together: if we have Christ for our Redeemer, then we have the Holy Spirit for our Indweller; but if we have not the Spirit, we are not Christ's. We may be members of His visible "church," we may be externally united to Him by association with his people, but unless we are partakers of that vital union which arises from the indwelling of the Spirit, we are His only by name. "The Spirit *visits* many who are unregenerate, with His motions, which they resist and quench; but in all that are sanctified He *dwells*: there He resides and rules. He is there as a man at his own house, where he is constant and welcome, and has the dominion. Shall we put this question to our hearts, Who dwells, who rules, who keeps house here? Which interest has the ascendant?" (M. Henry).

The Spirit belongs to Christ (Heb. 1:9; Rev. 3:1) and proceeds from Him (John 1:23; 15:26; Luke 24:49). The Spirit is sent by Christ as Mediator (Acts 2:33). He is given to God's people in consequence of Christ's having redeemed them from the curse of the law (Gal. 3:13, 14). We have nothing but what we have in and from the Son. The Spirit is given to Christ immediately, to us derivatively. He dwells in Christ by radication, in us by operation. Therefore is the Spirit called "the Spirit of Christ" (Rom. 8:9) and "the Spirit of his Son" (Gal. 4:6); and so it is Christ who "liveth in" us (Gal. 2:30). Christ is the great Fountain of the waters of life, and from Him proceeds every gift and grace. It is our glorious Head who communicates or sends from Himself that Spirit who quickens, sanctifies, and preserves His people.

What high valuation we set upon the blessed person and work of the Holy Spirit, when we learn that He is the gift, yea the dying legacy which Christ bequeathed unto His disciples to supply His absence. "How would some rejoice if they could possess any relic of anything that belonged unto our Saviour in the days of His flesh, though of no use or benefit unto them. Yea, how great a part of men, called Christians, do boast in some pretended parcels of the tree whereon He suffered. Love abused by superstition lies at the bottom of this vanity, for they would embrace anything left them by their dying Saviour. But He left them no such things, nor did ever bless and sanctify them unto any holy or sacred ends; and therefore hath the abuse of them been punished with blindness and idolatry. But this *is* openly testified unto in the gospel: when His heart was overflowing with love unto His disciples and care for them, when He took a holy prospect of what would be their condition, work, and temptations in the world, and thereon made provision of all that they could stand in need of, He promised to leave and give unto them *His Holy Spirit* to abide with them forever" (John Owen).

Plain and express are the declarations of Holy Writ on this wondrous and glorious subject. "Know ye not that ye are the temple of God, and that the Spirit of God *dwelleth in* you?" (I Cor. 3:16). "Because ye are sons, God hath sent forth the Spirit of his Son into your hearts, crying, Abba, Father" (Gal. 4:6). "Observe where the Spirit is said to dwell: not in the understanding — the fatal error of many — but in the heart. Most certainly He enlightens the understanding with the truth, but He does not rest there. He makes His way to, and takes up His abode in, the renewed and sanctified *heart*. There He sheds abroad the love of God. There He inspires the cry of 'Abba, Father.' And be that cry ever so faint, it yet is the breathing of the indwelling Spirit, and meets a response in the heart of God.

"How affecting are Paul's words to Timothy, 'That good thing which was committed unto thee *by the Holy Spirit which dwellth in us*' (II Tim. 1:14). Timothy had no spiritual strength of his own. The apostle therefore reminds him of a truth which, in his conscious weakness, was well calculated to cheer his heart and encourage him to cultivate and use for Christ's glory the spiritual gift bestowed upon him, namely, the power of the indwelling Spirit. That self-same Spirit dwells in all true believers. Let it constrain us to stir up our spiritual gifts and graces — so prone to slumber and become inert — and employ them more devotedly for the Lord" (O. Winslow).

> "Dear Lord, and shall Thy Spirit rest,
>   In such a heart as mine?
> Unworthy dwelling! glorious Guest
>   Favor astonishing, Divine."

The basis upon which the Spirit takes up His abode within the believer is twofold: first, on the ground of redemption. This is illustrated most blessedly in the cleansing of the leper — figure of the sinner. "And the priest shall take some of *the blood* of the trespass offerings, and the priest shall put it upon the tip of the right ear of him that is to be cleansed, and upon the thumb of his right hand, and upon the great toe of his right foot. . . . And of the rest of *the oil* that is in his hand shall the priest put upon the tip of the right ear of him that is to be cleansed, and upon the thumb of his right hand, and upon the great toe of his right foot, *upon the blood* of the trespass offering" (Lev. 14:14, 17). Wondrous type was that: the "oil" (emblem of the Holy Spirit) was placed "upon the blood" — only on the ground of atonement accomplished could the Holy Spirit take up His abode in sinners: this at once sets aside human merits.

There must be *moral fitness* as well. The Spirit of God will not tabernacle with unbelieving rebels. "*After* [or "when"] that ye believed, ye were sealed with that Holy Spirit of promise" (Eph. 1:13). It is to those who obey the command "Be ye not unequally yoked together" that God promises "I will dwell in them" (II Cor. 6:16). When by repudiating all idols, receiving Christ as Lord, trusting in the merits of His sacrifice, the heart is prepared, the Spirit of God enters to take possession for Christ's use. When we give up ourselves to the Lord, He owneth the dedication by making our bodies the temples of the Holy Spirit, there to maintain His interests against all the opposition of the Devil.

In considering the Spirit indwelling believers we need to be on our guard against entertaining any conception of this grand fact which is gross and dishonoring to His person. He does not so indwell as to impart His *essential* properties or perfections — such as omniscience or omnipotence; it would be blasphemy so to speak; but His saving and sanctifying operations are communicated to us as the sun is said to enter a room, when his bright beams and genial warmth are seen and felt therein. Further, we must not think that the grace and benign influence of the Spirit abide in us in the selfsame manner and measure they did in Christ: no, for God "giveth not the Spirit by measure unto Him" (John 3:34) — in Him all fulness dwells.

Let us now point out that what has been before us lays the basis of the most solemn appeal and powerful exhortation. Is my body a temple of the Holy Spirit? then how devoted should it be to God and His service! Am I indwelt by the Spirit of Christ? Then how I ought to lend my ear to His softest whisper, my will to His gentlest sway, my heart to His sacred influence. In disregarding His voice, in not yielding to His promptings, He is grieved, Christ is dishonored, and we are the losers. The greatest blessing we possess is the indwelling Spirit: let us seek grace to conduct ourselves accordingly.

"But ye are not in the flesh, but in the Spirit, if so be that the Spirit of God *dwell in you*" (Rom. 8:9). Three things are denoted by the Spirit's "indwelling." First, *intimacy*. As the inhabitant of a house is more familiar there than elsewhere, so is the Spirit in the hearts of Christ's redeemed. God the Spirit is omnipresent, being everywhere essentially, being excluded nowhere: "Whither shall I go from thy Spirit? or whither shall I flee from thy presence?" (Ps. 139:7). But as God is said more especially to be there where He *manifests* His power and presence, as Heaven is "His dwelling place," so it is with His Spirit. He is in believers not simply by the effects of common providence, but by His gracious operations and familiar presence. "Even the Spirit of truth: whom the world cannot receive, because it seeth Him not, neither knoweth Him; but ye know Him; for He dwelleth with you, and shall be in you" (John 14:17). The world of natural men are utter strangers to the Spirit of God, not being acquainted with His sanctifying operations, but He intimately discovers His presence to those who are quickened by Him.

Second, *constancy*: "dwelling" expresses a permanent abode. The Spirit does not affect the regenerate by a transient action only, or come "upon" them occasionally as He did the prophets of old, when He endowed them for some particular service above the measure of their ordinary ability; but He abides in them by working such effects as are lasting. He comes to the believer not as a Visitor, but as an Inhabitant: He is within us "a well of water, springing up into everlasting life" (John 4:14). He liveth in the renewed heart, so that by His constant and continual influence He maintains the life of grace in us. By the blessed Spirit Christians are "sealed unto the day of redemption" (Eph. 4:30).

Third, *sovereignly*: this is also denoted under the term "dwell." He is owner of the house, and not an underling. From the fact that the believer's body is the temple of the Holy Spirit, the apostle points out the necessary implication that he is "not his own" (I Cor. 6:19). Previously he was possessed by another owner, even Satan — the evil spirit says "I will return into *my* house" (Matt. 12:44). But the Spirit has dispossessed him, and the sanctified heart has become *His* "house," where He commands and governs after His own will. Take again the figure of the sanctuary: "Know ye not that ye are the temple of God, and the Spirit of God dwelleth in you" (I Cor. 3:16). A "temple" is a sacred dwelling, employed for the honor and glory of God, where He is to be revered and worshipped, and from which all idols must be excluded.

The indwelling Spirit is *the bond by which believers are united to Christ*. If therefore we find the Holy Spirit abiding in us, we may warrantably conclude we have been "joined to the Lord." This is plainly set forth in those words of the Saviour's, "And the glory which thou gavest me, I have given them: that they may be one even as we are one: I in them, and thou in me, that they may be made perfect in one" (John 17:22, 23). The "glory" of Christ's humanity was its union with the Godhead. How was it united? By the Holy Spirit. This very "glory" Christ has given His people: "I in them," which He is by the sanctifying Spirit — the bond of our union with Him.

The indwelling Spirit is *the sure mark of the believer's freedom from the covenant of works*, under which all Christless persons stand; and our title to the special privileges of the new covenant, in which none but Christ's are interested; which is another way of saying they are "not under the law, but under grace" (Rom. 6:14). This is plain from the apostle's reasoning in Galatians 4:6, 7, "Because ye are sons God hath sent forth the Spirit of his Son into your hearts, crying, Abba, Father. Wherefore thou art no more a servant, but a son." The spirit of the old covenant was a servile one, a spirit of fear and bondage, and those under the same were not "sons," but *servants*: but the spirit of the new covenant is a free one, that of *children*, inheriting the blessed promises and royal immunities contained in the charter of grace.

The indwelling Spirit is *the certain pledge and earnest of eternal salvation*. The execution of the eternal decree of God's electing love — "drawn" (Jer. 31:3), and the application of the virtues and benefits of the death of Christ by the Spirit (Gal. 3:13, 14), must needs be a sure evidence of our personal interest in the Redeemer. This is plain from I Peter 1:2: "Elect according to the foreknowledge of God the Father, through sanctification of the Spirit, unto obedience and sprinkling of the blood of Jesus Christ." God's eternal decree is executed and the blood of Christ is sprinkled upon us, when we receive the Spirit of sanctification. The Spirit's residing in the Christian is the guarantee and earnest of the eternal inheritance: "Who hath also sealed us, and given the earnest of the Spirit in our hearts" (II Cor. 1:22).

What are the evidences and fruits of the Spirit's habitation? First, wherever the Spirit dwells, He, in some degree, mortifies and subdues the evils of the soul in which He resides. "The Spirit lusteth against the flesh" (Gal. 5:17), and believers "through the Spirit, do mortify the deeds of the body" (Rom. 8:13). This is one special part of His sanctifying work. Though He kills not sin in believers, He subdues it; though He does not so subdue the flesh so that it never troubles or defiles them again, its dominion is taken away. Perfect freedom from its very presence awaits them in Heaven; but even now, animated by their holy Indweller, Christians deny themselves and use the means of grace which God has appointed for deliverance from the reigning power of sin.

Second, wherever the Spirit dwells, He produces a spirit of prayer and supplication. "Likewise the Spirit also helpeth our infirmities, for we know not what we should pray for as we ought; but the Spirit itself maketh intercession for us with groanings which cannot be uttered" (Rom. 8:26). The two things are inseparable: wherever He is poured out as the Spirit of *grace*, He is also poured out as the Spirit of *supplication* (Zech. 12:10). He helps Christians *before* they pray, by stirring up their spiritual affections and stimulating holy desires. He helps them *in* prayer, by teaching them to ask for those things which are according to God's will. He it is who humbles the pride of their hearts, moves their sluggish wills, and out of weakness makes them strong. He helps them *after* prayer, by quickening hope and patience to wait for God's answers.

Third, where the Spirit dwells, He works a heavenly and spiritual frame of mind. "They that are after the flesh do mind the things of the flesh; but they that are after the Spirit, the things of the Spirit. For to be carnally-minded is death; but to be spiritually-minded is life and peace" (Rom. 8:5-6). The workings of every creature follow the being and bent of its nature. If God, Christ, Heaven, engage the thoughts and affections of the soul, the Spirit of God is there. There are times in each Christian's life when he exclaims, "How precious also are *thy* thoughts unto me, O God! how great is the sum of them! If I should count them, they are more in number than the sand: when I awake, I am still with thee" (Ps. 139:17, 18) — such holy contemplation is the very life of the regenerate.

But, says the sincere Christian, If the Spirit of God dwelt in me, could my heart be so listless and averse to spiritual duties? Answer, the very fact that you are exercised and burdened over this sad state evidences the presence of spiritual life in your soul. Let it be borne in mind that there is a vast difference between spiritual death and spiritual deadness; the former is the condition of the unregenerate, the latter is the disease and complaint of thousands of the regenerate. Note it well that nine times over, David, in a single Psalm (119) prayed, "Quicken me!" Though it be so *often*, it is not so *always* with thee: there are seasons when the Lord breaks in upon thy heart, enlarges thy affections, and sets thy soul at liberty — clear proof thou art not deserted by the Comforter!

19

The Spirit Teaching

"But the Comforter, the Holy Spirit, whom the Father will send in my name, he shall *teach you* all things" (John 14:26). Those words received their first fulfilment in the men to whom they were immediately addressed: the apostles were so filled and controlled by the Holy Spirit that their proclamation of the gospel was without flaw, and their writings without error. Those original ambassadors of Christ were so taught by the third Person in the Trinity that what they delivered was the very mind of God. The second fulfilment of the Saviour's promise has been in those men whom He called to preach His gospel throughout the Christian era. No new revelations have been made to them, but they were, and are, according to their varied measure, and the particular work assigned to them, so enlightened by the Spirit that the truth of God has been faithfully preached by them. The third and widest application of our Lord's words are to the entire Household of Faith, and it is in this sense we shall now consider them.

It is written, "And *all* thy children shall be taught of the Lord" (Isa. 54:13 and cf. John 6:45). This is one of the great distinguishing marks of the regenerate: all of them are "taught *of the Lord.*" There are multitudes of unregenerate religionists who are taught, numbers of them well taught, in the letter of the Scriptures. They are thoroughly versed in the historical facts and doctrines of Christianity; but their instruction came only from human media — parents, Sunday School teachers, or through reading religious books. Their intellectual knowledge of spiritual things is considerable, sound, and clear, yet is it unaccompanied by any heavenly unction, saving power, or transforming effects. In like manner, there are thousands of preachers, who abhor the errors of "Modernists" and who contend earnestly for the faith. They were taught in Bible institutes, and theological schools, yet it is to be feared that many of them are total strangers to a *miracle of grace* being wrought in the heart. How it behooves each *of us* to test ourselves rigidly at this point!

It is a common fact of observation — which anyone may test for himself — that a very large percentage of those who constitute the membership of evangelical denominations were first taken there in childhood by their parents. The great majority in the Presbyterian churches today had a father or mother who was a Presbyterian and who instructed the offspring in their beliefs. The same is true of the Baptists, the Methodists, and those who are in fellowship at the Brethren Assemblies. The present

97

generation has been brought up to believe in the doctrines and religious customs of their ancestors. Now we are far from saying that
because a man who is a Presbyterian today had parents and grand-
parents that were Presbyterians and who taught him the Westminster
Catechism, therefore all the knowledge he possesses of Divine things is
but traditional and theoretical. No indeed, yet we do say that such a
training in the letter of the Truth makes it more difficult, and calls for
a more careful self-examination, to ascertain whether or not he has been
taught *of the Lord.*

Though we do not believe that Grace runs in the blood, yet we are
convinced that, *as a general rule* (having many individual exceptions),
God does place His elect in families where at least one of the parents
loves and seeks to serve Him, and where that elect soul will be nurtured
in the fear and admonition of the Lord. At least three-fourths of those
Christians whom the writer has met and had opportunity to question,
had a praying and Scripture-reading father or mother. Yet, on the other
hand, we are obliged to acknowledge that three-fourths of the empty
professors we have encountered also had religious parents, who sent
them to the Sunday School and sought to have them trained in their
beliefs: and these now rest upon their intellectual knowledge of the
Truth, and mistake it for *a saving experience* of the same. And it is *this*
class which it is the hardest to reach; it is much more difficult to
persuade such to *examine themselves* as to whether or not they have
been taught *of God,* than it is those who make no profession at all.

Let it not be concluded from what has been pointed out that, where
the Holy Spirit teaches a soul, He dispenses with all human instrumentality. Not so. It is true the Spirit is sovereign, and therefore works
where He pleases and when He pleases. It is also a fact that He is
Almighty, tied down to no means, and therefore works as He pleases
and how He pleases. Nevertheless, He frequently condescends to employ means, and to use very feeble instruments. In fact, this generally
seems to characterize His operations: that He works through men and
women, and sometimes through little children. Yet, let it be said emphatically, that no preaching, catechising, or reading, produces any vital
and spiritual results unless God the Spirit is pleased to bless and apply
the same unto the heart of the individual. Thus there are many who
have passed from death unto life and been brought to love the Truth
under the Spirit's application of a pious parent's or Sunday School teacher's instruction; while there are some who never enjoyed such privileges
yet have been truly and deeply taught by God.

From all that has been said a very pertinent question arises, How
may I know whether or not *my* teaching has been by the Holy Spirit?
The simple but sufficient answer is, *By the effects produced.* First, that
spiritual knowledge which the teaching of the Holy Spirit imparts is an
operative knowledge. It is not merely a piece of information which adds
to our mental store, but is a species of inspiration which stirs the soul
into action. "For God, who commanded the light to shine out of darkness, hath shined *in our hearts,* to give the light of the knowledge of the

glory of God in the face of Jesus Christ" (II Cor. 4:6). The light which the Spirit imparts reaches the heart. It warms the heart, and sets it on fire for God. It masters the heart, and brings it into allegiance to God. It molds the heart, and stamps upon it the image of God. Here, then, is a sure test: how far does the teaching you have received, the knowledge of Divine things you possess, *affect your heart?*

Second, that knowledge which the teaching of the Spirit imparts is *a soul-humbling* knowledge. "Knowledge puffeth up" (I Cor. 8:1), that is a notional, theoretical, intellectual knowledge, which is merely received from men or books in a natural way. But that spiritual knowledge which comes from God reveals to a man his empty conceits, his ignorance and worthlessness, and abases him. The teaching of the Spirit reveals our sinfulness and vileness, our lack of conformity to Christ, our unholiness; and makes a man little in his own eyes. Among those born of women was not a greater than John the Baptist; wondrous were the privileges granted him, abundant the light with which he was favored. What effect had it on him? "He it is who, coming after me, is preferred before me, whose shoe's latchet *I am not worthy* to unloose" (John 1:27). Who granted such an insight into heavenly things as Paul! Did he herald himself as "The greatest Bible teacher of the age"? No; "unto me who am less than the least of all saints" (Eph. 3:8). Here, then, is a sure test: how far does the teaching you have received *humble* you?

Third, that knowledge which the teaching of the Holy Spirit imparts is a *world-despising* knowledge. It makes a man have poor, low, mean thoughts of those things which his unregenerate fellows (and which he himself, formerly) so highly esteem. It opens his eyes to see the transitoriness and comparative worthlessness of earthly honors, riches, and fame. It makes him perceive that all under the sun is but vanity and vexation of spirit. It brings him to realise that the world is a flatterer, a deceiver, a liar, and a murderer, which has fatally deceived the hearts of millions. Where the Spirit reveals eternal things, temporal things are scorned. Those things which once were gain to him, he now counts as loss; yea, as dross and dung (Phil. 3:4-9). The teaching of the Spirit raises the heart high above this poor perishing world. Here is a sure test: does *your* knowledge of spiritual things cause you to hold temporal things with a light hand, and despise those baubles which others hunt so eagerly?

Fourth, the knowledge which the teaching of the Spirit imparts is a *transforming* knowledge. The light of God shows how far, far short we come of the standard Holy Writ reveals, and stirs us unto holy endeavors to lay aside every hindering weight, and run with patience the race set before us. The teaching of the Spirit causes us to deny "ungodliness and worldly lusts," and to "live soberly, righteously, and godly in this present world" (Titus 2:12). "But we all, with open face, beholding as in a glass, the glory of the Lord, *are changed into the same image,* from glory to glory, as by the Spirit of the Lord" (II Cor. 3:18). Here, then, is a sure test: how far does my knowledge of spiritual things influence my heart, govern my will, and regulate my life? Does increasing light lead to a more tender conscience, more Christlike character and conduct? If not, it is vain, worthless, and will only add to my condemnation.

"But the Comforter, the Holy Spirit, whom the Father will send in my name, he shall *teach you* all things" (John 14:26). How urgently we need a Divine Teacher! A natural and notional knowledge of Divine things may be obtained through men, but a spiritual and experimental knowledge of them can only be communicated by God Himself. I may devote myself to the study of the Scriptures in the same way as I would to the study of some science or the mastering of a foreign language. By diligent application, persevering effort, and consulting works of reference (commentators, etc.), I may steadily acquire a comprehensive and accurate acquaintance with the letter of God's Word, and become an able expositor thereof. But I cannot obtain a heart-affecting, a heart-purifying, and a heart-molding knowledge thereof. None but the Spirit of truth can write God's law on my heart, stamp God's image upon my soul, and *sanctify* me by the Truth.

"You may listen to the preacher,
God's own truth be clearly shown;
But you need a greater Teacher,
From the everlasting throne:
Application is the work of God alone."

Conscience informs me that I am a sinner; the preacher may convince me that without Christ I am eternally lost; but neither the one nor the other is sufficient to move me to receive Him as my Lord and Saviour. One man may lead a horse to the water, but no ten men can make him drink when he is unwilling to do so. The Lord Jesus Himself was "anointed to preach the gospel" (Luke 4:18), and did so with a zeal for God's glory and a compassion for souls such as none other ever had; yet He had to say to His hearers, "Ye will not come unto me that ye might have life" (John 5:40). What a proof is that, that something more is required above and beyond the outward presentation of the truth. There must be *the inward application* of it to the heart with Divine power, if the will is to be moved. And *that* is what the teaching of the Spirit consists of: it is an effectual communication of the Word which works powerfully *within* the soul.

Why is it that so many professing Christians change their views so easily and quickly? What is the reason there are so many thousands of unstable souls who are "tossed to and fro, and carried about with every wind of doctrine, by the sleight of men and cunning craftiness, whereby they lie in wait to deceive" (Eph. 4:14)? Why is it that this year they sit under a man who preaches the Truth and claim to believe and enjoy his messages; while next year they attend the ministry of a man of error and heartily embrace his opinions? It must be because they were *never taught of the Spirit.* "I know that whatsoever God doeth it shall be forever; nothing can be put to it, nor anything taken from it" (Eccles. 3:14). What the Spirit writes on the heart remains: "The anointing which ye have received of him *abideth in you*" (I John 2:27), and neither man nor devil can efface it.

Why is it that so many professing Christians are unfruitful? Month after month, year after year, they attend upon the means of grace, and yet remain unchanged. Their store of religious information is greatly increased, their intellectual knowledge of the truth is much advanced, but their lives are not transformed. There is no denying of self, taking up their cross, and following a despised Christ along the narrow way of personal holiness. There is no humble self-abasement, no mourning over indwelling sin, no mortification of the same. There is no deepening love for Christ, evidenced by a running in the way of His command-ments. Such people are "ever learning, and never able to come to the knowledge of the truth" (II Tim. 3:7), i.e., *that* "knowledge" which is vital, experimental, affecting, and transforming. They are not *taught of the Spirit*.

Why is it in times of temptation and death that so many despair? Because their house is not built upon *the rock*. Hence, as the Lord Jesus declared, "the rain descended, and the floods came, and the winds blew, and beat upon the house, and it *fell*" (Matt. 7:27). It could not endure the testing: when trouble and trial, temptation and tribulation came, its insecure foundation was exposed. And note the particular character Christ there depicted: "every one that heareth these sayings of mine [His precepts in the much-despised "Sermon on the Mount"] and *doeth them not*, shall be likened unto a man that built his house upon the sand." Men may go on in worldly courses, evil practices, sinful habits, trusting in a head-knowledge of Christ to save them, but when they reach "the swelling of Jordan" (Jer. 12:5) they will prove the insufficiency of it.

Ah, dear reader, a saving knowledge is not a knowledge of Divine things, but is a Divinely-imparted knowledge. It not only has God for its Object, but God for its Author. There not only must be a knowledge of spiritual things, but a *spiritual* knowledge of the same. The light which we have of them must be answerable to the things themselves; we must see them by their own light. As the things themselves are spiritual, they must be imparted and opened to us by the Holy Spirit. Where there is a knowledge of the Truth which has been wrought in the heart by the Spirit, there is an experimental knowledge of the same, a sensible con-sciousness, a persuasive and comforting perception of their reality, an assurance which nothing can shake. The Truth then possesses a sweet-ness, a preciousness. No inducement can cause the soul to part with it.

Now as to *what* it is which the Spirit teaches us, we have intimated, more or less, in previous chapters. First, He reveals to the soul "the exceeding sinfulness of sin" (Rom. 7:13), so that it is filled with horror and anguish at its baseness, its excuselessness, its turpitude. It is one thing to read of the excruciating pain which the gout or gall stones will produce, but it is quite another thing for me to experience the well-nigh unbearable suffering of the same. In like manner, it is one thing to hear others talking of the Spirit convicting of sin, but it is quite another for Him to teach me that I am a rebel against God, and give me a taste of His wrath burning in my conscience. The difference is as great as looking at a painted fire, and being thrust into a real one.

Second, the Spirit reveals to the soul the utter futility of all efforts to save itself. The first effect of conviction in an awakened conscience is to attempt the rectification of all that now appears wrong in the conduct. A diligent effort is put forth to make amends for past offenses, painful penances are readily submitted to, and the outward duties of religion are given earnest attendance. But by the teaching of the Spirit the heart is drawn off from resting in works of righteousness which we have done (Titus 3:5), and this, by His giving increasing light, so that the convicted soul now perceives he is a mass of corruption within, that his very prayers are polluted by selfish motives, and that unless God will save him, his case is beyond all hope.

Third, the Spirit reveals to the soul the suitability and sufficiency of Christ to meet its desperate needs. It is an important branch of the Spirit's teaching to open the gospel to those whom He has quickened, enlightened, and convicted; and to open their understanding and affections to take in the precious contents of the gospel. "He shall glorify me," said the Saviour, "for he shall receive of mine, and shall show it unto you" (John 16:14). This is His prime function; to magnify Christ in the esteem of "his own." The Spirit teaches the believer many things, but His supreme subject is *Christ*: to emphasize His claims, to exalt His person, to reveal His perfections, to make Him superlatively attractive. Many things in Nature are very beautiful, but when the sun shines upon them, we appreciate their splendor all the more. Thus it is when we are enabled to view Christ in the light of the Spirit's teaching.

The Spirit *continues to teach* the regenerate throughout the remainder of their lives. He gives them a fuller and deeper realization of their own native depravity, convincing them that in the flesh there dwelleth no good thing, and gradually weaning them from all expectation of improving the same, He reveals to them "the beauty of holiness," and causes them to pant after and strive for an increasing measure of the same. He teaches them the supreme importance of *inward piety*.

20

The Spirit Cleansing

THE title of this chapter may possibly surprise some readers, who have supposed that cleansing from sin is by the blood of Christ alone. Judicially it is so, but in connection with experimental purging certain distinctions need to be drawn in order to have a clearer understanding. Here, the gracious operation of the Holy Spirit is the efficient cause, the blood of Christ is the meritorious and procuring cause, faith's appropriation of the Word is the instrumental cause. It is by the Holy Spirit our eyes are opened to see and our hearts to feel the enormity of sin, and thus are we enabled to perceive our need of Christ's blood. It is by the Spirit we are moved to betake ourselves unto the "fountain" which has been opened for sin and for uncleanness. It is by the Spirit we are enabled to trust in the sufficiency of Christ's sacrifice now that we realize what Hell-deserving sinners we are. All of which is preceded by His work of regeneration whereby He capacitates the soul to see light in God's light and appropriate the provisions of His wondrous mercy.

It is not now our purpose to trace out the various aspects of the Spirit's work in purging the souls of believers, for we do not wish to anticipate too much the ground we hope to yet cover in the chapter on "Sanctification." But this is an important phase of the Spirit's operations. We shall therefore restrict ourselves to a single branch of the subject, which is sufficiently comprehensive as to include in it all that we now feel led to say thereon, namely, that of *mortification*.

"For if ye live after the flesh, ye shall die: but if ye through the Spirit do mortify the deeds of the body, ye shall live" (Rom. 8:13). A most solemn and searching verse is this, and one which we greatly fear has very little place in present-day preaching. Five things in it claim attention. First, the persons addressed. Second, the awful warning here set before them. Third, the duty enjoined upon them. Fourth, the efficient Helper provided. Fifth, the promise made. Those here addressed are regenerated believers, Christians, as is evident from the whole context: the apostle denominates them "brethren" (v. 12).

Our text, then, belongs to the Lord's own people, who "are debtors, not to the flesh, to live after the flesh" (v. 12); rather are they "debtors" to Christ (who redeemed them) to live for His glory, "debtors" to the Holy Spirit (who regenerated them) to submit themselves to His absolute control. But if an apprehension of their high privilege (to please their Saviour) and a sense of their bounden duty (to Him who has brought them from death unto life) fail to move them to godly living, perhaps an apprehension of their awful danger may influence them thereto: "For if ye live after the flesh, ye shall die" — die spiritually, die eternally, for "life" and "death" in Romans always signifies far more than natural life and death. Moreover, to restrict "ye shall die" to physical dissolution would be quite pointless, for *that* experience is shared by sinners and saints alike.

It is to be noted that the apostle did not say "If ye *have* lived after the flesh ye shall die," for every one of God's children did so before He delivered them from the power of darkness and translated them into the kingdom of His dear Son. No, it is "If ye live after the flesh" now. It is a continual course, a steady perseverance in the same, which is in view. To "live after the flesh" means to persistently follow the inclinations and solicitations of inward corruption, to be wholly under the dominion of the depravity of fallen human nature. To "live after the flesh" is to be in love with sin, to serve it contentedly, to make self-gratification the trade and business of life. It is by no means limited to the grosser forms of wickedness and crime, but includes as well the refinement, morality, and religiousness of the best of men, who yet give God no real place in their hearts and lives. And the wages of sin is *death.*

"For if ye live after the flesh, ye shall die." That is a rule to which there is no exception. No matter what your experience or profession, no matter how certain of your conversion or how orthodox your belief: "be not deceived, God is not mocked: for whatsoever a man soweth, *that* shall he also reap; for he that soweth to his flesh shall of the flesh reap corruption" (Gal. 6:7, 8). O the madness of men in courting eternal death rather than leave their sinful pleasures and live a holy life. O the folly of those who think to reconcile God and sin, who imagine they can please the flesh, and yet be happy in eternity notwithstanding. "How much she hath glorified herself and lived deliciously, so much torment and sorrow give her" (Rev. 18:7) — so much as the flesh is gratified, so much is the soul endangered. Will you, my reader, for a little temporal satisfaction run the hazard of God's eternal wrath? Heed this solemn warning, fellow-Christian: God means what He says, "If ye live after the flesh, *ye* shall die."

Let us now consider the duty which is here enjoined: "do mortify the deeds of the body." In this clause, "the body" is the same as "the flesh" in the previous one, they are equivalent terms for the corruption of nature. The emphasis here is placed upon the body because it is the tendency of indwelling sin to pamper and please our baser part. The soul of the unregenerate acts for no higher end than does the soul of a beast — to gratify his carnal appetites. The "deeds of the body," then, have reference not only to the outward actions, but also the springs from which they proceed. Thus, the task which is here assigned the Christian is to "mortify" or put to death the solicitations to evil within him. The life of sin and the life of grace are utterly inconsistent and repellent: we must die to sin in order to live unto God.

Now there is a threefold power in sin to which we must die. First, its damning or condemning power, whereby it brings the soul under the wrath of God. This power it has from the law, for "the strength of sin is the law" (I Cor. 15:56). But, blessed be God, the sentence of the Divine law is no longer in force against the believer, for that was executed and exhausted upon the head of his Surety: consequently "we are delivered from the law" (Rom. 7:6). Though sin may still hale Christians before God, accuse them before Him, terrify the conscience and make them acknowledge their guilt, yet it cannot drag them to Hell or adjudge them to eternal wrath. Thus, by faith in Christ sin is "mortified" or put to death as to its condemning power (John 5:24).

Second, sin has a ruling and reigning power, whereby it keeps the soul under wretched slavery and continual bondage. This reign of sin consists not in the multitude, greatness, or prevalence of sin, for all those are consistent with a state of grace, and may be in a child of God, in whom sin does not and cannot reign. The reign of sin consists in the inbeing of sin *unopposed by a principle of grace.* Thus, sin is effectually "mortified" in its reigning power at the first moment of re-generation, for at the new birth a principle of spiritual life is implanted, and this lusteth against the flesh, opposing its solicitations, so that sin is unable to dominate as it would (Gal. 5:17); and this breaks its tyranny. Our conscious enjoyment of this is dependent, mainly, upon our obedience to Romans 6:11.

Third, sin has an indwelling and captivating power, whereby it con-tinually assaults the principle of spiritual life, beating down the Chris-tian's defenses, battering his armor, routing his graces, wasting his con-science, destroying his peace, and at last bringing him into a woeful captivity *unless it be mortified.* Corruption does not lie dormant in the Christian: though it reigns not supreme (because of a principle of grace to oppose it) yet it molests and often prevails to a very considerable extent. Because of this the Christian is called upon to wage a constant warfare against it: to "mortify" it, to struggle against its inclinations and deny its solicitations, to make no provision for it, to walk in the Spirit so that he fulfill not the lusts of the flesh.

Unless the Christian devotes all his powers to a definite, uncompromis-ing, earnest, constant warfare upon indwelling sin; unless he diligently seeks to weaken its roots, suppress its motions, restrain its outward eruptions and actions, and seeks to put to death the enemy within his soul, he is guilty of the basest ingratitude to Christ. Unless he does so, he is a complete failure in the Christian life, for it is impossible that both sin and grace should be healthy and vigorous in the soul at the same time. If a garden be overrun with weeds, they choke and starve the profitable plants, absorbing the moisture and nourishment upon which they should feed. So, if the lusts of the flesh absorb the soul, the graces of the spirit cannot develop. If the mind be filled with worldly or filthy things, then meditation on holy things is crowded out. Oc-cupation with sin deadens the mind for holy duties.

But who is sufficient for such a task? Who can expect to gain the victory over such a powerful enemy as indwelling sin? Who can hope to put to death that which defies every effort the strongest can make against it? Ah, were the Christian left entirely to himself the outlook would be hopeless, and the attempt useless. But, thank God, such is not the case. The Christian is provided with an efficient Helper: "greater is he that is in you, than he that is in the world" (I John 4:4). It is only *"through the Spirit"* we can, in any measure, successfully "mortify the deeds of the body."

Though the real Christian has been delivered from condemnation and freed from the reigning power of sin, yet there is a continual need for him to "mortify" or put to death the principle and actings of indwelling corruption. His main fight is against suffering sin to bring him into captivity to the lusts of the flesh. "Have *no* fellowship with the unfruitful works of darkness" — enter into no truce, form no alliance with — "but rather reprove them" (Eph. 5:11). Say with Ephraim of old, "What have I to do any more with idols"? (Hos. 14:8). No real communion with God is possible while sinful lusts remain unmortified. Allowed sin draws the heart from God, entangles the affections, discomposes the soul, and provokes God to close His ears against our prayers (see Ezek. 14:3).

Now it is most important that we should distinguish between mock mortification and true, between the counterfeit resemblances of this duty and the duty itself. There is a *pagan* "mortification," which is merely suppressing such sins as nature itself discovers and from such reasons and motives as nature suggests (Rom. 2:14). This tends to hide sin rather than mortify it. It is not a recovering of the soul from the world unto God, but only acquiring a fitness to live with less scandal among men. There is a *popish* and superstitious "mortification" which consists in the neglect of the body, abstaining from marriage, certain kinds of meat, and apparel. Such things have "a show of wisdom" and are highly regarded by the carnal world, but not being commanded *by God* they have no spiritual value whatsoever. They mascerate the natural man instead of mortifying the old man. There is also a *protestant* "mortification" which differs nothing in principle from the popish: certain fanatics eschew some of God's creatures; others demand abstinence when God requires temperance.

True mortification consists, first, in *weakening* sin's root and principle. It is of little avail to chop off the heads of weeds while their roots remain in the ground; nor is much accomplished by seeking to correct outward habits while the heart be left neglected. One in a high fever cannot expect to lower his temperature while he continues to eat heartily, nor can the lusts of the flesh be weakened so long as we feed or "make provision for" (Rom. 13:14) them. Second, in *suppressing* the risings of inward corruptions by turning a deaf ear to their voice, by crying to God for grace so to do, by pleading the blood of Christ for deliverance. Make conscience of evil thoughts and imaginations: do not regard them as inevitable, still less cherish them; turn the mind to holy objects. Third, in *restraining* its outward actings: "denying un-godliness," etc. (Titus 2:12).

Though grace be wrought in the hearts of the regenerate, it is not in their power to act it: He who implanted it, must renew, excite and marshal it. "If ye *through the Spirit* do mortify." First, He it is who discovers the sin that is to be mortified, opening it to the view of the soul, stripping it of its deceits, exposing its deformity. Second, He it is who gradually weakens sin's power, acting as "the Spirit of burning" (Isa. 4:4), consuming the dross. Third, He it is who reveals and applies the efficacy of the cross of Christ, in which there is contained a sin-mortifying virtue, whereby we are "made conformable unto His death" (Phil. 3:14). Fourth, He it is who strengthens us with might in the inner man, so that our graces — the opposites of the lusts of the flesh — are invigorated and called into exercise.

The Holy Spirit is the effective Helper. Men may employ the aids of inward rigor and outward severity, and they may for a time stifle and suppress their evil habits; but unless the Spirit of God work in us, nothing can amount to true mortification. Yet note well it is not "If the Spirit do mortify," nor even "If the Spirit through you do mortify," but "If *ye* through the Spirit do mortify!" The Christian is not passive, but active in this work. We are bidden to "cleanse ourselves from all filthiness of the flesh and spirit" (II Cor. 7:1). We are exhorted to "build up ourselves on our most holy faith" and "keep ourselves in the love of God" (Jude 20, 21). Paul could say, "I keep under my body, and bring it into subjection" (I Cor. 9:27). It is by yielding to the Spirit's impulses, heeding His strivings, submitting ourselves unto His government, that any measure of success is granted us in this most important work.

The believer is not a cipher in this work. The gracious operations of the Spirit were never designed to be a substitute for the Christian's discharge of his duty. True, His influence is indispensable, though it relaxes us not from our individual responsibility. "Little children, keep yourselves from idols" (I John 5:20) emphasises our obligation, and plainly intimates that God requires from His people something more than a passive waiting for Him to stir them into action. O my reader, beware of cloaking a spirit of slothful indolence under an apparent jealous regard for the honor of the Spirit. Is no self-effort required to escape the snares of Satan by refusing to walk in those paths which God has forbidden? Is no self-effort to be made in breaking away from the evil influence of godless companions? Is no self-effort called for to dethrone an unlawful habit? Mortification is a task to which every Christian must address himself with a prayerful and resolute earnestness. Nevertheless it is a task far transcending *our* feeble powers.

It is only "through the Spirit" that any of us can acceptably and effectually (in any degree) "mortify the deeds of the body." He it is who works in us a loathing of sin, a mourning over it, a turning away from it. He it is who presses upon us the claims of Christ, reminding us that inasmuch as He died *for* sin, we must spare no efforts to die *to* sin —

"striving against sin" (Heb. 12:4), confessing it (I John 1:9), forsaking it (Prov. 28:13). He it is who preserves us from giving way to despair, and encourages us to renew the conflict, assuring us that ultimately we shall be more than conquerors through Him that loved us. He it is who deepens our aspirations after holiness, causing us to cry "Create in me a clean heart, O God" (Ps. 51:10), and moving us to "forget the things which are behind and reach forth unto those things which are before" (Phil. 3:12).

"If ye through the Spirit do mortify the deeds of the body, *ye shall live.*" Here is the encouraging promise set before the sorely-tried contestant. God will be no man's debtor: He is a rewarder of them that diligently seek Him (Heb. 11:6). If, then, by grace, we deny the flesh and co-operate with the Spirit, if we strive against sin and strive after holiness, richly shall we be recompensed. To say that Christians are unable to concur with the Spirit is to deny there is any real difference between the renewed and those who are dead in sin. It is true that without Christ we can do nothing (John 15:5), yet it is equally true (though far less frequently quoted) that "I can do all things through Christ which strengtheneth me" (Phil. 4:13). Mortification and vivification are inseparable: dying to sin and living unto God are indissolubly connected: the one cannot be without the other. If we through the Spirit do mortify the deeds of the body then, but only then, we shall "live" — live a life of grace and comfort here, and live a life of eternal glory and bliss hereafter.

Some have a difficulty here in that Romans 8:13 conditions "life" upon *our* performance of the duty of mortification. "In the Gospel there are promises of life upon the condition of our obedience. The promises are not made to the work, but to the worker, and to the worker not for his work, but for Christ's sake according to his work. As for example, promise of life is made not to the work of mortification, but *to him* that mortifieth the flesh, and that not for his mortification, but because he is in Christ, and his mortification is the token *or evidence thereof.* And therefore it must be remembered that all promises of the Gospel that mention works include in them reconciliation with God in Christ" (W. Perkins, 1604). The conditionality of the promise, then, is neither that of causation or uncertainty, but of coherence and connection, or means and end. The Highway of Holiness is the only path that leads to Heaven: "He that soweth to the Spirit shall of the Spirit reap life everlasting" (Gal. 6:8).

But let it be pointed out that the sowing of a field with grain is not accomplished in a few minutes, it is a lengthy and laborious task, calling for diligence and patience. So it is with the Christian: mortification is a *lifelong* task. A neglected garden is neither easily nor quickly rid of weeds, and much care is required for the cultivation of herbs and flowers. Nor is a long-neglected heart, with its indwelling corruptions and powerful lusts, brought into subjection to the Spirit by a few spasmodic efforts and prayers. It calls for painful and protracted effort, the daily denying of self, application of the principles of the Cross to our daily walk, earnest supplication for the Spirit's help. So *"Be not weary . . ."* (Gal. 6:9).

In conclusion let us seek to meet the objection of the discouraged Christian. "If a true mortification must be not only a striving against the motions of inward corruption, but also the weakening of its roots, then I fear that all my endeavors have been in vain. Some success I have obtained against the outbreakings of lust, but still I find the temptation of it as strong as ever. I perceive no decays in it, but rather does it grow more violent each day." Answer, "That is because you are more conscious and take more notice of corruption than formerly. When the heart is made tender by a long exercise of mortification, a less temptation troubles it more than a greater did formerly. This seeming strengthening of corruption is not a sign that sin is not dying, but rather an evidence that you are spiritually alive and more sensible of its motions." (Condensed from *Ezekiel*, Hopkins, 1680, to whom we are indebted for several leading thoughts in this chapter.)

21

The Spirit Leading

"For as many as are led by the Spirit of God, they are the sons of God" (Rom. 8:14). This verse presents to us another aspect of the varied work of the blessed Holy Spirit. In addition to all His other functions, He performs the office of Guide unto the godly. Nor is this peculiar to the present dispensation: He so ministered during the Old Testament times. This is brought out clearly in Isaiah 63, "Where is he that brought them up out of the sea with the shepherd of his flock? where is he that put his Holy Spirit within him? That led them by the right hand of Moses with his glorious arm, dividing the water before them, to make himself an everlasting name? That led them through the deep as a horse in the wilderness, that they should not stumble? As a beast goeth down into the valley, *the Spirit of the Lord* caused him to rest; *so* didst thou *lead* thy people to make thyself a glorious name" (vv. 11-14). Moses was no more able by his own power to induce the Hebrews to pass between the divided waters of the Red Sea and to cross the trackless desert, than by the mere extending of the rod he could divide those waters. Moses was simply the human instrument: the Holy Spirit was the efficient Agent.

In the above passage we have more than a hint of *how* the Holy Spirit "leads": it is by means of an inward impulse, as well as by external directions. Among his comments upon Romans 8:14 Matthew Henry says, "Led by the Spirit as a scholar in his learning is led by his tutor, as a traveller in his journey is led by his guide, as a soldier in his engagements is led by his captain." But such analogies are inadequate, for they present only the *external* side, leaving out of account the internal operations of the Spirit, which are even more essential. "O Lord, I know that the way of man is not in himself: it is not in man that walketh to direct his steps" (Jer. 10:23). By nature we are not only ignorant of God's way, but reluctant to walk therein even when it is shown us, and therefore we find the church praying, "*Draw* me, we will run after thee" (Song of Sol. 1:4). Ah, we never seek unto God, still less "run after Him," till we are Divinely drawn.

This humbling truth was well understood by David of old. First, he prayed, "Teach me, O Lord, the way of thy statutes. . . . Give me understanding" (Ps. 119:33, 34). But second, he realized that something more than Divine illumination was needed by him: therefore did he add, "*Make me to go* in the path of thy commandments. . . . *Incline my heart unto* thy testimonies" (vv. 35, 36). By nature our hearts are

110

averse from God and holiness. We can be worldly of ourselves, but we cannot be heavenly of ourselves. The power of sin lies in the love of it, and it is only as our affections are Divinely drawn unto things above that we are delivered from sin's dominion. Moreover, our *wills* are perverse, and only as supernatural grace is brought to bear upon them are they "inclined" Godwards. Thus, to be "*led* by the Spirit of God" is to be *governed* by Him from within, to be subject to His secret but real impulses or strivings.

Not only are our hearts inclined *by nature* to temporal, material, worldly, and evil things, rather than to eternal, spiritual, heavenly and holy things, but they are by inveterate *custom*, too. As soon as we are born we follow the bent of our natural appetites, and the first few years of our life are governed merely by sense; and the pleasures begotten by gratifying our senses become deeply ingrained in us. Moreover, by constant living in the world and long contact with material things, the tendency increases upon us and we become more strongly settled in a worldly frame. "Can the Ethiopian change his skin, or the leopard his spots? Then may ye also do good, that are *accustomed* to do evil" (Jer. 13:23). Custom becomes a "second nature" to us: the more we follow a certain course of life, the more we delight in it, and we are only weaned from it with very great difficulty.

Natural lusts and appetites, being born and bred in us from infancy, continue to cry out for indulgence and satisfaction. The will has become bent to a carnal course and the heart craves material pleasures. Hence when the claims of God are presented to us, when the interests of our *souls* and the things of *eternity* are brought before us, when the "beauty of *holiness*" is presented to our view, they find our wills already biased in the contrary direction and our heart prepossessed with other inclinations, which by reason of long indulgence bind us to them. The heart, being deeply engaged with a delighting in temporal and worldly things, is quite unable to respond to the dictates of reason and set itself upon that which is heavenly and Divine; and even the voice of conscience is unheeded by the soul, which prefers the insidious lullaby of Satan. Naught but the Almighty power of the Holy Spirit can turn ("lead") the heart in a contrary direction.

Now the heart is *inclined* toward God when the habitual bent of our affections is more to holiness than to worldly things. As the power of sin lies in the love of it, so it is with indwelling grace. Grace prevails over us when we so love the things of God that the bent of the will and the strength of our affections is carried after them. When the course of our desires and endeavors, and the strength and stream of our souls, runs out after holiness, then the heart is "inclined" Godwards. And how is this brought to pass? How does God reduce our rebellious hearts and mold them to the obedience of His will? The answer is, by His Word and by His Spirit; or putting it another way, by moral persuasion and by gracious power.

"And I will put my Spirit within you, and *cause* you to walk in my statutes" (Ezek. 36:27). This God does by combining together invincible might and gentle inducements. God works upon us morally, not physically, because He will preserve our nature and the principles thereof. He does not force us against our wills, but sweetly draws us. He presents weighty reasons, casting into the mind one after another, till the scales be turned and then all is made efficacious by His Spirit. Yet this is not a work which He does in the soul once for all, but is often renewed and repeated; and that because the "flesh" or sinful nature remains in us, unchanged, even after regeneration. Therefore do we need to ask God to *continue* inclining our hearts toward Himself.

This brings us to notice the intimate connection which exists between our present text and the verse immediately preceding it. "For if ye live after the flesh, ye shall die; but if ye through the Spirit do mortify the deeds of the body, ye shall live" (Rom. 8:13). If we yield ourselves to the Spirit's impulses to restrain our evil propensities and our proneness to indulge them, then Heaven will be our portion, "For as many as are led by the Spirit of God, they are the sons of God." Thus, Romans 8:14 is said in confirmation and amplification of verse 13; only those who are *ruled by* the Spirit give evidence that they are the "sons of God." To be "led by the Spirit," then, means, as the whole context clearly shows, to "walk not after the flesh, but after the Spirit" (v. 4), to "mind the things of the Spirit" (v. 5), to "through the Spirit mortify the deeds of the body" (v. 13). Suitably did Calvin remark on Romans 8:14, "Thus the empty boasting of hypocrites is taken away, who without any reason assume the title of sons of God."

Thus we are "led by the Spirit" both actively and passively: actively, with respect to His prompting; passively on our part, as we submit to those promptings; actively, by His pressing upon us the holy requirements of the Scriptures; passively, as we yield ourselves to those requirements. The Spirit is our Guide, but we must obey His motions. In the immediate context it is His *restraining* motives which are in view, moving us to the mortifying of sin. But His "leading" is not to be restricted to that: He exercises *inviting* motives, encouraging us to the perfecting of holiness. And this being guided and governed by the Holy Spirit is an infallible proof that we are living members of God's family.

It is the office of Jehovah the Spirit in the covenant of redemption, after He has called the elect out of the world, to place Himself at their head and undertake their future guidance. He knows the only path which leads to Heaven. He knows the difficulties and dangers which beset us, the intricate maze of life's journey, the numerous false routes by which Satan deceives souls, and the proneness of the human heart to follow that which is evil; and therefore He, in His infinite grace, takes charge of those who are "strangers and pilgrims" in this scene, and conducts them safely to the Celestial Country. O what praise is due to this heavenly Guide! How gladly and thankfully should we submit ourselves to His directions! How hopeless would be our case without Him! With what alacrity should we follow His motions and directions!

As we have already pointed out, the blessed Spirit of God "leads" both objectively and subjectively: by pointing us to the directive precepts of the Word, that our actions may be regulated thereby; and by secret impulses from within the soul, impressing upon us the course we should follow — the evils to be avoided, the duties to be performed. The Spirit acts upon His own life in the renewed soul. He works in the Christian a right disposition of heart relating to Truth and duty. He maintains in the believer a right disposition of mind, preparing and disposing him to attend unto the revealed will of God. He speaks effectually to the conscience, enlightens the understanding, regulates the desires, and orders the conduct of those who submit themselves to His holy suggestions and overtures. To be "led by the Spirit of God" is to be under His guidance and government.

The wayward child and the self-willed youth is guided by his own unsanctified and unsubdued spirit. The man of the world is controlled by "the spirit of the world." The wicked are governed by Satan, "the spirit that now worketh in the children of disobedience" (Eph. 2:2). But the Christian is to yield himself to "the still small voice" of the Holy Spirit. Yet a word of caution is needed at this point, for in our day there are many fanatics and impious people who do that which is grossly dishonoring to God under the plea that they were "prompted by the Spirit" so to act. To be "led by the Spirit of God" does not mean being influenced by unaccountable suggestions and uncontrollable impulses which result in conduct displeasing to God, and often injurious to ourselves and others. No, indeed; not so does the Spirit of God "lead" any one.

There is a safe and sure criterion by which the Christian may gauge his inward impulses, and ascertain whether there proceeds from his own restless spirit, an evil spirit, or the Spirit of God. That criterion is the written Word of God, and *by it* all must be measured. The Holy Spirit never prompts anyone to act contrary to the Scriptures. How could He, when He is the Author of them! *His* promptings are always unto obedience to the precepts of Holy Writ. Therefore, when a man who has not been distinctly called, separated, and qualified by God to be a minister of His Word, undertakes to "preach," no matter how strong the impulse, it proceeds not from the Holy Spirit. When a woman "feels led" to pray in public where men are present (I Cor. 14:34), she is moved by "another spirit" (II Cor. 11:4), or if one claimed "guidance" in assuming an unequal yoke by marrying an unbeliever (II Cor. 6:14), would prove conclusively that it was *not* the "guidance" of the Holy Spirit.

The Holy Spirit fulfils His office of Guide by three distinct operations. First, He communicates life and grace, a new "nature"; second, He stirs that life unto action, and gives "more grace"; third, He directs the action into performance of duty. Life, motion and conduct are inseparable in nature and grace alike. First, the Holy Spirit quickens us into newness of life, infusing gracious habits into the soul: "A new heart will I give you, and a new spirit will I put within you" (Ezek. 36:26). Second, He moves upon the soul and assists the new nature to act according to its own gracious habits and principles: He "worketh in us both to will and to do of His good pleasure" (Phil. 2:13). Third, He *directs* our actions by enlightening our understandings, guiding our inclinations, and moving our wills to do that which is pleasing to God. It is the last two we are now considering.

Divine direction is *promised* the saints: "The meek will he guide in judgment, and the meek will he teach his way" (Ps. 25:9): and this not only by general directions, but by particular excitations. "I am the Lord thy God which teacheth thee to profit, which leadeth thee by the way that thou shouldest go" (Isa. 48:17). Divine guidance is *desired* by the saints as a great and necessary blessing: "Show me thy ways, O Lord; teach me thy paths. Lead me in thy truth and teach me: for thou art the God of my salvation; on thee do I wait all the day" (Ps. 25:4, 5). Mark the earnestness of this prayer: "show me, teach me, lead me." Note the argument: "Thou art the God of my salvation," and as such, pledged to undertake for me. Observe the importunity: "on thee do I wait all the day," as if he would not be left for a moment to his own poor wisdom and power. Even the "new nature" is utterly dependent upon the Holy Spirit.

Though the children of God are "light in the Lord" (Eph. 5:8) and have a general understanding of the way of godliness, yet much ignorance and darkness still remains in them, and therefore in order to keep a steady and constant course of obedience they need to be guided by the Holy Spirit, so that their light may be both directive and persuasive. Though Christians have a general understanding of their duty, yet to perform it in particular cases much grace from God is needed by them. If left to themselves, their own corruptions would blind and govern them, and therefore do they pray, "Order my steps in thy Word, and let not any iniquity have dominion over me" (Ps. 119:133). The way to Heaven is a "narrow" one, hard to find and harder still to be kept, except God teach us *daily* by His Spirit. Wisdom from on High is continually needed to know how to apply the rules of Scripture to all the varied details of our lives. The Holy Spirit is the only fountain of holiness, and to Him we must constantly turn for directions.

But something more than knowledge is needed by us: the Spirit must persuade and incline our hearts, and move our wills. How strong are our inclinations to sin, how easily fleshly impulses override our better judgment, how weak we are before temptation! We know what we *should* do, but are carried away by corrupt affections to the contrary. It is at *this* point the Holy Spirit governs from within. First, by His restraining motions, bidding us to avoid and mortify sin; second, by His quickening motions, inviting us to the pursuit of holiness. And just so far as we *yield* to His "strivings" are we "*led* by the Spirit of God." As moral agents we are responsible to co-operate with the Spirit and respond to His gentle sway over us. Alas, we so often fail to do so. But though He suffers this up to a certain point — for our humbling — yet by His invincible power He prevents our making shipwreck of the faith, and after many chastenings, conducts us safely to Glory.

In conclusion we will seek to supply the answer to the following question: *How* may Christians know whether they be among those who are "led by the Spirit of God" (Rom. 8:14)? In general, those who are directed by this Divine Guide are moved to examine their hearts and take frequent notice of their ways, to mourn over their carnality and perverseness, to confess their sins, to earnestly seek grace to enable them to be obedient. They are moved to search the Scriptures daily to ascertain the things which God has prohibited and the things which He enjoins. They are moved to an increasing conformity to God's holy Law, and an increasing enablement to meet its requirements is wrought in them by the Spirit blessing to them the means of grace. But to be more specific.

First, just so far as we are governed by the Spirit of God are we *led from ourselves*: from confidence in our own wisdom, from dependence upon our own strength, and from trust in our own righteousness. We are led from self-will, self-pleasing, self-aggrandizement. The Spirit conducts away from self unto God. Yet let it be pointed out that this weaning us from ourselves is not accomplished in a moment, but is a perpetual and progressive thing. Alas, at best God has but a portion of our affections. It is true there are moments when we sincerely and ardently desire to be fully and unreservedly surrendered to him, but the ensnaring power of some rival object soon discovers how partial and imperfect our surrender has been.

Second, just so far as we are governed by the Spirit of God are we *brought to occupation with Christ*. To whom else, in our deep need, can we go? Who so well-suited to our misery and poverty? Having severed us in some degree from ourselves, the Spirit brings us into a closer realization of our union with the Saviour. Are we conscious of our filth and guilt? The Spirit leads to the blood of Christ. Are we sorely tried and oppressed? The Spirit leads unto Him who is able to succor the tempted. Are we mourning our emptiness and barrenness? The Spirit leads to the One in whom dwelleth all the fulness of the Godhead bodily. It is the special office of the Spirit to take of the things of Christ and show them to us.

Third, just so far as we are governed by the Spirit of God are we *conducted along the highway of holiness*. The Spirit leads the Christian away from the vanities of the world, to the satisfying delight which is to be found in the Lord. He turns us from the husks which the swine feed upon to spiritual realities, drawing our affections to things above. He moves us to seek after more intimate and more constant communion with God, which can only be obtained by separation from that which He abhors. His aim is to conform us more and more to the image of Christ. Finally, He will conduct us to Heaven, for of it the Spirit is both the pledge and the earnest.

22

The Spirit Assuring

WE do not propose to treat of the Spirit assuring in a topical and general way, but to confine ourselves to His inspiring the Christian with a sense of his adoption into the family of God, limiting ourselves to two or three particular passages which treat specifically thereof. In Romans 8:15 we read, "For ye have not received the spirit of bondage again to fear; but ye have received the Spirit of adoption, whereby we cry, Abba, Father." The eighth chapter of Romans has ever been a great favorite with the Lord's people, for it contains a wide variety of cordials for their encouragement and strengthening in the running of that heavenly race which is marked out and set before them in the Word of God. The apostle is there writing to such as have been brought, by the grace and power of the Holy Spirit, to know and believe on the Lord Jesus, and who by their communion with Him are led to set their affection upon things above.

First, let us observe that Romans 8:15 opens with the word "For," which not only suggests a close connection with that which precedes, but intimates that a proof is now furnished of what had just been affirmed. In verse 12 the apostle had said, "Therefore, brethren, we are debtors, not to the flesh, to live after the flesh": the "Therefore" being a conclusion drawn from all the considerations set forth in verses 1-11. Next, the apostle had declared, "For if ye live after the flesh, ye shall die: but if ye through the Spirit do mortify the deeds of the body, ye shall live" (v. 13); which means, first, ye shall *continue* to "live" a life of *grace* now; and second, this shall be followed by a "life" of *glory* throughout eternity. Then the apostle added, "For as many as are led by the Spirit of God, they are the sons of God" (v. 14), which is a confirmation and amplification of verse 13: none live a life of grace save those who are "led by the Spirit of God" — are inwardly controlled and outwardly governed by Him: for they only are "the sons of God."

Now, in verse 15, the apostle both amplifies and confirms what he had said in verse 14: there he shows the reality of that relationship with God which our regeneration makes manifest — obedient subjection to Him as dear children; here he brings before us further proof of our Divine sonship — deliverance from a servile fear, the exercise of a filial confidence. Let us consider the negative first: "For ye have not received the spirit of bondage again to fear." By nature we were in "bondage" to sin, to Satan, to the world; yet they did not work in us a spirit of "fear," so they cannot be (as some have supposed) what the apostle had reference to: rather is it what the Spirit's convicting us of sin wrought in us. When He applies the law to the conscience our complacency is shattered, our false peace is destroyed, and we are terrified at the thought of God's righteous wrath and the prospect of eternal punishment.

When a soul has received life and light from the Spirit of God, so that he perceives the infinite enormity and filthiness of sin, and the total depravity and corruption of every faculty of his soul and body, that spirit of *legality* which is in all men by nature, is at once stirred up and alarmed, so that the mind is possessed with secret doubts and suspicions of God's mercy in Christ to save; and thereby the soul is brought into a state of legal bondage and fear. When a soul is first awakened by the Holy Spirit, it is subject to a variety of fears; yet it does not follow from thence that *He* works those fears or is the Author of them: rather are they to be ascribed to our own unbelief. When the Spirit is pleased to convict of sin and gives the conscience to feel the guilt of it, it is to show him his need of *Christ*, and not to drive unto despair.

No doubt there is also a dispensational allusion in the passage we are now considering. During the Mosaic economy, believing Israelites were to a considerable extent under the spirit of legal bondage, because the sacrifices and ablutions of the Levitical institutions could not take away sins. The precepts of the ceremonial law were so numerous, so various, so burdensome, that the Jews were kept in perpetual bondage. Hence, we find Peter referring to the same as "a yoke which neither our fathers nor we were able to bear" (Acts 15:10). Much under the Old Testament dispensation tended to a legal spirit. But believers, under the gospel, are favored with a clearer, fuller, and more glorious display and revelation of God's grace in the person and work of the Lord Jesus Christ, the Evangel making known the design and sufficiency of His finished work, so that full provision is now made to deliver them from all servile fear.

Turning now to the positive side: believers have "received the Spirit of adoption, whereby they cry, Abba, Father": they have received that unspeakable Gift which attests and makes known to them their adoption by God. Before the foundation of the world God predestinated them "unto the adoption of children by Jesus Christ to himself" (Eph. 1:5). But more: the elect were not only predestinated *unto* the adoption of children — to actually and openly enjoy this inestimable favor in time — but this blessing was itself provided and bestowed upon them in the Everlasting Covenant of grace, in which they not only had promise of this relationship, but were given in that covenant to Christ under that very character. Therefore does the Lord Jesus say, "Behold I and the children which God hath given me" (Heb. 2:13).

It is to be carefully noted that God's elect are spoken of as "children" *previous to* the Holy Spirit's being sent into their hearts: "Because ye *are* sons, God hath sent forth the Spirit of His Son into your hearts" (Gal. 4:6). They are not, then, made children by the new birth. They were "children" before Christ died for them: "he prophesied that Jesus should die for that nation; And not for that nation only, but that also he should gather together in one *the children* of God that were scattered abroad" (John 11:51, 52). They were not, then, made children by what Christ did for them. Yea, they were "children" before the Lord Jesus became incarnate: "Forasmuch then as *the children* are partakers of flesh and blood, he also himself likewise took part of the same" (Heb. 2:14). Thus it is a great mistake to confound adoption and regeneration: they are two distinct things; the latter being both the effect and evidence of the former. Adoption was by an act of God's will in eternity; regeneration is by the work of His grace in time.

Had there been no adoption, there would be no regeneration: yet the former is not complete without the latter. By adoption the elect were put into *the relation* of children; by regeneration they are given *a nature* suited to that relation. So high is the honor of being taken into the family of God, and so wondrous is the privilege of having God for our Father, that some extraordinary benefit is needed by us to assure our hearts of the same. This we have when we receive the Spirit of adoption. For God to give us His Spirit is far more than if He had given us all the world, for the latter would be something *outside* Himself, whereas the former *is* Himself. The death of Christ on the cross was a demonstration of God's love for His people, yet that was done without them; but in connection with what we are now considering "the love of God is shed abroad *in our hearts* by the Holy Spirit which is given unto us" (Rom. 5:5).

Wondrous and blessed fact that God manifests His love to the members of His Church in precisely the same way that He evidenced His love to its Head when He became incarnate, namely, by the transcendent gift of His Spirit. The Spirit came upon Jesus Christ as the proof of God's love to Him and also as the visible demonstration of His Sonship. The Spirit of God descended like a dove and abode upon Him, and then the Father's voice was heard saying, "This is my beloved Son, in whom I am well pleased" (compare John 3:34, 35). In fulfillment of Christ's prayer, "I have declared to them thy name, and will declare it; that the love wherewith thou hast loved me may be *in them*" (John 17:26) the Spirit is given to His redeemed, to signify the sameness of the Father's love to His Son and to His sons. Thus, the inhabitation of the Spirit in the Christian is both the surest sign of God's fatherly love and the proof of his adoption.

"Because ye are sons, God hath sent forth the Spirit of his Son into your hearts, crying, Abba, Father" (Gal. 4:6). Because they had been eternally predestinated unto the adoption of sons (Eph. 1:4, 5); because they were actually given to Christ under that character in the Everlasting Covenant (John 11:52; Heb. 2:13), at God's appointed time the Holy Spirit is sent into their hearts to give them a knowledge of the wondrous fact that they have a place in the very family of God and that God is their Father. This it is which inclines their hearts to love Him, delight in Him, and place all their dependence on Him. The great design of the gospel is to reveal the love of God to His people, and thereby recover their love to God, that they may love Him again who first loved them. But the bare revelation of that love in the Word will not secure this, until "the love of God is shed abroad in our hearts by the Holy Spirit which is given unto us" (Rom. 5:5).

It is by the gracious work of the Holy Spirit that the elect are recovered from the flesh and the world unto God. By nature they love themselves and the world above God; but the Holy Spirit imparts to them a new nature, and Himself indwells them, so that they now love God and live to Him. This it is which prepares them to believe and appropriate the gospel. The effects of the Spirit's entering as the Spirit of adoption are liberty, confidence, and holy delight. As they had "received" from the first Adam "the spirit of bondage" — a legalistic spirit which produced "fear"; their receiving the Spirit of adoption is all the more grateful: liberty being the sweeter because of the former captivity. The Law having done its work in the conscience, they can now appreciate the glad tidings of the gospel — the revelation of the amazing love and grace of God in Jesus Christ. A spirit of love is now bred in them by the knowledge of the same.

The blessed fruit of receiving the Spirit of adoption is that there is born in the heart a childlike affection toward God and a childlike confidence in Him: "Whereby we cry, Abba, Father." The apostle employs in the original two different languages. "Abba," being Syrian, and "Father," being Greek, the one familiar to the Jews, the other to the Gentiles. By so doing he denotes that believing Jews and Gentiles are children of one family, alike privileged to approach God as their Father. "Christ, our peace, having broken down the middle wall of partition between them; and now, at the same mercyseat, the Christian Jew and the believing Gentile, both one in Christ Jesus, *meet*, as the rays of light converge and blend in one common centre — at the feet of the reconciled Father" (O. Winslow).

As the Spirit of adoption, the Holy Spirit bestows upon the quickened soul a filial spirit: He acts in unison with the Son and gives a sense of our relationship as sons. Emancipating from that bondage and fear which the application of the law stirred up within us, He brings into the joyous liberty which the reception of the gospel bestows. O the blessedness of being delivered from the Covenant of Works! O the bliss of reading our sentence of pardon in the blood of Immanuel! It is by virtue of our having received the Spirit of adoption that we cry "Father! Father!" It is the cry of our own heart, the desire of our soul going out to God. And yet *our* spirit does not originate it: without the immediate presence, operation, and grace of the Holy Spirit we neither would nor could know God as our "Father." The Spirit is the Author of everything in us which goes out after God.

This filial spirit which the Christian has received is evidenced in various ways. First, by a holy *reverence* for God our Father, as the natural child should honor or reverence his human parent. Second, by *confidence* in God our Father, as the natural child trusts in and relies upon his earthly parent. Third, by *love* for our Father, as the natural child has an affectionate regard for his parent. Fourth, by *subjection to*

God our Father, as the natural child obeys his parent. This filial spirit prompts him to approach God with spiritual freedom, so that he clings to Him with the confidence of a babe, and leans upon Him with the calm repose of a little one lying on its parent's breast. It admits to the closest intimacy. To God *as his "Father"* the Christian should repair at all times, casting all his care upon Him, knowing that He careth for him (I Peter 5:7). It is to be manifested by an affectionate subjection (obedience) to Him "as dear children" (Eph. 5:1).

"The Spirit of adoption is the Spirit of God, who proceedeth from the Father and the Son, and who is sent by Them to shed abroad the love of God in the heart, to give a real enjoyment of it, and to fill the soul with joy and peace in believing. He comes to testify of Christ; and by taking of the things which are His, and showing them to His people, He draws their heart to Him; and by opening unto them the freeness and fullness of Divine grace, and the exceeding great and precious promises which God has given unto His people, He leads them to know their interest in Christ; and helps them in His name, blood, and righteousness, to approach their heavenly Father with holy delight" (S. E. Pierce).

John Gill observes that the word "Abba" reads backwards the same as forwards, implying that God is the Father of His people in adversity as well as prosperity. The Christian's is an inalienable relationship: God is as much his "Father" when He chastens as when He delights, as much so when He frowns as when He smiles. God will never disown His own children or disinherit them as heirs. When Christ taught His disciples to pray He bade them approach the mercyseat and say, "Our Father which art in heaven." He Himself, in Gethsemane, cried, "Abba, Father" (Mark 14:36) — expressive of His confidence in and dependency upon Him. To address God as "Father" encourages faith, confirms hope, warms the heart, and draws out its affections to Him who is Love itself.

Let it next be pointed out that this filial spirit is subject to the state and place in which the Christian yet is. Some suppose that if we have received the Spirit of adoption there must be produced a steady and uniform assurance, a perpetual fire burning upon the altar of the heart. Not so. When the Son of God became incarnate, He condescended to yield unto all the sinless infirmities of human nature, so that He hungered and ate, wearied and slept. In like manner, the Holy Spirit deigns to submit Himself to the laws and circumstances which ordinarily regulate human nature. In Heaven the man Christ Jesus is glorified; and in Heaven the Spirit in the Christian will shine like a perpetual star. But on earth, He indwells our hearts like a flickering flame; never to be extinguished, but not always bright, and needing to be guarded from rude blasts, or why bid us "quench not the Spirit" (I Thess. 5:19)?

The Spirit, then, does not grant the believer assurance irrespective of his own carefulness and diligence. "Let your loins be girded, your lights *burning*" (Luke 12:35): the latter being largely determined by the former. The Christian is not always in the enjoyment of a childlike confidence. And why? Because he is often guilty of "grieving" the Spirit, and then He withholds much of His comfort. Hereby we may ascertain our communion with God and when it is interrupted, when He be pleased or displeased with us — by the motions or withdrawings of the Spirit's consolation. Note the order in Acts 9:31, "Walking in the fear of the Lord and in the comfort of the Holy Spirit"; and again in Acts 11:24, "He was a good man and full of the Holy Spirit." Hence, when our confidence toward "the Father" is clouded, we should search our ways and find out what is the matter.

Empty professors are fatally deluded by a false *confidence,* a complacent taking for granted that they are real Christians when they have never been born again. But many true possessors are plagued by a *false diffidence,* a doubting whether they be Christians at all. None are so inextricably caught in the toils of a false confidence as they who suspect not their delusion and are unconscious of their imminent danger. On the other hand, none are so far away from that false confidence as those who tremble lest *they* be cherishing it. True diffidence is a distrust of *myself.* True confidence is a leaning wholly upon *Christ,* and *that* is ever accompanied by utter renunciation of myself. Self-renunciation is the heartfelt acknowledgment that my resolutions, best efforts, faith and holiness, are nothing before God, and that Christ must be my All.

In all genuine Christians there is a co-mingling of real confidence and false diffidence, because as long as they remain on this earth there is in them the root of faith and the root of doubt. Hence their prayer is "Lord, I believe; help thou mine unbelief" (Mark 9:24). In some Christians *faith* prevails more than it does in others; in some *unbelief* is more active than in others. Therefore some have a stronger and steadier assurance than others. The presence of the indwelling Spirit is largely evidenced by our frequent recourse to the Father in prayer — often with sighs, sobs, and groans. The consciousness of the Spirit of adoption within us is largely regulated by the extent to which we yield ourselves to His government.

23

The Spirit Witnessing

THE Holy Spirit is first a witness *for* Christ, and then He is a witness *to* His people of Christ's infinite love and the sufficiency of His finished work. "But when the Comforter is come, whom I will send unto you from the Father, the Spirit of Truth, which proceedeth from the Father, he shall testify ["bear witness"] of me" (John 15:26). The Spirit bears His testimony to us in our renewed minds. He is a Witness for the Lord Jesus by all that is revealed in the Sacred Volume concerning Him. He bears witness to the abiding efficacy of Christ's offering: that sin is effectually put away thereby, that the Father hath accepted it, that the elect are forever perfected thereby, and that pardon of sins is the fruit of Christ's oblation.

The sufficiency of the Spirit to be Witness for Christ unto His people appears, first, from His being a Divine Person; second, from His being present when the everlasting covenant was drawn up; third, from His perfect knowledge of the identity of each member of the election of grace. When the ordained hour strikes for each one to be quickened by Him, He capacitates the soul to receive a spiritual knowledge of Christ. He shines upon the Scriptures of Truth and into the renewed mind. He enables the one born again to receive into his heart the Father's record concerning His beloved Son, and to give full credit to it. He enables him to realize that the Father is everlastingly well pleased with every one who is satisfied with the person, righteousness, and atonement of His co-equal Son, and who rests his entire hope and salvation thereon. Thereby He assures him of the Father's acceptance of him in the Beloved.

Now the Spirit is a Witness unto God's people both objectively and subjectively: that is to say, He bears witness *to* them, and He also bears witness *in* them; such is His wondrous grace toward them. His witness to them is in and through and by means of the Scriptures. "By one offering He hath perfected forever them that are sanctified: whereof the Holy Spirit also is a witness to us" (Heb. 10:14, 15), which is explained in what immediately follows. A quotation is made from the prophet Jeremiah, who had spoken as he was moved by the Holy Spirit (II Peter 1:21). The Lord declares of His people "their sins and iniquities will I remember no more." Whereupon the Holy Spirit points out, "Now where remission of these is, there is no more offering for sin." Thus does He witness to us, through the Word, of the sufficiency and finality of Christ's one offering.

But something more is still required by God's needy people, for they are the subjects of many fears, and Satan frequently attacks their faith. It is not that they have any doubt about the Divine inspiration of the Scriptures, or the unerring reliability of everything recorded therein, nor is it that they are disposed for a moment to call into question the infinite sufficiency and abiding efficacy of the sacrifice of Christ. No; that which occasions them such deep concern is, whether *they* have a saving interest therein. Not only are they aware that there is a faith (such as the demons have — James 2:19) which obtains no salvation, not only do they perceive that the faith of which many empty professors boast so loudly is *not evidenced* by their works, but they discover so much in themselves that appears to be altogether incompatible with their being new creatures in Christ, until they often fear their own conversion was but a delusion after all.

When an honest soul contemplates the amazing greatness of the honor and the stupendousness of the relation of regarding itself as a joint-heir with Christ, it is startled and staggered. What, *me* a child of God! God *my* Father! Who am I to be thus exalted into the Divine favor? Surely it cannot be so. When I consider my fearful sinfulness and unworthiness, the awful depravity of my heart, the carnality of my mind, such rebellion of will, so prone to evil every moment, and such glaring flaws in all I undertake — surely I cannot have been made a partaker of the Divine nature. It seems impossible; and Satan is ever ready to assure me that I am not God's child. If the reader be a stranger to such tormenting fears, we sincerely pity him. But if his experience tallies with what we have just described, he will see how indispensable it is that the Holy Spirit should bear witness to him *within*.

But there are some who say that it is a sin for the Christian to question his acceptance with God because he is still so depraved, or to doubt his salvation because he can perceive little or no holiness within. They say that such doubting is to call God's Truth and faithfulness into question, for He has assured us of His love and His readiness to save all who believe in His Son. They affirm it is not our duty to examine our hearts, that we shall never obtain any assurance by so doing; that we must look to Christ alone, and rest on His naked Word. But does not Scripture say, "For our rejoicing is this: *the testimony of our conscience,* that in simplicity and godly sincerity, not with fleshly wisdom but by the grace of God we have had our conversation in the world" (II Cor. 1:12)? And again; we are told, "Let us not love in word, neither in tongue; but in deed and in truth. And *hereby* we know that we are of the truth, and shall *assure our hearts* before him" (I John 3:18, 19).

But it is insisted that Scripture forbids all doubting: "O thou of little faith, wherefore didst thou doubt?" (Matt. 14:31). Yes, but Christ was *not* there blaming Peter for doubting his spiritual *state,* but for fearing he would be drowned. Yet Christ "upbraided them with their unbelief" (Mark 16:14): true, for not believing He was risen from the dead — not for calling into question their regeneration. But Abraham is commended because "against hope [all appearances] he believed in hope" (Rom. 4:18): yes, and that was that he should have a son! How is that relevent to what we are now discussing? But "we walk by faith, and not by sight" (II Cor. 5:7): yes, the conduct of the apostles was governed by a realization of that which is to come (see v. 11). But "Whatsoever is not of faith is sin" (Rom. 14:23): but this is nothing to the purpose; if a man does not believe it is right to do some act, and yet ventures to do it, he sins.

Let us define more closely the point now under discussion. We may state it thus: Does God require anyone to believe he has been born again when he has no clear *evidence* that such be the case? Surely, the question answers itself: the God of Truth never asks any one to believe a lie. If my sins have *not* been pardoned, then the more firmly convinced I am that they *have been,* the worse for me; and very ready is Satan to second me in my self-deception! The Devil would have me assured that all is well with me, *without* a diligent search and thorough examination for sufficient *evidence* that I am a new creature in Christ. O how many he is deceiving by making them believe it is wrong to challenge their profession and put their hearts to a real trial.

True, it *is* a sin for a real Christian so to live that his evidences of regeneration are not clear; but it is no sin for him to be honest and impartial, or to doubt when, in fact, his evidences are not clear. It is sin to darken my evidences, but it is no sin to discover that they *are* darkened. It is a sin for a man, by rioting and drunkenness, to make himself ill; but it is no sin to *feel* he is sick, or, if there be grounds for it, to doubt if he will survive his sickness. Our sins bring upon us *inward* calamities as well as outward, but these are chastisements rather than sins. It is the Christian's sins which lay the foundation for doubts, which occasions them; yet those doubtings are not themselves sins.

But it will be said, believers are exhorted to "hold fast the confidence and rejoicing of the hope firm unto the end" (Heb. 3:6) and that "we are made partakers of Christ if we hold the beginning of our confidence steadfast unto the end" (v. 14). Yes, but *that* "confidence" is, that Jesus is the Christ, together with a true faith in Him, as is clear from the whole context there. Nothing is more absurd then to say that professing Christians are made partakers of Christ by holding fast the confidence *that they are saved,* for that is what many a *deceived* soul does, and does to the very end (Matt. 7:22). There can be no well-grounded confidence unless it rests upon clear evidence or reliable testimony. And for *that,* there must be not only "the answer of a good conscience" (I Peter 3:21), but the confirmatory witness of the Spirit.

The Holy Spirit who dwelleth in Christ, the great and eternal Head of His people, dwelleth also in all the living members of His mystical Body, to conform them to Him and to make them like Him in their measure. He it is who takes possession of every quickened soul, dwelling in them as the Spirit of life, of grace, of holiness, of consolation, of glory. He who made them alive *in* the Lord, now makes them alive *to* the Lord. He gives them to know the Father in the Son, and their union with

Christ. He leads them into communion with the Father and the Son, and fulfills all the good pleasure of His will in them and the work of faith with power (II Thess. 1:11). In the carrying on of His "good work" in the soul — commenced in regeneration, and manifested in conversion to the Lord — the Spirit is pleased to act and perform the office of Witness: "The Spirit itself beareth witness with our spirit, that we are the children of God" (Rom. 8:16).

Now the office of a "witness" is to bear testimony or supply evidence for the purpose of adducing proof. The first time this term occurs in the epistle to the Romans is in 2:15, "Which show the work of the law written in their hearts, their conscience also *bearing witness*, and their thoughts the meanwhile accusing or else excusing." The reference is to the Heathen: though they had not recieved from God a written revelation (like the Jews had), nevertheless, they were His creatures, responsible creatures, subject to His authority, and will yet be judged by Him. The grounds upon which God holds them accountable are, first, the revelation which He has given them of Himself in creation, which renders them "without excuse" (Rom. 1:19, 20); and second, the work of His law written in their hearts, that is, their rationality or "the light of nature." But not only do their moral instincts instruct them in the difference between right and wrong, and warn them of a future day of reckoning, but their conscience also bears witness — it is a Divine monitor within, *supplying evidence* that God is their Governor and Judge.

But while the Christian ever remains a creature accountable to his Maker and Ruler, he is also a child of God, and, normally (that is, while he is sincerely endeavoring to walk as such), his renewed conscience bears witness to — supplies evidence of — the fact; we say "renewed conscience," for the Christian has been renewed throughout the whole of his inner man. The genuine Christian is able to say, "We trust we have a good conscience, in all things *willing* to live honestly" (Heb. 13:18); the bent of his heart is for God and obedience to Him. Not only is there a desire to please God, but there are answerable *endeavors*: "Herein do I exercise myself to have always a conscience void of offense toward God and men" (Acts 24:16). When these endeavors are carried on there is inward assurance of our state: "For our rejoicing is this, the testimony of our conscience" (II Cor. 1:12).

Thus, the Christian's sincerity is evidenced by his conscience. It is true that there is also "another law in his members, warning against the law of his mind, and bringing him into captivity to the law of sin" (Rom. 7:23); yet *that* is his grief, and not his joy; his burden, and not his satisfaction. It is true that "to will is present with him, but how to perform that which is good [how to attain unto what he ardently desires and prays for] he finds not," yea, the good that he loves to do, he often does not; and the evil which he hates, he often falls into (Rom. 7:18, 19). Even so; yet, blameworthy and lamentable though such things be, it in no wise alters the fact that the one whose experience it is, can call God Himself to witness that he wishes with all his heart it were otherwise; and his own conscience testifies to his sincerity in expressing such a desire.

It is most important that the Christian should be quite clear as to *what it is* his own "spirit" or conscience bears witness to. It is *not* to the eradication of evil from his heart, nor is it to any purification of or improvement in his carnal nature — anyone whose conscience bears witness to *that*, bears witness to *a lie*, for "if we say we have no sin we deceive ourselves, and the truth is not in us" (I John 1:8). So long as the Christian remains on earth, "the flesh [the principle of sin] lusteth against the Spirit" [the principle of grace]" (Gal. 5:17). Moreover, the more our thoughts are formed by the Word, the more do we discover how full of corruption we are; the closer we walk with God, the more light we have, and the more are the hidden (unsuspected) things of darkness within discovered to our horrified gaze. Thus, the Christian's assurance that he is a regenerate person by no means signifies he is conscious that he is more and more dying to the presence and activities of indwelling sin. God does not intend that we should be in love with ourselves.

That which the renewed conscience of the Christian bears witness to is the fact that he is a child of God. Side by side with the sink of iniquity which indwells the believer — of which he becomes increasingly conscious, and over which he daily groans — is the spirit of adoption which has been communicated to his heart. That filial spirit draws out his heart in love to God, so that he craves after the conscious enjoyment of His smiling countenance, and esteems fellowship with Him high above all other privileges. That filial spirit inspires confidence toward God, so that he pleads His promises, counts on His mercy, and relies on His goodness. The filial spirit begets reverence for God, so that His ineffable majesty is held in awe, His high authority is respected, and he trembles at His Word. That filial spirit produces subjection to God, so that he desires to obey Him in all things, and sincerely endeavors to walk according to His commands and precepts.

Now here are definite marks by which the Christian may test himself. True, he is yet very far from being what he *should* be or what he *would* be could his earnest longings only be realised; nevertheless, is not his present case very different from what it once was? Instead of seeking to banish God from your thoughts, is it not now the desire of your heart for your mind to be stayed upon Him, and is it not a joy to meditate upon His perfections? Instead of giving little or no concern as to whether your conduct honored or dishonored the Lord, is it not now your sincere endeavor to please Him in all your ways? Yes. Instead of paying no attention to indwelling sin, has not the plague of your heart become your greatest burden and grief? Yes. Well, then, these very things *evidence* you are a child of God. They were not in you by nature, so they must have been implanted by the Holy Spirit. Those graces may be very feeble, yet their *presence* — struggling amid corruptions — are marks of the new birth.

If with honesty of purpose, lowliness of heart, and prayerful inquiry,

I find myself breathing after holiness, panting after conformity to Christ, and mourning over my failures to realize the same, then so far from it being presumption for me to conclude I am a child of God, it would be wilful blindness to refuse to recognize the work of the Spirit in my soul. If my conscience bears witness to the fact that I honestly desire and sincerely endeavor to serve and glorify God, then it is wrong for me to deny, or even to doubt, that God has "begun a good work" in me. Take note of your health, dear reader, as well as of your disease. Appropriate to yourself the language of Christ's Spouse, "I sleep, but my heart waketh" (Song of Sol. 5:2) — grace is to be owned amid infirmities; that which is a cause for humiliation, must not be made a ground for doubting.

But notwithstanding the evidences which a Christian has of his Divine sonship, he finds it no easy matter to be assured of his sincerity, or to establish solid comfort in his soul. His moods are fitful, his frames variable. Grace in the best of us is but small and weak, and we have much cause to mourn the feebleness of our faith, the coldness of our love, and the grievous imperfections of our obedience. But it is at this very point the blessed Spirit of God, in His wondrous grace and infinite condescension, helps our infirmities: He adds *His* witness to the testimony of our renewed conscience, so that (at times) the conviction is confirmed, and the trembling heart is assured. It is at such seasons the Christian is able to say, "My conscience also bearing me witness in the Holy Spirit" (Rom. 9:1).

The question which most deeply exercises a genuine saint is not, Have I repented, have I faith in Christ, have I any love for God? But rather, Are my repentance, faith and love *sincere and genuine?* He has discovered that Scripture distinguishes between repentance (I Kings 21: 27) and repentance "not to be repented of" (II Cor. 7:10); between faith (Acts 8:13) and "faith unfeigned" (I Tim. 1:5), between love (Matt. 26:49) and "love in sincerity" (Eph. 6:24); and only by the gracious enabling of the Holy Spirit can any soul discern between them. He who bestowed upon the Christian repentance and faith must also make him to *know* the things which are freely given to him of God (I Cor. 2:12). Grace can only be known by grace, as the sun can only be seen in its own light. It is only by the Spirit Himself that we can be truly assured we have been born of Him.

Rightly did Jonathan Edwards affirm, "Many have been the mischiefs that have arisen from that false and delusory notion of the witness of the Spirit, that it is a kind of inward voice, suggestion, or revelation from God to man, that he is beloved of Him, and that his sins are pardoned — sometimes accompanied with, sometimes without a text of Scripture; and many have been the false and vain (though very high) affections that have arisen from hence. It is to be feared that multitudes of souls have been eternally undone by it." Especially was this so in the past, when fanaticism made much of the Spirit witnessing *to* souls.

An affectionate and dutiful child has within his own bosom the proof of the peculiar and special relationship in which he stands to his father.

So it is with the Christian: his filial inclinations and aspirations after God prove that he is His child. In addition to this, the Holy Spirit gives assurance of the same blessed fact by shedding abroad in his heart the love of God (Rom. 5:5). The Holy Spirit's indwelling of the Christian is the sure mark of his adoption. Yet the Spirit cannot be discerned by us in His essence: only by means of His operations is He to be known. As we discern His work, we perceive the Worker; and *how* His work in the soul can be *ascertained* without diligent examination of our inward life and a careful comparison of it with the Scriptures, we know not. The Spirit reveals Himself to us by that spirit which He begets in us.

"The Spirit itself beareth witness with our spirit, that we are the children of God" (Rom. 8:16). Let it be carefully noted that this verse does not say the Spirit bears witness *to* our spirit (as it is so often misquoted), but "*with*" — it is a single word in the Greek (a compound verb) "beareth witness with." It is deeply important to notice this distinction: the witness of the Spirit is not so much a revelation which is made to my spirit, considered as the recipient of the testimony, as it is a *confirmation* made in or with my spirit, considered as co-operating in the testimony. It is not that my spirit bears witness that I am a child of God, and that then the Spirit of God comes in by a distinguishable process with a separate testimony, to say Amen to my assurance; but it is that there is a single testimony which has a conjoint origin.

The "witness" of the Spirit, then, is *not* by means of any supernatural vision nor by any mysterious voice informing me I am a child of God — for the devil tells many a hypocrite that. "This is not done by any immediate revelation or impulse or merely by any text brought to the mind (for all these things are equivocal and delusory); but by coinciding with the testimony of their own consciences, as to their uprightness in embracing the Gospel and giving themselves up to the service of God. So that, whilst they are examining themselves concerning the reality of their conversion, and find scriptural evidence of it, the Holy Spirit from time to time shines upon His own work, excites their holy affections into lively exercise, renders them very efficacious upon their conduct, and thus puts the matter beyond all doubt" (T. Scott).

First, the Spirit's witness is in strict accord with the teaching of Holy Writ. In the Word He has given certain marks by which the question may be decided as to whether or not I am a child of God: He has described certain features by which I may identify myself (see John 8:39; Rom. 4:12 and 8:14 and contrast John 8:44 and Eph. 2:2, 3). It is by the Truth that the Spirit enlightens, convicts, comforts, feeds, and guides the people of God; and it is by and through the Truth that He bears witness with their spirit. There is a perfect harmony between the testimony of Scripture and the varied experiences of each renewed soul, and it is by revealing to us this harmony, by showing us the correspondency between the history of our soul and the testimony of the Word that He persuades us we are born again: "Hereby we know that we are of the truth, and shall assure our hearts before Him" (I John 3:19).

Second, He works such graces in us as are peculiar to God's children, and thereby evidences our interest in the favor of God. He makes the Christian to feel "poor in spirit," a pauper dependent upon the charity of God. He causes him to "mourn" over much which gives the worldling no concern whatever. He bestows a spirit of "meekness" so that the rebellious will is, in part, subdued, and God's will is submitted unto. He gives a "hunger and thirst after righteousness" and gives the soul to feel that the best this perishing world has to offer him is unsatisfying and but empty husks. He makes him "merciful" toward others, counteracting that selfish disposition which is in us by nature. He makes him "pure in heart" by giving him to pant after holiness and hate that which is vile (Matt. 5:3-8, etc.). By His own fruit in the soul, the Spirit makes manifest His indwelling presence.

Third, He helps us to discern His work of grace in our souls more clearly. Conscience does its part, and the Spirit confirms the same. The conjoint witness of the Spirit gives vigor and certainty to the assurance of our hearts. When the flood-waters of a land mingle themselves with a river they make one and the same stream, but it is now more rapid and violent. In like manner, the united testimonies of our own conscience and of the Spirit make but one witness, yet it becomes such as to break down our fears and overcome our doubts. When the blessed Spirit shines upon His own work of grace and holiness in our souls, then in His light we "see light" (Ps. 36:9). Inward holinesss, a filial spirit, an humble heart, submission to God, is something that the devil cannot imitate.

Fourth, He helps us not only to see grace, but to judge of the sincerity and reality of it. It is at this point many honest souls are most sorely exercised. It is much easier to prove that we believe, than to be assured that our faith is a saving one. It is much easier to conclude that we love Him in sincerity and for what He is in Himself. Our hearts are fearfully deceitful, there are such minglings of faith and unbelief (Mark 9:24), and grace in us is so feeble, that we hesitate to pronounce positively upon our state. But when the Spirit increases our faith, rekindles our love, strengthens us with might in the inner man, He enables us to come to a definite conclusion. First He sanctifies and then He certifies.

The deceits of Satan, though often plausible imitations up to a point, are, in their tendency and outcome, always opposed to that which God enjoins. On the other hand, the operations of the Spirit are ever in unison with the written Word. Here, then, is a sure criterion by which we may test *which* spirit is at work within us. The three truths of Scripture which more directly concern us are, our ruin by nature, our redemption by grace, and the duties we owe by virtue of our deliverance. If then, our beliefs, our feelings, our assurance, tend to exalt depraved nature, depreciate Divine grace, or lead to a licentious life, they are certainly not of God. But if they have quite the opposite tendency, convincing us of our wretchedness by nature, making Christ more precious to us, and leading us into the duties He enjoins, they are of the Holy Spirit.

It only remains for us to ask, Why does not the Holy Spirit grant unto the Christian a strong and comforting assurance of his Divine sonship *at all times?* Various answers may be given. First, we must distinguish between the Spirit's *work* and His *witness*: often it is His office to convict and make us miserable, rather than to impart comfort and joy. Second, His assuring consolation is often withheld because of our slackness: we are bidden to "make your calling and election sure" and "*be diligent* that ye may be found of Him in peace" (II Peter 1:10; 3:14) — the comforts of the Spirit drop not into lazy souls. Third, because of our sins: "The Holy Spirit fell on all them which heard the word" (Acts 10:44) — not while they were walking in the paths of unrighteousness. His witness is a *holy* one. He will not put a jewel in a swine's snout (Prov. 11:22). Keep yourselves in the love of God (Jude 21) and the Spirit's witness will be yours.

24

The Spirit Sealing

CLOSELY connected with the Spirit's work of witnessing with the Christian's spirit that he is a child of God, is His operation in sealing. This appears clearly from II Corinthians 1:19-22 and Ephesians 1:13.

The riches of the Christian are found in the promises of God, and these are all "Yea and Amen" in Christ: unless, then, our faith be built upon *them*, it is worthless. It is not sufficient that the promises be sure, we must be "established" upon them. No matter how firm the foundation (be it solid rock), unless the house be connected therewith, actually built thereon, it is insecure. There must be a *double* "Amen": one in the promises, and one in us. There must be an echo in the Christian's own heart: *God* says these things, so they must be true; faith appropriates them and says they *are for me*. In order to have assurance and peace it is indispensable that we be established in and on the Divine promises.

The Christian's *riches* lie in the promises of God: his *strength and comfort* in his faith being built upon them. Now the same Divine power which delivered the Christian from the kingdom of Satan and brought him into a state of grace, must also deliver him from the attacks of the enemy upon his faith and *confirm* him in a state of grace. Only God can produce stability: only He can preserve that spark of faith amid the winds and waves of unbelief, and this He is pleased to do — "He which hath begun a good work in you *will finish it*" (Phil. 1:6). Therefore are we told "Now he which *stablisheth* us with you in Christ . . . is God." Observe carefully it is *not* "hath stablished," but "stablisheth" — it is a continuous process throughout the Christian's life on earth.

In what follows the apostle shows us what this "stablishing" consists of, or how it is accomplished: "and hath *anointed* us . . . who hath also *sealed* us, and given the *earnest* of the Spirit in our heart" (II Cor. 1:22). Each of these figures refers to the same thing, and has to do with the "stablishing" or assuring of our hearts. Under the Old Testament economy prophets, priests, and kings were authorized and confirmed in their office by "anointing" (Lev. 8:11; II Sam. 5:3; I Kings 19:16). Again; contracts and deeds of settlement were ratified by "sealing" (Esth. 8:8; Jer. 32:8-10). And a "pledge" or "earnest" secured an agreement or bargain (Gen. 38:17, 18; Deut. 24:10). Thus *the sure estate* of the Christian is first expressed under the general word "stablisheth," and then it is amplified under these three figurative terms

131

"anointed, sealed, earnest." It is with the second of them we are now concerned.

It may be asked, But what need has the Christian of attestation or confirmation of his state in Christ — is not faith itself sufficient proof? Ah, often our faith and the knowledge we have of our believing in Christ is severely shaken; the activities of indwelling sin stir up a thick cloud of doubt, and Satan avails himself of this to tell us our profession is an empty one. But in His tender grace, God has given us the Holy Spirit, and from time to time He "seals" or *confirms* our faith by His quickening and comforting operations. He draws out our hearts anew unto God and enables us to cry "Abba, Father." He takes of the things of Christ, shows them to us, and brings us to realize that we have a personal interest in the same.

The same blessed truth is found again in Ephesians 1:13. It is important to note the order of the three things there predicated of saints: they "heard," they "believed," they were "sealed": thus the sealing is quite distinct from and follows the believing, as the believing does the hearing. There are two things, and two only, upon which the Spirit puts His seal, namely, two mighty and efficacious works: first, the finished work of Christ, whereby He put away sin by the sacrifice of Himself; and second, upon His own work in the hearts of those who believe. In legal documents the writing always precedes the witnessing and sealing: so here, the Spirit writes God's laws on the heart (Heb. 8:10), and then He seals the truth and reality of His own work to the consciousness of the recipient.

The main intent of "sealing" is to assure, to certify and ratify. First, the Holy Spirit conveys an assurance of the *truth* of God's promises, whereby a man's understanding is spiritually convinced that the promises are from God. Neither the light of reason nor the persuasive power of a fellow-mortal can bring any one to rest his heart upon the Divine promises: in order to do that, there must be the direct working of the Holy Spirit — "Our gospel came not unto you in word only, but also in power, and in the Holy Spirit, and in much assurance" (I Thess. 1:5): the "much assurance" comes last! Second, He gives the believer an assurance of his own *personal interest* in those promises: and this again is something which none but the Spirit can impart. We do not say that this sealing excludes all doubting, but it is such an assurance as *prevails* over doubts.

There are many uses of a "seal" such as proprietorship, identification, confirmation, secrecy, security; but in Ephesians 1:13 the immediate thing stated is *the sealing of an inheritance*: we have obtained an inheritance by faith, and having believed we are "sealed." What is the specific use of a "seal" in connection with an inheritance? It may either be the making of the inheritance *sure* to a man in itself, or making the man *know* that it is *his* — assuring him of the fact. Now it cannot be the former, for nothing is needed to make Heaven sure once a sinner truly believes — the moment he lays hold of Christ, the inheritance is certain. So it must be the latter: to make *us* sure, to persuade our hearts the inheritance is ours. It is this the Spirit accomplishes in His "seal."

The Holy Spirit is never called a "Seal" as He is an "Earnest" (II Cor. 5:5): it is only in relation to an *act* of sealing that this figure is associated with Him; thus it is a distinct operation of His "in our hearts" (II Cor. 1:22). It is not the stamping of God's image upon the soul (as many of the Puritans supposed) that is referred to in Ephesians 1:13, for that is done *before* believing, and not after. The order of truth in that verse is very simple and decisive: in the gospel salvation is offered — it *may* be mine; faith accepts that offer so as to *make* salvation mine; the Spirit seals or confirms my heart that salvation *is* mine. Thus in "sealing" the Spirit authenticates, certifies, ratifies.

Observe that He does this in His special character as "the Spirit of promise." He is so designated because, first, the Spirit was the great and grand promise of the New Testament (John 14:26; 15:26, etc.) as Christ was of the Old Testament. Second, because He works by means of the promises. Third, because in His whole work He acts according to the everlasting covenant, which, as it respects the elect, is a Covenant of Promise (Eph. 2:12). When He seals home a sense of the love of God and gives the soul a view of its interest in Christ, it is done by means of the Word of Promise. It was so when He "sealed" Christ (John 6:27) and consecrated Him to the work of redemption. The Father said by an audible voice from Heaven, "This is my beloved Son, in whom I am well pleased": this was repeating what had been pronounced in the purpose of Jehovah the Father concerning the Mediator (Isa. 42:1); this the Holy Spirit brought home in power or "sealed" upon the mind of Jesus at that time.

The "sealing" or assuring operations of the Spirit are known to the believer in two ways. First, *inferentially*: by enabling him to perceive His work in the soul and from it conclude his regeneration. When I see smoke I must infer a fire, and when I discern spiritual graces (however feeble) I reason back to the Producer of them. When I feel a power within combatting my corruptions, and often thwarting my intentions to indulge the lusts of the flesh, I conclude it is the Spirit resisting the flesh (Gal. 5:17). Second, intuitively: by a Divine light in the heart, by a Divine authority felt, by the love of God shed abroad therein. If I have any hope wrought in me, either by looking to Christ's blood or perceiving grace in me, it is by the power of the Spirit (Rom. 15:13).

The Spirit brings to the mind of the Christian the sacred promises. He shows us the good contained in them, the grace expressed in them, the perfection and freeness of Christ's salvation declared by them; and thereby He seals them on our mind and enables us to rest thereon. He shows us the veracity and faithfulness of God in the promises, the immutability of the everlasting covenant, the eternity of God's love, and that He hath by two immutable things (His word and His oath), in which it is impossible for Him to lie, given a firm foundation for strong consolation to us who have fled for refuge to lay hold upon the hope set before us in the gospel (Heb. 6:18). It is in this way that "the God of all grace" doth, by the Spirit, "stablish, strengthen, settle us" (I Peter 5:10). It is by the Spirit's operations that the Christian's fears are quietened, his doubts subdued, and his heart assured that a "good work" (Phil. 1:6) has been Divinely begun *in him*. The Spirit indwelling us is Christ's seal (mark of identification) that we are His sheep; the Spirit authenticating His own blessed work in our souls, by revealing to us our "title" to Heaven, is His *sealing* us.

25

The Spirit Assisting

A child of God oppressed, suffering sorely, often driven to his wit's end — what a strange thing! A joint-heir with Christ financially embarrassed, poor in this world's goods, wondering where his next meal is coming from — what an anomaly! An object of the Father's everlasting love, and distinguishing favor tossed up and down upon a sea of trouble, with every *apparent* prospect of his frail barque capsizing — what a perplexity! One who has been regenerated and is now indwelt by the Holy Spirit daily harassed by Satan, and frequently overcome by indwelling sin — what an enigma! Loved by the Father, redeemed by the Son, his body made the temple of the Holy Spirit, yet left in this world year after year to suffer affliction and persecution, to mourn and groan over innumerable failures, to encounter one trial after another, often to be placed in far less favorable circumstances than the wicked; to sigh and cry for relief, yet for sorrow and suffering *to increase* — what a mystery! What Christian has not felt the force of it, and been baffled by its inscrutability.

Now it was to cast light upon this pressing problem of the sorely tried believer that Romans 8 was written. There the apostle was moved to show that "the sufferings of this present time" (v. 18) are *not inconsistent* with the special favor and infinite love which God bears unto His people. First, because by those sufferings the Christian is brought into personal and experimental fellowship with the sufferings of Christ (v. 17; cf. Phil. 3:10). Second, severe and protracted as our afflictions may be, yet there is an immeasurable disproportion between our present sufferings and the future Glory (vv. 18-23). Third, our very sufferings provide occasion for the exercise of hope and the development of patience (vv. 24, 25). Fourth, Divine aids and supports are furnished us under our afflictions (vv. 26, 27) and it is *these* we would now consider.

"Likewise the Spirit also helpeth our infirmities" (Rom. 8:26). Not only does "hope" (a sure expectation of God's making good His promises) support and cheer the suffering saint, leading him to patiently wait for deliverance from his afflictions, but the blessed Comforter has also been given to him in order to supply help to this very end. By His gracious aid the believer is preserved from being totally submerged by his doubts and fears. By His renewing operations the spark of faith is maintained, despite all the fierce winds of Satan which assail. By His mighty enabling the sorely harassed and groaning Christian is kept from sinking into complete skepticism, abject despair, and infidelity. By His quickening power hope is still kept alive, and the voice of prayer is still faintly heard.

And how is the gracious help of the Spirit *manifested?* Thus: seeing the Christian bowed down by oppression and depression, His compassion is called forth, and He strengthens with His might in the inner man. Every Christian is a living witness to the truth of this, though he may not be conscious of the Divine process. Why is it, my afflicted brother, my distressed sister, that you have not made shipwreck of your profession long ere this? What has kept you from heeding that repeated temptation of Satan's to totally abandon the good fight of faith? Why has not your manifold "infirmities" annihilated your faith, extinguished your hope, and cast a pall of unrelieved gloom upon the future? The answer is, because the blessed Spirit silently, invisibly, yet sympathetically and effectually *helped* you. Some precious promise was sealed to your heart, some comforting view of Christ was presented to your soul, some whisper of love was breathed into your ear, and the pressure upon your spirit was reduced, your grief was assuaged, and fresh courage possessed you.

Here, then, is real light cast upon the problem of a suffering Christian, the most perplexing feature of that problem being how to harmonize sore sufferings with the love of God. But if God had ceased to care for His child, then He had deserted him, left him to himself. Very far from this, though, is the actual case: the Divine Comforter is given to help his infirmities. Here, too, is the sufficient answer to an objection which the carnal mind is ready to make against the inspired reasoning of the apostle in the context: How can we who are so weak in ourselves, so inferior in power to the enemies confronting us, bear up under our trials which are so numerous, so protracted, so crushing? We could not, and therefore Divine grace has provided for us an all-sufficient Helper. Without His aid we had long since succumbed, mastered by our trials. Hope looks forward to the Glory to come; in the weary interval of waiting, the Spirit supports our poor hearts and keeps grace alive within us.

"Our infirmities": note the plural number, for the Christian is full of them, physically, mentally and spiritually. Frail and feeble are we in ourselves, for "*all* flesh is grass, and all the goodliness thereof is as the flower of the field" (Isa. 40:6). We are "compassed with infirmity" (Heb. 5:2) both within and without. When trials and troubles come we are often bewildered by them and faint beneath them. When opposition and persecution break out against us because of our cleaving to the Truth and walking with Christ, we are staggered. When the chastening rod of our Father falls upon us, how we fret and fume. What a little thing it takes to disturb our peace, stifle the voice of praise and cause us to complain and murmur. How easily is the soul cast down, the promises of God forgotten, the glorious future awaiting us lost sight of. How ready are we to say with Jacob "All these things are against me," or with David "I shall now perish one day at the hand of Saul."

The "infirmities" of Christians are as numerous as they are varied. Some are weak in faith, and constantly questioning their interest in Christ. Some are imperfectly instructed in the Truth, and therefore ill-prepared to meet the lies of Satan. Some are slow travellers along the path of obedience, frequently lagging in the rear. Others groan under the burden of physical afflictions. Some are harassed with a nervous temperament which produces a state of perpetual pessimism, causing them to look only on the dark side of the cloud. Others are weighed down with the cares of this life, so that they are constantly depressed. Others are maligned and slandered, persecuted and boycotted, which to those of a sensitive disposition is well-nigh unbearable. "Our infirmities" includes all that causes us to groan and renders us the objects of the Divine compassion.

But "the Spirit also helpeth our infirmities." Here is a Divine revelation, for we had known nothing about it apart from the Scriptures. We are not left alone to endure our infirmities: we have a helper, a Divine Helper; One not far off, but with us; nay, *in* us. The Greek word here for "helpeth" is a striking one: it signifies to "take part with" or to "take hold with one." It occurs in only one other passage, namely, "bid Mary therefore that she help me" (Luke 10:40), where the obvious thought is, that Martha was asking for her sister's assistance to *share* the burden of the kitchen, that she might be eased. The Spirit "helpeth" the Christian's infirmities not only by a sympathetic regard, but by personal participation, supporting him beneath them, like a mother "helps" her child when he is learning to walk, or a friend gives his arm to an aged person to lean upon.

In his comments on this clause Calvin says, "The Spirit takes on Himself a part of the burden by which our weakness is oppressed, so that He not only succors us, but lifts us up, as though He went under the burden with us." Oh, how this should endear the blessed Spirit of God to us. We worship the Father, whence every mercy has its rise; we adore the Son, through whom every blessing flows; but how often we overlook the Holy Spirit, *by whom* every blessing is actually communicated and applied. Think of His deep compassion, His manifold succorings, His tender love, His mighty power, His efficacious grace, His infinite forbearance; all these challenge our hearts and should awaken fervent praises from us. They *would* if we meditated more upon them.

The Spirit does not remove our "infirmities," any more than the Lord took away Paul's thorn in the flesh; but He enables us to bear them. Constrained by a love which no thought can conceive, moved by a tenderness no tongue can describe, He places His mighty arm beneath the pressure and sustains us. Though He has been slighted and grieved by us a thousand times, receiving at our hands the basest requital for His tenderness, and grace, yet when a sword enters our soul or some fresh trouble bows us down to the ground, He again places beneath us the arms of his everlasting love and prevents our sinking into hopeless despair.

It is a great infirmity or weakness for the Christian to faint in the day of adversity, yet such is often the case. It is a sad thing when, like Rachel of old weeping for her children, he "refuses to be comforted" (Jer. 31:15). It is most deplorable of all when he so gives way to unbelief that the Lord has to say to him, "How is it, that ye have no faith?" (Mark 4:40). Terrible indeed would be his end if God were to leave him entirely to himself. This is clear from what is said in Mark 4:17, "when affliction or persecution ariseth for the word's sake, immediately they are offended," or as Luke says, "Which for a while believe, and in time of temptation fall away" (8:13). And *why* does the stony-ground hearer apostatize? Because he is *without* the assistance of the Holy Spirit! Writer and reader would do the same if no Divine aid were forthcoming!

But thank God, the feeble and fickle believer is not left to himself: "the Spirit also helpeth our infirmities" (Rom. 8:26). That "help" is as manifold as our varied needs; but the apostle singles out one particular "infirmity" which besets all Christians, and which the blessed Spirit graciously helps: "for we know not what we should pray for as we ought; but the Spirit itself maketh intercession for us." How this Divine declaration should humble us into the dust; so depraved is the saint that in the hour of need he is incapable of asking God aright to minister unto him. Sin has so corrupted his heart and darkened his understanding that, left to himself, he cannot even discern *what* he should ask God for. Alas, that pride should so blind us to our real condition and our deep, deep need.

In nothing do the saints more need the Spirit's presence and His gracious assistance than in their addresses of the Throne of Grace. They know that God in His persons and perfections is the Object of their worship; they know that they cannot come unto the Father but by Christ, the only Mediator; and they know that their access to Him must be by the Spirit (Eph. 2:18). Yet such are their varying circumstances, temptations, and wanderings, so often are they shut up in their frames and cold in their affections, such deadness of heart is there toward God and spiritual things, that at times they know not what to pray for as they ought. But it is *here* that the Spirit's love and grace is most Divinely displayed: He helpeth their infirmities and maketh intercession for them!

One had thought that if ever there is a time when the Christian would really *pray*, earnestly and perseveringly, and would know what to ask for, it should be when he is sorely tried and oppressed. Alas, how little we really know ourselves. Even a beast will cry out when suffering severe pain, and it is *natural* (not spiritual!) that we should do the same. Of degenerate Israel of old God said, "they have not cried unto me with their *heart* when they *howled* upon their beds" (Hos. 7:14): no, *relief* from their sufferings was all they thought about. And by nature *our* hearts are just the same! So long as we are left to ourselves (to try us and manifest what we are: II Chron. 32:31), when the pressure of sore trial comes upon us, we are concerned only with *de-*

liverance from it, and not that God may be glorified or that the trial may be sanctified to our souls.

Left to himself, man asks God for what would be curses rather than blessings, for what would prove to be snares rather than helps to him spiritually. Have we not read of Israel that, "They tempted God in their heart by asking meat for their lust" (Ps. 78:18); and again, "He gave them their request: but sent leanness into their soul" (Ps. 106:15). Perhaps someone replies, But they were not regenerate souls. Then have we not read in James, "Ye ask, and receive not, because ye *ask amiss*, that ye may consume it upon your lusts" (4:3). This is a truth which is very unpalatable to our proud hearts. Did not Moses "ask" the Lord that he might be permitted to enter Canaan (Deut. 3:26, 27)? Did not the Apostle Paul thrice beseech the Lord for the removal of this thorn in the flesh? What *proofs* are these that "we *know not* what we should pray for as we ought!"

"The Spirit also helpeth our infirmities." This being so, surely the least that we can do is to *seek* His aid, to definitely ask Him to undertake for us. Alas, how rarely we do so. As intimated above, when the pressure of trouble first presses upon us, usually it is *nature* which cries out for relief. At other times the soul is so cast down that even the voice of natural "prayer" is stifled. Often there is so much rebellion at work in our hearts against the providential dispensations of God toward us that we feel it would be a mockery to seek *His* face; yea, we are ashamed to do so. Such at least has been the experience of the writer more than once, and that not long ago, though he blushes to acknowledge it. O the infinite patience and forbearance of our gracious God.

"We know not what we should pray for as we ought." And why? First, because we are so blinded by *self-love* that we are unable to discern what will be most for God's glory, what will best promote the good of our brethren (through some of the dross being purged out of us), and what will advance our own spiritual growth. O what wretched "prayers" (?) we put up when we are guided and governed by *self-interests*, and what cause do we give the Lord to say "ye know not what manner of spirit ye are of" (Luke 9:55). Alas, how often we attempt to make God the Servant of our carnal desires. Shall we ask our heavenly Father for worldly success? Shall we come to Him who was born in a stable and ask Him for temporal luxuries or even comforts?

Why is it that "we know not what we should pray for as we ought?" Second, because our minds are so discomposed by the trial and the suffering it brings, and then we have to say with one of old "I am so troubled that I cannot speak" (Ps. 77:4): so you see dear "brother and companion in tribulation" (Rev. 1:9) that *you* are not the first to experience spiritual dumbness! But it is most blessed to link with this such a promise as "For the Holy Spirit shall teach you in the same hour what ye ought to say" (Luke 12:12). *Why* is it that "we know not what we should pray for as we ought?" Third, because oftentimes our tongues are tied as the result of the leanness of our souls. It is "out of the abundance of the heart" that "the mouth speaketh" (Matt. 12:40), and if the Word of Christ be not dwelling in us "richly" (Col. 3:16), how can we expect to have the right petition to present to God in the hour of our need!

"The Spirit also helpeth our infirmities," but He does so silently and secretly, so that we are not conscious of His assistance at the time He renders it. That gracious and effectual help is manifested to us by *the effects* which it has produced in us; though so perverse are our hearts and so great is our pride, we often attribute those effects to our own willpower or resolution. Have we suddenly, or even gradually, emerged from the slough of despond? it was *not* because *we* had "come to our senses" or "regained our poise," rather was it solely due to the Spirit's renewing us in the inner man. Has the storm within us — which God's crossing of our will occasioned — been calmed? it was because the Spirit deigned to subdue our iniquities. Has the voice of true prayer again issued from us? it was because the Spirit had made intercession for us.

Lord God the Spirit, to whom Divine honor and glory belongeth, equally as to the Father and the Son, I desire to present unto Thee unfeigned praise and heartfelt thanksgiving. O how deeply am I indebted to Thee: how patiently hast Thou borne with me, how tenderly hast Thou dealt with me, how graciously hast Thou wrought in me. Thy love passeth knowledge, Thy forbearance is indeed Divine. O that I were more conscientious and diligent in seeking not to slight and grieve Thee.

26

The Spirit Interceding

IF left to himself, the believer would never see (by faith) the all-wise hand of God in his afflictions, still less would his heart ever honestly say concerning them *"Thy* will be done." If left to himself, he would never seek grace to patiently endure the trial, still less would he hope that afterwards, it would produce the peaceable fruit of righteousness (Heb. 12:11). If left to himself, he would continue to chafe and kick like "a bullock unaccustomed to the yoke" (Jer. 31:18), and would curse the day of his birth (Job 3:1). If left to himself, he would have no faith that his sufferings were among the "all things" working together for his ultimate good, still less would he "glory in his infirmity that the power of Christ might rest upon him" (II Cor. 12:9). Such holy exercises of heart are not the product of poor fallen human nature; instead, they are nothing less than the immediate, gracious, and lovely fruits of the Holy Spirit — brought forth amid such uncongenial soil. What a marvel!

"Likewise the Spirit also helpeth our infirmities, for we know not what we should pray for as we ought" (Rom. 8:26). At no one point is the Christian made more conscious of his "infirmities" than in connection with his prayer-life. The effects of indwelling corruption are such that often prayer becomes an irksome task rather than the felt delight of a precious privilege; and strive as he may, he cannot always overcome this fearful spirit. Even when he endeavors to pray, he is handicapped by wanderings of mind, coldness of heart, the intrusion of carnal cares; while he is painfully conscious of the *unreality* of his petitions and *unfelt* confessions. How cold are the effusions of our hearts in secret devotions, how feeble our supplications, how little solemnity of mind, brokenness of heart. How often the prayer exercises of our souls seem a mass of confusion and contradiction.

"But the Spirit itself maketh intercession for us with groanings which cannot be uttered" (Rom. 8:26). It is particularly the help which the blessed Comforter gives the Christian in his prayer-life, in the counteracting of his "infirmities" which is now to engage our attention. In Zechariah 12:10 He is emphatically styled "The Spirit of grace and of *supplications,*" for He is the Author of every spiritual desire, every holy aspiration, every outgoing of the heart after God. Prayer has rightly been termed "the breathing of the newborn soul," yet we must carefully bear in mind that its respiration is wholly determined by the stirrings of the Holy Spirit within him. As the person, work and intercession of Christ are the foundation of all our confidence in approaching the Fa-

141

ther, so every spiritual exercise in prayer is the fruit of the Spirit's operations and intercession.

First, when the believer is most oppressed by outward trials and is most depressed by a sense of his inward vileness, when he is at his wit's end and ready to wring his hands in despair, or is most conscious of his spiritual deadness and inability to express the sinfulness of his case, the Spirit stirs him in the depths of his being: "The Spirit itself maketh intercession for us with groanings which cannot be uttered." There has been some difference of opinion as to whether this refers directly to groanings of the Spirit Himself, or indirectly to the spiritual groanings of the Christian, which are prompted and produced by Him. But surely there is no room for uncertainty: the words "*cannot* be uttered" could not apply to a Divine person. That which He *produces* in and through the believer is *ascribed to* the Spirit — the "fruit" of Galatians 5:22 and 4:6 compared with Romans 8:15.

As it is the Spirit who illumines and gives us to see the exceeding sinfulness of sin and the depravity of our hearts, so He is the One who causes us to groan over the same. The conscience is pierced, the heart is searched, the soul is made to *feel* something of its fearful state. The conscious realization of "the plague of our hearts" (I Kings 8:38) and its "putrifying sores" (Isa. 1:6), produces unutterable anguish. The painful realization of our remaining enmity against God, the rebellion of our wills, the woeful lack of heart-conformity to His holy Law, so casts down the soul that it is temporarily paralysed. Then it is that the Spirit puts forth His quickening operations, and we "groan" so deeply that we cannot express our feelings, articulate our woe, or unburden our hearts. All that we can do is to sigh and sob inwardly. But such tears of the heart are precious in the sight of God (Ps. 56:8) because they are produced by His blessed Spirit.

Second, when the soul is so sorely oppressed and deeply distressed the Spirit reveals to the mind *what* should be prayed for. He it is who pours oil on the troubled waters, quietens in some measure the storm within, spiritualizes the mind, and enables us to perceive the nature of our particular need. It is the Spirit who makes us conscious of our *lack* of faith, submissiveness, obedience, courage, or whatever it may be. He it is who gives us to see and feel our spiritual wants, and then to make them known before the Throne of Grace. The Spirit helps our infirmities by subduing our fears, increasing our faith, strengthening our hope, and drawing out our hearts unto God. He grants us a renewed sense of the greatness of God's mercy, the changelessness of His love, and the infinite merits of Christ's sacrifice before Him on our behalf.

Third, the Spirit reveals to cast-down saints that the *supplies of grace* for their varied needs are all expressed in the *promises* of God. It is those promises which are the measure of prayer, and contain the matter of it; for what God has promised, all that He has promised, but nothing else are we to ask for. "There is nothing that we really stand in need of, but God hath promised the supply of it, in such a way and under such limitations as may make it good and useful to us. And there is nothing that God hath promised but we stand in need of it, or are some way or other concerned in it as members of the mystical body of Christ" (John Owen). But at this point also the help of the Spirit is imperative, "that we might know the things that are freely given us of God" (I Cor. 2:12).

It is thus *that* the Spirit bears up the distressed minds of Christians: *by* directing their thoughts to those promises most suited to their present case, by impressing a sense of them upon their hearts, by giving them to discern that those precious promises contain in them the fruits of Christ's meditation, by renewing their faith so that they are enabled to lay hold of and plead them before God. Real prayer is in faith: faith necessarily respects God's promises: therefore if we understand not the *spiritual import* of the promises, the suitability of them to our varied cases, and reverently urge the actual fulfillment of them to us, then we have not *prayed* at all. But for *that* sight and sense of the promises, and the appropriation of them, we are entirely dependent upon the Holy Spirit.

Fourth, the Spirit helps the Christian to direct his petitions *unto right ends*. Many prayers remain unanswered because of our failure at this point: "Ye ask, and receive not, because ye ask amiss; that ye may consume it upon your lusts" (James 4:3). The "ask amiss" in that passage means, to ask for something with a wrong end in view, and were we left entirely to ourselves, this would *always* be the case with us. Only three ends are permissible: that God may be glorified, that our spirituality may be promoted, that our brethren may be blessed. Now none but the Spirit can enable us to subordinate all our desires and petitions unto *God's* glory. None but the Spirit can bring us to make our *advancement in holiness* our end — the reason why we ask God *to* grant our requests. This He does by putting into our minds a high valuation of conformity to God, a deep longing in the heart that His image may be more manifestly stamped upon us, a strong inclination of will to diligently seek the same by the use of all appointed means.

It is by the Spirit the sin-troubled Christian is helped to apprehend God as his Father, and his heart is emboldened to approach Him as such. It is by the Spirit we are granted a conscious access to the Throne of Grace. He it is who moves us to plead the infinite merits of Christ. He it is who strengthens us to pray in a holy manner, rather than from carnal motives and sentiments. He it is who imparts any measure of fervor to our hearts so that we "cry" unto God — which respects not the loudness of our voices, but the earnestness of our supplications. He it is who gives us a spirit of importunity, so that we are enabled (at times) to say with Jacob, "I will not let Thee go, except Thou bless me" (Gen. 32:26). And He it is who *prepares the heart* to receive God's answer, so that what is bestowed is a real blessing to us and not a curse.

In conclusion let it be pointed out that the motions of the Spirit in the saint are a "help" *to* prayer, but *not* the rule or reason *of* prayer. There are some who say that they never attempt to pray unless conscious that the Spirit moves them to do so. But this is wrong: the Spirit is given to help us in the performance of duty, and not in the neglect of it! God commands us to pray: *that* is our "rule" — "always to pray" (Luke 18:1), "in everything by prayer and supplication" (Phil. 4:6). For many years past, the writer has made it a practice of beginning his prayers by definitely and trustfully *seeking* the Spirit's aid: see Luke 11:13. Do not conclude that lack of words and suitable expressions is a proof that the Spirit is withholding His help. Finally, remember that He is a sovereign: "the wind bloweth where it listeth" (John 3:8).

God's Word is designed to have a twofold effect upon the Christian: a distressing and a comforting. As we appropriate the Scriptures to ourselves, pride will be abased and the old man cast down; on the other hand faith will be strengthened and the new man built up. Our poor hearts first need humbling, and then exalting; we must be made to mourn over our sins, and then be filled with praise at the realization of God's amazing grace. Now in Romans 8:26, 27 there is that which should produce *both* these effects upon us. First, we are reminded of "our *infirmities*" or weaknesses: note the plural number, for we are full of them — how our apprehension of this should "hide pride from us!" Yet, second, here is also real ground for comfort and hope: "the Spirit also *helpeth* our infirmities." The frail and erring believer is not left to himself: a gracious, all-powerful, ever-present Helper is given to support and assist him. How this blessed fact should rejoice our hearts!

The tones of Scripture, then, fall upon the ear of God's children in ever alternating keys: the minor and the major. So it is in the passage before us, for next we read "*we know not* what we should pray for as we ought." What a pride-withering word is that! one which is in direct variance with what is commonly supposed. The general belief is that men *do know* well enough what they should pray for, but they are so careless and wicked they do not discharge this duty; but God says, they "*know not*." Nor can the godliest saint or wisest minister help the unregenerate at this point, by drawing up for them a form of words, which suitably expresses their needs, for it is one thing to have Scriptural words upon our lips, but it is quite another for the soul to *feel* his dire need of what he asks for; it is out of the abundance of the heart the mouth speaketh in prayer, or God will not hear.

But the words of our text are yet more searching and solemn: it refers not to the unregenerate (though of course it *is* true of them), but to the regenerate: "*we* [Christians] know not what we should pray for as we ought." And again we say, what a heart-humbling word is this. Now that we are partakers of the Divine nature, now that a way has been opened for us into the presence of God, now that we have access to the Throne of Grace itself, now that we are invited to "make known our requests"; yet so fearfully has sin darkened our judgment, so deceitful and wicked are our hearts, so blind are we as to what would truly promote the manifestative glory of God and what would really be for our highest good, that "we know not what we should pray for as we ought." Do you actually *believe this,* my reader? If you *do,* it must bring you into the dust before the One with whom we have to do.

"We know not what we should pray for as we ought." No, we "know not" even with the Bible in our hands, in which are full instructions to direct praying souls; in which are so many inspired prayers for our guidance. No, we "know not," even after the Lord Himself has graciously supplied us with a pattern prayer, after which ours should be modeled. Sin has so perverted our judgments, self-love has so filmed our eyes, worldliness has so corrupted our affections, that even with a Divine manual of prayer in our hands, we are quite incapable (of ourselves) of discerning *what* we should ask for — supplies of Divine grace to minister to our *spiritual* needs; and are unable to present our suit in a spiritual manner, acceptable to God. How the recognition of this fact should empty our hearts of conceit! how the realization of it should fill us with shame! What need have we to cry, "Lord, teach us *to* pray"!

But now on the other side: lest we should be utterly cast down by a sense of our excuseless and guilty ignorance, we are Divinely informed, "the Spirit itself *maketh intercession for us.*" Wondrous indeed, unspeakably blessed, is this. Instead of turning away from us in disgust because of our culpable ignorance, God has not only provided us with an Intercessor at *His* right hand (Heb. 7:25): but what is to the writer even more remarkable, God has given His needy people a Divine Intercessor at *their* right hand, even the Holy Spirit. How this glorious fact should raise our drooping souls, revolutionize our ideas of prayer, and fill our hearts with thanksgiving and praise for this unspeakable Gift. If it be asked, Why has God provided *two* Intercessors for His people, the answer is: *To bridge the entire gulf between Him and us.* One to represent *God* to us, the Other to represent *us* before God. The One to *prompt* our prayers, the Other to *present* them to the Father. The One to ask blessings *for* us, the Other to convey blessings *unto* us.

It is indeed striking to observe this alternation between the minor and major keys running all through our passage, for next we are told, "the Spirit maketh intercession for us with *groanings* which cannot be uttered." This, as we have seen, refers to the inward anguish which the Spirit produces in the believer. Here, then, is further ground for self-abasement. Even when a sense of need has been communicated to us, so sottish are we that our poor hearts are overwhelmed, and all we can do is to sigh and groan. Even when the Spirit has convicted us of our corruptions and imparted a deep yearning for Divine grace, we are incapable of articulating our wants or expressing our longings. Rather is our case then like the Psalmist's, "I was *dumb* with silence" (39:2). If left to ourselves the distress occasioned by our felt sinfulness would quite *disable* us to pray.

It may be objected, To what purpose is it that the Spirit should stir up such "groanings," which the Christian can neither understand nor express? Ah, this brings us to the brighter side again: "He that searcheth the hearts *knoweth what* is the mind of the Spirit" (Rom. 8:27). *God* knows what those groanings mean, for He discerns the very thoughts and intents of our hearts. How comforting is this: to realize in prayer we are coming to One who thoroughly understands us! How blessed to be assured that God will rightly interpret every motion the Spirit prompts within us. God "knows" the "mind of the Spirit" — His intention in producing our anguish. God is able to distinguish between the moanings of mere nature and the "groanings" of which the Spirit is the Author.

There is a fourfold "spirit" which works in prayer. First, the natural spirit of man, which seeks his own welfare and preservation. This is not sinful, as may be seen from the case of Christ in Gethsemane: the innocent desire of human nature to be delivered from the awful pressure upon Him; and then subjecting His will to the Father's. Second, a carnal and sinful spirit: "your brethren that hated you, that cast you out for my name's sake, said, *Let the Lord be glorified*" (Isa. 66:5), but God did not answer them in the way they meant. Third, the new nature in the believer, which has holy aspirations, but is powerless of itself to express them. Fourth, "praying in the Holy Spirit" (Jude 21) — by His prompting and power. Now God discerns between the motions of nature, the lustings of the flesh, the longings of grace, and the desires wrought by the Spirit. This it is which explains "The Lord weigheth the spirits" (Prov. 16:2) — the fourfold "spirit" mentioned above.

None but God *is able* to thus distinguish and interpret the "groanings" of the Spirit in the saint. A striking proof of this is found in, "Now Hannah, she spake in her heart; only her lips moved, but her voice was not heard: therefore Eli thought she had been drunken" (I Sam. 1:13). Even the high priest of Israel was incapable of discerning the anguish of her heart and what the Spirit had prompted within her. "He that searcheth the hearts *knoweth* what is the mind of the Spirit," signifies far more than that He understands: God *approves* and *delights in* — for *this* use of the word "know" see Psalm 1:6; Amos 3:2; John 10:14; I Corinthians 8:3. And *why* is it that God thus finds perfect complacency in the mind of our Helper? Because as the Father and the Son are one, so the Father and the Spirit are *one* — one in nature, in purpose, in glory.

"Because He maketh intercession for the saints according to the will of God." Here is additional ground for our encouragement. The words "the will of" are in italics, which means they are not in the Greek, but have been supplied by our translators. They interpose a needless limitation. That which the Spirit produces in the saint is, first, in accord with God's *nature* — spiritual and holy. Second, it is according to God's Word, for the Spirit ever prompts us to ask for what has been revealed or promised. Third, it is according to God's *purpose*, for the Spirit is fully cognizant of all the Divine counsels. Fourth, it is according to God's *glory*, for the Spirit teaches us to make *that* our end in asking. O what encouragement is here: the Spirit creates within us holy desires, the Son presents them, the Father understands and approves them! Then let us "*come boldly* to the Throne of Grace."

"Come, Holy Spirit, come
with energy Divine:
And on this poor benighted soul
with beams of mercy shine."

Just as there are certain verses in the Old Testament and the Gospels which give us a miniature of the redemptive work of Christ for God's people — such, for example, as Isaiah 53:5 and John 3:16 — so in the Epistles there are some condensed doctrinal declarations which express in a few words the entire work of the Spirit in reforming, conforming, and transforming believers. II Corinthians 3:18 is a case in point: "But we all, with open face, beholding as in a glass the glory of the Lord, are changed into the same image from glory to glory, even as by the Spirit of the Lord." This important passage supplies a brief but blessed summary of the progressive work of grace which is wrought in the Christian by the indwelling Spirit. It focuses to a single point the different rays which are emitted by the various graces which He communicates to them, namely, that wherein the saint is slowly but surely conformed unto and transfigured into the very image of the Lord.

There are many parts in and aspects of the Spirit's work in reforming, conforming, and transforming the believer, but they are here epitomised in one brief but most comprehensive statement, which we now propose to examine and expound. As an aid to this, let us proceed to ask our verse a number of questions. First, exactly what is meant by "the glory of the Lord," into "the same image" of which all believers "are changed"? — are, not "shall be." Second, what is "the glass" in which we are beholding this glory? Third, what is denoted in the "we are changed into the same image from glory to glory"? Fourth, what is the force of "we all with open face" are beholding this glory? Finally, how does the Spirit of the Lord effect this great change in believers? Are they entirely passive therein, or is there an active co-operation on their part?

Perhaps it will help the reader most if we first give brief answers to these questions and then supply amplifications of the same in what follows. The "glory of the Lord" here signifies His moral perfections, the excellences of His character. The "glass" in which His glory is revealed and in which those with anointed eyes may behold it, is the Holy Scriptures. Our being "changed into the same image" has reference to our salvation, viewed from the experimental side; that it is here said to be "from glory to glory" intimates it is a gradual and progressive work. Our beholding that glory with "open face" means that the veil of darkness, of prejudice, of "enmity," which was over our depraved hearts by nature, has been removed, so that in God's light we now see light. The Spirit effects this great change both immediately and mediately, that is, by His direct actions upon the soul and also by blessing to us our use of the appointed means of grace.

"The glory of the Lord." This we have defined as His moral perfections, the excellences of His character. The best theologians have classified God's attributes under two heads: incommunicable and communicable. There are certain perfections of the Divine Being which are peculiar to Himself, which in their very nature cannot be transmitted to the creature: these are His eternity, His immutability, His omnipotence, His omniscience, His omnipresence. There are other perfections of the Divine Being which He *is* pleased to communicate, in measure, to the unfallen angels and to the redeemed from among men: these are His goodness, His grace, His mercy, His holiness, His righteousness, His wisdom. Now, obviously, it is the latter which the apostle has before him in II Corinthians 3:18, for believers are not, will not, and cannot be changed into the "same image" of the Lord's omniscience, etc. Compare "we beheld His glory . . . full of *grace and truth*" (John 1:14) — His *moral* perfections.

The "glass" in which the glory of the Lord is revealed and beheld by us is His written Word, as is clear by a comparison with James 1:22-25. Yet let it be carefully borne in mind that the Scriptures have *two* principal parts, being divided into two Testaments. Now the contents of those two testaments may be summed up, respectively, in the law and the gospel. That which is outstanding in the Old Testament is *the law;* that which is pre-eminent in the New Testament is *the gospel.* Thus, in giving an exposition or explanation of the "glass" in which believers behold the Lord's glory, we cannot do better than say, It is in the law and the gospel His glory is set before us. It is absolutely essential to insist on this amplification, for a *distinctive* "*glory* of the Lord" is revealed in each one, and to *both* of them is the Christian conformed (or "changed") by the Spirit.

Should anyone say that we are "reading our own thoughts into" the meaning of the "glass" in which the glory of the Lord is revealed, and object to our insisting this signifies, first, *the law,* we would point out this is fully borne out by the immediate context of II Corinthians 3:18, and what is found there *obliges* us to take this view. The apostle is there comparing and contrasting the two great economies, the Mosaic and the Christian, showing that the pre-eminence of the one over the other lay in the former being an *external* ministration (the "letter"), whereas the latter is *internal* (the "spirit"), in the heart; nevertheless, he affirms that the former ministration "was *glorious*" (v. 7), and "if the ministration of condemnation be *glorious*" (v. 9), "for even that which is made *glorious*" (v. 10), "if that which was done away was *glorious*" (v. 11) — all being explained by the fact that the glory of the Lord was exhibited therein.

In the "glass" of the law the Lord gave a most wondrous revelation of His "glory." The law has been aptly and rightly designated "a transcript of the Divine nature," though (as is to be expected) some of our moderns have taken serious exception to that statement, thereby setting themselves in opposition to the Scriptures. In Romans 8:7 we are told "the carnal mind is enmity against God," and the proof furnished of this declaration is "*for* it is not subject to *the law* of God," which, manifestly, is only another way of saying that the law is a transcript of the very character of God. So again we read, "The law is holy, and the commandment holy, and just, and good" (Rom. 7:12): what is that but a summarized description of the Divine perfections. If God Himself is "holy and just and good" and the law be an immediate reflection of His very nature, then it will itself be "holy and just and good." Again, if God Himself be "love" (I John 4:8) and the law is a glass in which His perfections shine, then that which the law requires, all that it requires, will be *love*, and that is exactly the case (Matt. 22:37-39).

What a word is that in Exodus 24:16, "And *the glory of the Lord* abode upon Mount Sinai." Yes, the glory of the Lord was as really and truly manifested at Sinai as it is displayed now at mount Sion — that man in his present state was unable to appreciate the awe-inspiring display which God there made of His perfections, it nowise alters the fact, for He is a God to be feared as well as loved. In the "glass" of the law we behold the glory of the Lord's majesty and sovereignty, the glory of His government and authority, the glory of His justice and holiness; yes, and the "glory" of His *goodness* in framing such a law which requires us to love Him with all our hearts, and for His sake, as His creatures, our neighbors as ourselves.

But the "glory of the Lord" is further manifested in the "glass" of *the gospel*, in which God has made a fuller and yet more blessed revelation of His moral perfections than He did at Sinai. Now the gospel necessarily implies or presupposes the following things. First, a broken law, and its transgressors utterly unable to repair its breach. Second, that God graciously determined to save a people from its curse. Third, that He purposes to do so without making light of sin, without dishonoring the law, and without compromising His holiness — otherwise, so far from the gospel being the best news of all, it would herald the supreme calamity. *How* this is effected, by and through Christ, the gospel makes known. In His own Son God shines forth in meridian splendor, for Jesus Christ is the brightness of His glory, the express image of His person. In Christ the veil is rent, the holy of holies is exposed to fullest view, for now we behold "The light of the knowledge of the glory of God in the face of Jesus Christ" (II Cor. 4:6).

In the gospel is displayed not only the amazing grace and infinite mercy, but also and mainly the "manifold *wisdom*" of God. Therein we learn how grace is exercised righteously, how mercy is bestowed honorably, how transgressors are pardoned justly. God did not deem it suitable to the honor of His majesty to sovereignly pardon sinners without a satisfaction being offered to Himself, and therefore did He appoint a Mediator to magnify the law and make it honorable. The great design of the incarnation, life and death of Christ, was to demonstrate in the most public manner that God was worthy of all that love, honor and obedience which the law required, and that sin was as great an evil as the punishment threatened supposed. The heart of the glorious gospel of Christ is *the Cross*, and *there* we see all the Divine perfections fully displayed: in the death of the Lord Jesus the law was magnified, Divine holiness vindicated, sin discountenanced, the sinner saved, grace glorified, and Satan defeated.

Though the glory of the Lord be so plainly revealed in the two-fold "glass" of the law and the gospel, yet the unregenerate appreciate it not: concerning the one it is said, "But even unto this day, when Moses is read, the veil is upon their heart" (II Cor. 3:15); and of the latter we read, "In whom the god of this world hath blinded the minds of them that believe not, lest the light of the glorious gospel of Christ, who is the image of God, should shine unto them" (II Cor. 4:4). The unregenerate are blind to the loveliness of the Divine character: not that they have no eyes to see with, but that they have deliberately "closed them" (Matt. 13:15); not that they are not intellectually convinced of the Divine perfections, but that their hearts are *unaffected* thereby. It is because man is a fallen, depraved and vicious creature that he is not won by "the beauty of holiness."

"Except a man be born again he *cannot see* the kingdom of God." Clearest possible proof of this was furnished when the Word became flesh and tabernacled among men. Those who had been "born of God" (John 1:13) could say, "we *beheld His glory*, the glory as of the Only begotten of the Father, full of grace and truth" (John 1:14); but different indeed was it with those who were left in their natural state. They, notwithstanding their education, culture, and religion, were so far from discerning any form or comeliness in Christ, that they cried "Thou art a Samaritan, and hast a demon" (John 8:48). Yet it is as plain as a sunbeam that the blindness of the Pharisees was due neither to the lack of necessary faculties nor to the want of outward opportunities, but entirely to the perverted state of their minds and the depraved condition of their hearts — which was altogether of a criminal nature.

From what has just been pointed out, then, it is plain when the apostle declares "but we all with open face *beholding* as in a glass the glory of the Lord" (II Cor. 3:18), that a miracle of grace had been wrought in them. As spiritual blindness consists in an absence of relish for holy beauty — which blindness is capable of being greatly increased and confirmed through the exercise and influence of the various corruptions of a wicked heart, and which Satan augments by all means in his power — so spiritual sight is the soul's delighting itself in Divine and spiritual things. In regeneration there is begotten in the soul a holy taste, so that the heart now goes out after God and His Christ. This is referred to in Scripture in various ways. It is the fulfilment of that promise "And the Lord thy God will circumcise thine heart, and the heart of thy seed, *to love* the Lord thy God" (Deut. 30:6).

This new relish for spiritual things which is begotten in the soul by the immediate operations of the Spirit is also the fulfilment of "A new heart also will I give you, and a new spirit will I put within you: and I will take away the stony heart out of your flesh, and I will give you a heart of flesh" (Ezek. 36:26); and of "I will give them a heart to know me, that I am the Lord; and they shall be my people" (Jer. 24:7). So also, "Then the eyes of the blind shall be opened, and the ears of the deaf shall be unstopped" (Isa. 35:5). Of Lydia we read, "Whose heart the Lord opened, that she attended unto the things which were spoken of Paul" (Acts 16:14). To the Corinthian saints, the apostle wrote "For God, who commanded the light to shine out of darkness, *hath shined in our hearts*" (II Cor. 4:6). In consequence thereof, the happy subjects of this work of Divine grace perceive and relish the holy character of God and are enamored with His perfections.

"But we all": that is, all who have been supernaturally brought from death unto life, out of darkness into God's marvellous light; "with open face," or "unveiled face" as it is in the Greek and as the Revised Version translates it: that is, with hearts from which "the veil" of prejudice (II Cor. 3:15) has been removed, from which that "covering cast over all people" (Isa. 25:7), the covering of enmity against God, has been destroyed; "beholding" — note carefully the present tense, for it is a continuous action which is here in view; "as in a glass" or "mirror," namely, the twofold glass of the law and the gospel: "the glory of the Lord," that is His communicable perfections, His moral character; "*are changed into the same image*," this clause it is which must next engage our careful attention.

Following our usual custom let us first give a brief definition and then amplify the same. To be changed into "the same image" means that the regenerated soul becomes conformed unto the Divine character, that answerable principles and affections are wrought in his heart, bringing him into harmony with the perfections of God. This *must* be the case, for since Divinely enlightened souls have a relish for holy beauty, for *such* beauty as there is in the character of God, then it necessarily follows that every Divine truth as it comes into their view will appear beautiful and will accordingly beget and excite holy affections corresponding with its nature. Or, more specifically, as the heart is occupied with the several perfections of God exhibited in the law and in the gospel, corresponding desires and determinations will be awakened in and exercised by that soul.

It would imply a contradiction to suppose that any heart should be charmed with a character just the opposite to its own. The carnal mind is enmity against God: resenting His authority, disliking His holiness, hating His sovereignty, and condemning His justice: in a word, it is immediately opposed to His glory as it shines in the glass of the law and the gospel. But one who has been Divinely enlightened loves the Truth, because he has a frame of heart answerable thereto — just as the unregenerate soul loves the world because it suits his depraved tastes. The regenerate discerns and feels that the law is righteous in requiring what it does, even though it condemn him for his disobedience. He perceives too that the gospel is exactly suited to his needs, and that its precepts are wise and excellent. Thus he is brought into conformity with the one and into compliance with the other.

Universal experience teaches us that characters appear aggreeable or disagreeable just as they suit our taste or not. To an angel, who has a taste for holy beauty, the moral character of God appears infinitely amiable; but to the Devil, who is a being of a contrary taste, God's moral character appears just the reverse. To the Pharisees, no character was more odious than that of the Lord Jesus; but at the same time Mary and Martha and Lazarus were charmed with Him. To the Jewish nation in general, who groaned under the Roman yoke, and longed for a Messiah to set them at liberty, to make them victorious, rich and honorable; a Messiah in the character of a temporal prince, who had gratified their desires — such an one had appeared glorious in their eyes, and they would have been changed into the same image; that is, every answerable affection had been excited in their hearts.

Now it is this moral transformation in the believer which is *the evidence* of his spiritual enlightenment: "beholding" he is "changed." Where a soul has been supernaturally illumined there will issue a corresponding conformity to the Divine image. But in so affirming many of our Christian readers are likely to feel that we are thereby cutting off their hopes; they will be ready to exclaim, Alas *my* character resembles the likeness of the Devil far more than it does the image of God. Let us, then, ease the tension a little. Observe, dear troubled souls, this transformation is not effected instantaneously, but by *degrees*: this great "change" is not accomplished by the Spirit in a moment, but is a gradual work. This is plainly signified in the "*from* glory *to* glory" which means, from one degree of it to another. Only as this fact is apprehended can our poor hearts be assured before God.

This expression "from glory to glory" is parallel with "the rain also filleth the pools: they go from strength to strength" (Ps. 84:6, 7), which means that under the gracious revivings of the Spirit believers are renewed again and again, and so go on from one degree of strength to another. So in Romans 1:17 we read of "from faith to faith," which means from little faith to more faith, until sometimes it may be said "your faith groweth exceedingly" (II Thess. 1:3). So it is with this blessed "change" which the Spirit works in believers. The first degree of it is effected at their *regeneration*. The second degree of it is accomplished during their progressive (practical) *sanctification*. The third and last degree of it takes place at their *glorification*. Thus "the path of the just is as the shining light, that shineth *more and more* unto the perfect day" (Prov. 4:18).

27

The Spirit Transforming

WE will give a brief digest of our previous exposition of II Corinthians 3:18, which is a verse that supplies a comprehensive summary of the Spirit's work in the believer. The "we all" are those that are indwelt by the Holy Spirit. The "with open face" signifies with minds from which their enmity against God has been removed, with hearts that are reconciled to Him. "Beholding" is a *repeated* act of the soul, which is the effect of its having been supernaturally enlightened. "As in a glass" refers to the revelation which God has made of Himself in the law and in the gospel. The "glory of the Lord" connotes His character or moral perfections. "Are changed into the same image" tells of the transformation which is effected in the believer by the Spirit. The "from glory to glory" announces that this great change of the heart's reformation and conformation to the image of God is produced gradually.

When the Spirit deals with an elect soul, He first brings him face to face with God's law, for "by the law is the knowledge of sin" (Rom. 3:20). He reveals to him the perfections of the law: its spirituality, its immutability, its righteousness. He makes him realize that the law is "holy, and just, and good" (Rom. 7:12) even though it condemns and curses him. He shows that the law requires that we should love the Lord our God with all our hearts, and our neighbors as ourselves; that it demands perfect and perpetual obedience in thought, word, and deed. He convinces the soul of the righteousness of such a demand. In a word, the one with whom the Spirit is dealing beholds "the glory of the Lord" — His majesty, His holiness, His justice — in the glass of the law. Only thus is the soul prepared and fitted to behold and appreciate the second great revelation which God has made of His moral perfections.

Next, the Spirit brings before the soul the precious gospel. He shows him that therein a marvellous and most blessed display is made of the love, the grace, the mercy, and the wisdom of God. He gives him to see that in His eternal purpose God designed to save a people from the curse of the law, and that, without flouting its authority or setting aside its righteous claims; yea, in such a way that the law is "magnified and made honorable" (Isa. 42:21) through its demands being perfectly met by the believing sinner's Surety. He unveils to his wondering gaze the infinite condescension of the Father's Beloved, who willingly took upon Him the form of a servant and became obedient unto death, even the death of the Cross. And the Spirit *so* works in his heart that, though the Cross be a stumbling block to the Jew and foolishness unto the

Greek, it appears to him to be the most wondrous, blessed, and glorious object in the universe; and by faith he thankfully rests the entire interests of his soul for time and eternity upon the atoning sacrifice which Christ offered thereon unto God.

Not only does the Spirit give that soul to behold "the glory of the Lord" as it shines first in the "glass" of the law, and second in the "glass" of the gospel, but He also causes him to be "*changed into* the same image," that is, He begets within him corresponding principles and affections, to the one and to the other. In other words, He brings his heart to a *conformity* to the law and to a *compliance* with the gospel. He causes the believer to "set . . . his seal" (John 3:33) to the whole Truth of God. He brings him to a full acquiescence with the law, consenting to its righteous claims upon him, and working in him a desire and determination to adopt the law as his rule of life or standard of conduct. So too the Spirit causes him to gladly embrace the gospel, admiring the consummate wisdom of God therein, whereby the perfect harmony of His justice and mercy are blessedly exhibited. He brings him to renounce all his own works, and rest alone on the merits of Christ for his acceptance with God.

"Beholding as in a glass" is literally "in a mirror." Now the mirrors of the ancients, unlike ours, were not made of glass, but of highly burnished metal, which reflected images with great brilliancy and distinctness, corresponding to the metal. If the mirror was of silver, a white light would be the result; if of gold, a yellow glow would be suffused. Thus an opaque object reflected the rays of the sun, and so became in a measure luminous. Here the apostle makes use of this as a figure of the Spirit's transforming the believer. The law and the gospel display various aspects of "the glory of the Lord," that is, of God Himself, and as anointed eyes behold the same, the soul is irradiated thereby and an answerable change is wrought in it.

As the soul by faith, with *broken* heart (and not otherwise), beholds the glory of the Lord, in the mirror of the *two* Testaments (and not in the New without the Old), he is by the continual operations of the Spirit in him (Phil. 1:6) "changed into the same image." The views thus obtained of the Divine character excite answerable affections in the beholder. Rational argument may convince a man that God is holy, yet that is a vastly different thing from his heart being brought to *love* Divine holiness. But when the Spirit removes the veil of enmity and prejudice from the mind and enables the understanding to see light in God's light, there is a genuine esteem of and delight in God's character. The heart is won with the excellency of His moral perfections, and he perceives the rightness and beauty of a life wholly devoted to His glory. Thus there is a radical change in his judgment, disposition and conduct.

In the glass of the law there shines the glory of God's holiness and righteousness, and in the glass of the gospel the glory of His grace and mercy, and as by the Spirit's enablement the believer is beholding them, there is wrought in him a love for the same, there is given to him an answerable frame of heart. He cordially owns God as righteous in all

His ways and holy in all His works. He acknowledges that God is just in condemning him, and equally just in pardoning him. He freely confesses that he is as evil as the law pronounces him to be, and that his only hope lies in the atoning sacrifice of the Lamb. Christ is now "The Fairest of ten thousand to his soul." He desires and endeavors to *exercise* righteousness and truth, grace and mercy, in all his dealings with his fellows. Thus a personal experience of the transforming power of the law and the gospel brings its subject into a conformity to their temper and tendency.

This being "changed into the same image" of the glory of the Lord, is but another way of saying that the law of God is now written on the heart (Heb. 8:10), for as we have said previously, the law is a transcript of the Divine nature, the very image of God. As the law was written in indelible characters on the tables of stone by the very finger of God, so at regeneration and throughout the entire process of sanctification views and dispositions in accord with the nature of the law become habitual in the heart, through the operation of the Holy Spirit, according to the measure of grace which He supplies. The genuine language of the soul now becomes, "How reasonable it is that I should love with all my heart such an infinitely glorious being as God, that I should be utterly captivated by His supernal excellency. How fitting that I should be entirely for Him, and completely at the disposal of Him who is Lord of all, whose rectitude is perfect, whose goodness and wisdom are infinite, and who gave His Son to die for me!"

This being "changed into the same image" of the glory of the Lord, is also the same as Christ being "formed" in the soul (Gal. 4:19). It is having in kind, though not in degree, the same mind that was in the Lord Jesus. It is being imbued with His spirit, being brought into accordance with the design of His mediatorial work, which was to honor and glorify God. In a word, it is being at heart the very disciples of Christ. This being "changed into the same image" of the glory of the Lord, is to be *"reconciled to* God" (II Cor. 5:20). Previously, we were at enmity against Him, hating His sovereignty, His strictness, His severity; but now we perceive the surpassing beauty of His every attribute and are in love with His whole person and character. No greater change than this can be conceived of: "Ye were sometime darkness, but now are ye light in the Lord" (Eph. 5:8). This great change is to "come unto" God (Heb. 11:6), causing us to diligently seek daily supplies of grace from Him.

"Mine eye affecteth mine heart" (Lam. 3:51). We are influenced by the objects we comtemplate, we become insensibly assimilated to those with whom we have much intercourse, we are molded by the books we read. This same law or principle operates in the spiritual realm: "But we all with open face beholding as in a glass the glory of the Lord, are changed into the same image from glory to glory, as by the Spirit of the Lord" (II Cor. 3:18) — beholding, we are changed. Here, then, is our responsibility: to *use* the means which God has appointed for

our growth in grace, to be daily occupied with spiritual objects and
heavenly things. Yet *our* study and contemplation of the Truth will not,
of itself, produce any transformation: there must be a *Divine application*
of the Truth to the heart. Apart from the Divine agency and blessing
all our efforts and use of the means amount to nothing, and therefore
is it added "We are changed . . . *by the Spirit.*"

Just as surely as Christ's all-mighty power will, on the resurrection
morning, transform the bodies of His people from mortality to life and
from dishonor to glory, so also does the Holy Spirit now exert a supernatural power in morally transforming the characters of those whom He
indwells. The great difference between these two — the future work of
Christ upon the bodies of the saints and the present work of the Spirit
upon their souls — is that the one will be accomplished instantaneously,
whereas the other is effected slowly and gradually; the one we shall be
fully conscious of, the other we are largely unconscious of. This being
"*changed* into the same image" of the glory of the Lord is a progressive
experience, as the "from glory to glory" plainly intimates — from one
degree of it to another. It is begun at regeneration, is continued throughout our sanctification, and will be perfected at our glorification.

Now that which deeply exercises and so often keenly distresses the
sincere Christian is, that as he seeks to honestly examine himself, he
discovers so very little evidence that he IS being "changed into" the
image of the Lord. He dare not take anything for granted, but desires
to "prove" himself (II Cor. 13:5). The moral transformation of which
we have been treating is that which supplies proof of spiritual illumination, and without at least a measure of it all supposed saving knowledge
of the Truth is but a delusion. We shall therefore endeavor now to
point out some of the leading features by which this transformation
may be identified, asking the reader to carefully compare himself with
each one.

First, where the Spirit has begun to transform a soul *the Divine Law
is cordially received as a rule of life,* and the heart begins to echo to the
language of Psalm 119 in its commendation. Nothing more plainly distinguishes a true conversion from a counterfeit than this: that one who
used to be an enemy to God's law is brought understandingly and
heartily to love it, and seek to walk according to its requirements.
"Hereby we do know that we know Him if we keep His commandments"
(I John 2:3). He who has been born again has a new palate, so that
he now relishes what he formerly disliked. He now begins to prove that
it is not only the fittest, but the happiest thing in the world, to aspire
to be holy as God is holy, to love Him supremely and live to Him entirely.

Second, *a life of self-loathing.* The regenerated soul perceives that
complete and constant subjection to God is His due, and that the gift of
His beloved Son has laid him under lasting obligations to serve, please,
and glorify Him. But the best of God's people are only sanctified in part
in this life and, realizing the law requires and that God is entitled to sinless perfection from us, what but a life of self-abhorrence must ensue?

Once, we are supernaturally enlightened to see that "the law is *spiritual*," the inevitable consequence *must be* for me to see and feel that "I am *carnal*, sold under sin (Rom. 7:14). And therefore there must be a continued sense of infinite blame, of self-loathing, of godly sorrow, of broken-heartedness, of hungering and thirsting after righteousness; of watching, praying, striving, or mourning because of frequent defeat.

Third, *genuine humility*. In view of what has just been pointed out, it is easy to see why humility is represented all through Scripture as a dominant feature of those who are quickened by the Spirit. A hypocrite, being experimentally ignorant of the Divine law — never having been slain by it (Rom. 7:9-11) — then, the more religious he is, the more proud and conceited he will be. But with a true saint it is just the opposite: for if the law be his rule of duty, and his obligations to conform thereto are infinite, and his blame for every defect is proportionately great; if the fault lie entirely in himself, and his lack of perfect love and obedience to God be wholly culpable, then he must be filled with low and mean thoughts of himself, and have an answerable lowliness of heart.

There is no greater proof that a man is ignorant of the Truth savingly, and a stranger to Christ experimentally, than for spiritual pride to reign in his heart. "Behold his soul is *lifted up*, is *not upright* in him" (Hab. 2:4). The graceless Pharisee, blind to the real character and purport of the law, was ready to say, "God, I thank thee, that I am not as other men"; while the penitent Publican, seeing himself in the light of God, dared not lift up his eyes to Heaven, but smote upon his breast (the seat of his spiritual leprosy) and cried "God *be merciful* to me, the sinner." The proud religionists of Christ's day exclaimed, "Behold, we see" (John 9:41); but the holy Psalmist prayed, "Open thou mine eyes, *that I may* behold wondrous things out of thy law." Thousands of deluded people who profess to be Christians prate about their consecration, victories, and attainments; but the apostle Paul said, "I count not myself to have apprehended" (Phil. 3:13).

Fourth, *a growing apprehension of the Divine goodness*. The more a quickened soul sees himself in the light of God, the more he discovers how much there still is in him which is opposed to His law, and in how many respects he daily offends. The more clearly he perceives how very far he comes short of the glory of God, and how unlike Christ he is in character and conduct, the deeper becomes his appreciation of the grace of God through the Mediator. The man who is of a humble, broken and contrite heart, finds the promises of the gospel just fitted to his case. None but One who is *"mighty* to save" (Isa. 63:1) can redeem such a wretch as he knows himself to be; none but the "God of *all* grace (I Peter 5:10) would show favor to one so vile and worthless. "Worthy is the Lamb" is now his song. "Not unto us, O Lord, not unto us, but unto thy name give glory; for thy mercy, for thy truth's sake" (Ps. 115:1) is his hearty acknowledgement. It is the Spirit's continued application of the law to the believer's conscience which prepares him to receive the comforts and consolations of the gospel.

When the mind is thoroughly convinced that God can, consistently with His honor, willingly receive to favor the most naked, forlorn, wretched, guilty, hell-deserving of the human race, and become a Father and Friend to him, he is happier than if all the world was his own. When God is his sensible Portion, everything else fades into utter insignificance. The fig tree may not blossom nor any fruit be in the vine, yet he will "joy in the God of his salvation" (Hab. 3:18). The apostle, Paul, although a prisoner at Rome, not in the least dejected, cries "Rejoice in the Lord, and again I say, rejoice" (Phil. 4:4). When God is chosen as our supreme Good, all earthly idols are rejected, and our treasure is laid up in Heaven. In proportion as grace flourishes in the heart our comforts will remain, let outward things go as they will; yea, it will be found that it is "*good* to be afflicted" (Ps. 119:71).

Here, then, are some of the principal effects produced by our being "changed," or reformed, conformed, and transformed by the Spirit of God. There is a growing realization of the ineffable holiness of God and of the righteousness and spirituality of the law, and the extent of its requirements. There is a deepening sense of our utter sinfulness, failure, and blameworthiness, and the daily loathing of ourselves for our hard-heartedness, our base ingratitude, and the ill returns we make to God for His infinite goodness to us. There is a corresponding self-abasement, taking our place in the dust before God, and frankly owning that we are not worthy of the least of His mercies (Gen. 32:10). There is an increasing appreciation of the grace of God and of the provision He has made for us in Christ, with a corresponding longing to be done with this body of death and conformed fully to the lovely image of the Lord; which longings will be completely realized at our glorification.

28

The Spirit Preserving

DURING recent years much has been written upon the eternal security of the saints, some of it helpful, but most of it superficial and injurious. Many Scriptures have been quoted, but few of them expounded. A great deal has been said about the *fact* of Divine preservation, but comparatively little on the *method* thereof. The preservation of the believer by the Father and by the Son has been given considerable prominence, but the work of the Spirit therein was largely ignored. The general impression conveyed to the thoughtful reader has been that, the "final perseverance" of the Christian is a mechanical thing rather than a spiritual process, that it is accomplished by physical force rather than by moral suasion, that it is performed by external might rather than by internal means — something like an unconscious non-swimmer being rescued from a watery grave, or a fireman carrying a swooning person out of a burning building. Such illustrations are radically faulty, utterly misleading, and pernicious in their tendency.

It may be objected that the principal thing for us to be concerned with is the blessed fact itself, and that there is no need for us to trouble ourselves about the modus operandi: let us rejoice in the truth that God *does* preserve His people, and not wrack our brains over *how* He does so. As well might the objector say the same about the redemptive work of Christ: let us be thankful that He did make an atonement, and not worry ourselves over the philosophy of it. But is it of no real importance, no value to the soul, to ascertain that Christ's atonement was a *vicarious* one, that it was a *definite* one, and not offered at random; that it is a *triumphant* one, securing the actual justification of all for whom it was made? Why, my reader, it is at this very point lies the dividing-line between vital truth and fundamental error. God has done something more than record in the gospels the historical fact of Christ's death: He has supplied in the Epistles an explanation of its nature and design.

So, too, God has given us far more than bald statements in His Word that none of His people shall perish: He has also revealed *how* He preserves them from destruction, and it is not only highly insulting to Him, but to our own great loss, if we ignore or refuse to ponder carefully what He has made known thereon. Was it without reason Paul prayed, "That the God of our Lord Jesus Christ, the Father of glory, may give unto you the spirit of wisdom and revelation in the knowledge of him: the eyes of your understanding being enlightened: *that ye may know* . . .

what is the exceeding greatness of his power to usward who believe, according to the working of his mighty power which he wrought in Christ, when he raised him from the dead and set him at his own right hand" (Eph. 1:17-20). Christians are "kept by the power of God" (I Peter 1:5), and evidently we can only know what that power is, and the greatness thereof, as we are spiritually enlightened concerning the same.

When we read that we are "kept by the power *of God* through faith unto salvation ready to be revealed in the last time" (I Peter 1:5), or "For it is *God* which worketh in you both to will and to do of His good pleasure" (Phil. 2:13), in such passages the immediate reference is always to *the Holy Spirit* — the "immediate," though not the exclusive. In the economy of redemption all is from the Father, through the Son, by the Spirit. All proceeds from the foreordination of the Father, all that comes to the believer is through Christ, that is, on account of His infinite merits: all is actually wrought by the Spirit, for He is the Executive of the Godhead, the active Agent in all the works of redemption. The believer is as truly and directly *preserved by the Spirit*, as he was quickened by Him; and only as this is duly recognized by us will we be inclined to render Him that thanks and praise which is His distinctive due.

The chief end for which God sends the Spirit to indwell His people is to deliver them from apostasy: to preserve them not only from the everlasting burnings, but from those things which would expose them thereto. Unless that be clearly stated, we justly lay ourselves open to the charge that this is a *dangerous* doctrine — making light of sin and encouraging careless living. It is not true that, if a man has once truly believed in Christ, no matter what enormities he may commit afterwards, nor what course of evil he follow, he cannot fail to reach Heaven. Not so is the teaching of Holy Writ. The Spirit does not preserve in a way of licentiousness, but only in the way of holiness. Nowhere has God promised His favor to dogs who go back to their vomit, nor to swine which return to their wallowing in the mire. The believer may indeed experience a fearful fall, yet he will not lie down content in his filth, any more than David did: "Though he fall, he shall not be utterly cast down: for the Lord upholdeth him with his hand" (Ps. 37:24).

That many Christians *have* persevered in holiness to the last moment of their lives, cannot be truthfully denied. Now their perseverance must have been obtained wholly of themselves, or partly of themselves and partly by Divine aid, or it must have been wholly dependent on the purpose and power of God. None who profess to believe the Scriptures would affirm that it was due entirely to their own efforts and faithfulness, for they clearly teach that progress in holiness is as much the work of the Spirit as is the new birth itself. To say that the perseverance of the saint is due, in part to himself, is to divide the credit, afford ground for boasting, and rob God of half His rightful glory. To declare that a life of faith and holiness is entirely dependent upon the grace and power of God, is but to repeat what the Lord told His disciples: "without me ye can do *nothing*" (John 15:5), and to affirm with the apostle "Not that we are sufficient of ourselves to think any thing as of ourselves; but our sufficiency *is of God*" (II Cor. 3:5).

Yet it needs to be pointed out that in maintaining His people in holiness, the power of God operates in quite another manner than it does in the maintenance of a river or the preservation of a tree. A river may (sometimes *does*) dry up, and a tree may be uprooted: the one is maintained by being replenished by fresh waters, the other is preserved by its being nourished and by its roots being held in the ground; but in each case, the preservation is by physical power, from without, entirely without their concurrence. In the case of the Christian's preservation it is quite otherwise. With him, God works from within, using moral suasion, leading him to a *concurrence* of mind and will with the Holy Spirit in this work. God deals with the believer as a moral agent, draws him "with cords of a man" (Hos. 11:4), maintains his responsibility, and bids him "work out your own salvation with fear and trembling, for it is God which worketh in you both to will and to do of His good pleasure" (Phil. 2:12-13).

Thus there is both preservation on God's part and perseverance in holiness on ours, and the former is accomplished by maintaining the latter. God does not deal with His people as though they were machines, but as rational creatures. He sets before them weighty considerations and powerful motives, solemn warnings and rich rewards, and by the renewings of His grace and the revivings of His Spirit causes them *to respond* thereto. Are they made conscious of the power and pollution of indwelling sin? Then they cry for help to resist its lustings and to escape its defilements. Are they shown the importance, the value, and the need of faith? Then they beg the Lord for an increase of it. Are they made sensible of that obedience which is due unto God, but aware too of the hindering drag of the flesh? Then they cry "Draw me, we will run after thee." Do they yearn to be fruitful? Then they pray "Awake, O north wind; and come, thou south; blow upon my garden, that the spices thereof may flow out. Let my Beloved come into his garden, and eat his pleasant fruits" (Song of Sol. 4:16).

His understanding having been savingly enlightened, the believer desires to grow in grace and the knowledge of his Lord, that he may abound in spiritual wisdom and good works. Every affection of his heart is stirred, every faculty of his soul called into action. And yet this concurrence is not such as to warrant us saying that his perseverance depends in any degree on himself, for every spiritual stirring and act on his part is but the effect of the Spirit's operation within him, "He which hath begun a good work in you will finish it" (Phil. 1:6). He who first enlightened, will continue to shine upon the understanding; He who originally convicted of sin, will go on searching the conscience; He who imparted faith, will nourish and sustain the same; He who drew to Christ, will continue to attract the affections toward Him.

There are two eminent benefits or spiritual blessings which comprehend all others, filling up the entire space of the Christian's life, from the moment of his quickening unto his ultimate arrival in Heaven, namely, his regeneration and his preservation. And as the renowned Puritan, Thomas Goodwin, says, "If a debate were admitted which of them is the greater, it would be found that no jury of mankind could determine on either side, but must leave it to God's free grace itself, which is the author and finisher of our faith, to decide." As the creating of the world at first and the upholding and governing of all things by Divine power and providence are yoked together (Heb. 1:2, 3), so are regeneration and preservation. "Faithful is He that *calleth* you, who also will do it" (I Thess. 5:24) — i.e., *preserve* (v. 23). "Blessed be the God and Father of our Lord Jesus Christ, which according to his abundant mercy hath *begotten* us again unto a living hope . . . to an inheritance incorruptible and undefiled . . . who are *kept* by the power of God through faith" (I Peter 1:3-5).

The same blessed linking together of these eminent benefits is seen in the Old Testament: "Do ye thus requite the Lord, O foolish people and unwise? is not he thy Father that hath bought thee? hath he not *made* thee and *established* thee?" (Deut. 32:6); "And even to your old age I am he; and even to hoar hairs will I carry you; I have *made*, and I will *bear*" (Isa. 46:4); "Which *holdeth* our soul in life, and suffereth not our feet to be moved" (Ps. 66:9) — the verb has a double meaning, as the margin signifies: "putteth" at the first, and "holdeth" or maintaineth afterwards. How wonderful is this in the natural: delivered from countless dangers, preserved from epidemics and diseases which carried off thousands of our fellows, recovered from various illnesses which had otherwise proven fatal. Still more wonderful is the spiritual preservation of the saint: kept from the dominion of sin which still indwells him; kept from being drawn out of the Narrow Way by the enticements of the world; kept from the horrible heresies which ensnare multitudes on every side; kept from being entirely overcome by Satan, who ever seeks his destruction.

What pleasure it now gives the Christian to hear of the varied and wondrous ways in which God *regenerates* His people! What delight will be ours in Heaven when we learn of the loving care, abiding faithfulness, and mighty power of God in the *preservation* of each of His own! What joy will be ours when we learn the details of how He made good His promise "When thou passest through the waters, I will be with thee; and through the rivers, they shall not overflow thee; when thou walkest through the fire, thou shalt not be burned, neither shall the flame kindle upon thee" (Isa. 43:2) — His providence working for us externally, His grace operating internally: preserving amid the tossings and tempests of life, recovering from woeful backslidings, reviving us when almost dead.

The preservation of God's people through all the vicissitudes of their pilgrim journey is accomplished, immediately by the Holy Spirit. He it is who watches over the believer. Delivering him when he knows it not; keeping him from living in the world's sinks of iniquity, lifting up a standard when the enemy comes like a flood against him (Isa. 59:19).

He it is who keeps him from accepting those fatal heresies which deceive and destroy so many empty professors. He it is who prevents his becoming contented with a mere "letter" ministry or satisfied with head-knowledge and notional religion. And *how* does the Spirit accomplish the Christian's preservation? By sustaining the new nature within him, and calling it forth into exercise and act. By working such graces in him that he becomes "stablished" (II Cor. 1:21). By keeping him conscious of his utter ruin and deep need of Christ. By bringing him to a concurrence with His gracious design, moving him to use appropriate means. But let us be more specific.

"Teach me, O Lord, the way of Thy statutes; and I shall keep it unto the end" (Ps. 119:33). We lost the way of true happiness when we fell in Adam, and ever since men have wandered up and down vainly seeking rest and satisfaction: "They are *all* gone out of the way" (Rom. 3:12). Nor can any man discover the way of holiness and happiness of himself: he must be *taught it* spiritually and supernaturally by God. Such teaching is earnestly desired by the regenerate, for they have been made painfully conscious of their perversity and insufficiency: "Surely I am more brutish than any man, and have not the understanding of a man" (Prov. 30:2) is their confession. It is by Divine and inward teaching that we are stirred into holy activity: "*I will* keep it" — that which is inwrought by the Spirit is outwrought by us. Thereby our final perserverance is accomplished: "I will keep it *to the end*" — because effectually taught of Jehovah.

"When wisdom entereth into thine heart, and knowledge is pleasant unto thy soul; *discretion shall preserve thee,* understanding shall keep thee" (Prov. 2:10, 11). For wisdom to enter into our hearts means that the things of God have such an influence upon us as to dominate our affections and move our wills. For knowledge to be pleasant to our souls signifies that we delight in the law of God after the inward man (Rom. 7:22), that submission to God's will is not irksome but desirable. Now where such really be the case, the individual possesses a discernment which enables him to penetrate Satan's disguises and perceive the barb beneath the bait, and is endowed with a discretion which makes him prudent and cautious, so that he shuns those places where alluring temptations abound and avoids the company of evil men and women. Thereby is he delivered from danger and secured from making shipwreck of the faith (see also Prov. 4:6; 6:22-24).

"I will make an everlasting covenant with them, that I will not turn away from them to do them good; but I will put *my fear* in their hearts that they shall *not depart* from me" (Jer. 32:40). This statement casts much light upon the means and method employed by God in the preserving of His people. The indwelling Spirit not only *constrains* the new nature by considerations drawn from the love of Christ (II Cor. 5:14), but He also *restrains* the old nature by a sense of God's majesty. He often drops an awe on the believer's heart, which holds him back from running into that excess of riot unto which his lusts would carry him. The Spirit makes the soul to realize that God is not to be trifled with, and delivers from wickedly presuming upon His mercy. He stimulates a spirit of filial reverence in the saint, so that he shuns those things which would dishonor his Father. He causes us to heed such a word as "Be not highminded, but fear: for if God spared not the natural branches, take heed lest He also spare not thee" (Rom. 11:20, 21). By such means does God fulfil His promise "I will put my Spirit within you, and *cause* you *to* walk in my statutes" (Ezek. 36:27).

"For we through the Spirit wait for the hope of righteousness by faith" (Gal. 5:5). It is the stirrings of hope, however faint, which keeps the soul alive in seasons of disappointment and despondency. But for the renewings of the gracious Spirit, the believer would relinquish his hope and sink into abject despair. "Then the eyes of the blind shall be opened, and the ears of the deaf shall be unstopped. Then shall the lame man leap as a hart, and the tongue of the dumb sing: for in the wilderness shall waters break out, and streams in the desert" (Isa. 35:5, 6): it is by fresh supplies of the Spirit (Phil. 1:19) that there comes not only further light, but new strength and comfort. Amid the perturbations caused by indwelling sin and the anguish from our repeated defeats, it is one of the Spirit's greatest works to sustain the soul by the expectation of things to come.

"Who are kept by the power of God *through faith*" (I Peter 1:5). Here again we are shown *how* the preservation of the saint is effected: through the influences of an exercised faith (compare I John 5:4). Now faith implies not only the knowledge and belief of the Truth, but also those pious affections and dispositions and the performance of those spiritual duties which constitute practical holiness. Without faith no man can attain unto that holiness, and without the power of God none can exercise this faith. Faith is the channel through which the mighty works of God are wrought — as Hebrews 11 so clearly shows — not the least of which is the conducting of His people safely through the enemy's land (I John 5:19).

Perseverance in grace, or continuance in holiness, is not promoted by a blind confidence or carnal security, but by watchfulness, earnest effort, and self-denial. So far from teaching that believers shall certainly reach Heaven whether or not they use the means of grace, Scripture affirms "If ye live after the flesh ye shall die: but if ye through the Spirit do mortify the deeds of the body, ye shall live" (Rom. 8:13). God has not promised that, no matter how loosely a saint may live or what vile habits he may persist in, he shall not perish; but rather does He assure us that He will preserve from such looseness and wickedness as would expose him to His wrath. It is by working grace in our hearts, by calling into exercise the faculties of our souls, by exciting fear and hope, hatred and love, sorrow and joy, that the saint is preserved.

29

The Spirit Confirming

In view of the preceding articles on the Spirit *preserving*, there was really no need for us to take up another aspect of the subject which so closely approximates thereto; yet a little reflection has persuaded us that it may be wise to do so. Some of our readers are fearful that the author wavers on the blessed truth of the eternal security of the Christian. Some Arminians, because of our strong emphasis upon the absolute supremacy and sovereignty of God and the total impotency of fallen men unto holiness, have charged us with denying human responsibility, when the fact is that we go much farther than they do in the holding and proclaiming of man's accountability. On the other hand, some Calvinists, because we insist so emphatically and frequently on the imperative necessity of treading the Highway of Holiness in order to escape the everlasting burnings, have questioned our soundness on the final perseverance of the saints; we believe this truth more *fully* than they do. Very few today hold the balance of the Truth.

That which we now desire to contemplate is the blessed Spirit viewed under the metaphor of an *"earnest."* This term is used of Him in the following passages: "Who hath also sealed us, and given the earnest of the Spirit in our hearts" (II Cor. 1:22); "Now he that hath wrought us for the self-same thing is God, who also hath given unto us the earnest of the Spirit" (II Cor. 5:5); "After that ye believed, ye were sealed with that Holy Spirit of promise, which is the earnest of our inheritance until the redemption of the purchased possession, unto the praise of his glory" (Eph. 1:13, 14). The figure is taken from an ancient custom (which is by no means obsolete today) of the method used in the clinching of a commercial bargain or compact. The seller agrees to make delivery at some future date of what has been agreed upon, and as a *guaranty of* this the purchaser receives an "earnest," that is, a sample or token, an insignificant instalment of what has been contracted for.

An "earnest," then, *supposes a compact* wherein two parties are agreed, the one who is ultimately to come into possession of what has been agreed upon being given a token of the other's good faith that he will abide by the terms of the bargain. It is a part of the price given beforehand, to assure the one to whom the "earnest" is given that at the appointed season he shall receive the whole of that which is promised. Now the right which the believer has to eternal life and glory comes in a way of *compact* or covenant. On the one side, the believer agrees to the terms specified (the forsaking of sin and the serving of the Lord), and yields himself to God by repentance and faith. On the other side, God binds Himself to give the believer forgiveness of sins and an inheritance among them which are sanctified by faith. This is clearly enough stated in "Incline your ear, and come unto me: hear, and your soul shall live; *and* I will [then] make an everlasting covenant with you, even the sure mercies of David" (Isa. 55:3) — upon our hearty consent to the terms of the gospel, God engages Himself to bestow upon us those inestimable blessings secured for His people by the spiritual or anti-typical David.

An "earnest" *intimates there is some delay* before the thing bargained for is actually bestowed: in the case of goods, deliverance at once is not agreed upon, in the case of property possession is not immediately entered into. It is for this reason that the token of good faith or pre-liminary instalment is given: because the promised deliverance is de-ferred, possession being delayed for a season, an "earnest" is bestowed as a pledge or confirmation of what is to follow. Now as soon as the believer really enters into covenant with God, he has a right to the everlasting inheritance, but his actual entrance into full blessedness is deferred. God does not remove us to Heaven the moment we believe, any more than He brought Israel into Canaan within a few days after delivering them from Egypt. Instead, we are left for a while in this world, and that for various reasons: one among them being that we may have opportunities for exercising faith and love; faith in *"looking for* that blessed hope and the glorious appearing of the great God and our Saviour Jesus Christ" (Titus 2:13); hope in *longing:* "ourselves also, which have received the first-fruits of the Spirit, even we ourselves groan within ourselves, *waiting for* the adoption" (Rom. 8:23).

An "earnest" is *a part,* though only a very small one, *of the whole* that has been agreed upon. If a contract was made for the delivery of a sum of money on a certain date, then a trifling instalment thereof was given; if it were the transfer of a piece of land, then a square of turf was cut and handed to its future possessor, that being a symbolic guarantee to assure him during the interval of waiting. So too, those comforts which the Spirit communicates to believers are the same in kind as the joys of Heaven though they are vastly inferior in their degree. The saving gifts and graces of the Spirit are but a small beginning and part of that glory which shall yet be revealed in and to us. Grace is glory begun, and they differ from each other only as an infant does from a fully matured adult. Holiness or purity of heart is a pledge of that sinless estate and full conformity to Christ which is promised the Christian in the future. That present loosing of our bonds is but a sample of our perfect and final freedom.

An "earnest" is given *for the security* of the party who receives it, and not for the benefit of him that bestows it. He who gives the earnest is legally bound to complete his bargain, but the recipient has this guarantee in hand for the confirming and comforting of his mind while he is waiting, it being to him a tangible pledge and sample of what as yet is only promised. Here again we may see the aptness and accuracy of the figure, for the spiritual earnest which Christians receive is given solely for *their benefit*, for there is no danger whatever of backing out on God's part. "Wherein God, willing more abundantly to show unto the heirs of promise the immutability of his counsel, confirmed it by an oath: that by two immutable things, in which it was impossible for God to lie, *we* might have *a strong consolation*, who have fled for refuge to lay hold upon the hope set before us" (Heb. 6:17, 18) — and this because believers commonly are assailed by many doubts and fears.

An "earnest" remains *the irrevocable possession* of its recipient until the bargain is consummated, and even then it is not taken from him. Therein an "earnest" differs from a "pledge," for when a pledged article is returned, the pledge is taken back again. So too the "earnest" which Christians receive is irrevocable and inalienable: "For the gifts and calling of God are without repentance" or "change of mind" on His part (Rom. 11:29). As the Lord Jesus declared, "I will pray the Father, and he shall give you another Comforter, that he may abide with you *forever*" (John 14:16). How blessedly and how positively this intimates the eternal security of God's elect! Jehovah has made with them "an everlasting covenant, ordered in all things *and sure.*" Even now they have received "the firstfruits of the Spirit," and that is the Divine certification of the glorious harvest, the plentitude of God's favor, yet to follow. Like Mary, the believer today, by yielding to the Lordship of Christ, has "chosen that good part which shall *never be taken away*" (Luke 10:42).

"Now he which stablisheth us with you in Christ, and hath anointed us, is God, who hath also sealed us, and given the earnest of the Spirit in our hearts" (II Cor. 1:21, 22). It is to be duly noted that both the sealing and the earnest are for our "stablishing." As one hymn-writer put it "What more can he *say* than to you he hath said, to you who to Jesus for refuge hath fled?" And what more can he *do*, we may ask, than what He has done to assure His people of the glorious inheritance awaiting them? We have the Lord Jesus Christ in Heaven *with our nature*, to show that our nature shall yet come there: "Whither the forerunner is for us entered, even Jesus" (Heb. 6:20). Nor is that all: we have the Holy Spirit sent down *into our hearts* as proof that we are not only children, but also the heirs of God (Rom. 8:14-17).

"Now he that hath wrought us for this selfsame thing is God, who also hath given unto us the earnest of the Spirit" (II Cor. 5:5). That "selfsame thing" is *not* to be restricted unto a resurrected body: it is the "far more exceeding and eternal weight of glory" of 4:17, the "things which are not seen" of 4:18. Having spoken of the everlasting bliss awaiting the saints on High, for which they now groan and earnestly long (5:3), the apostle mentions two of the principal grounds on which such a hope rests. God has "wrought us for" the same, that is, He has regenerated us, giving us a holy and heavenly nature which fully capacitates us to be with Himself. Then, He has given us "the earnest of the Spirit" as a guaranty of this glorious estate. Thus are we fitted for, and thus are we assured of the infinitely better life awaiting us.

"After that ye believed, ye were sealed with that Holy Spirit of promise, which is the earnest of our inheritance, until the redemption of the purchased possession, unto the praise of his glory" (Eph. 1:13, 14). In this passage (1:3-14) the apostle describes those wondrous and numerous blessings with which the saints are blest in Christ. Eternal election (v. 4), membership in God's family (v. 5), acceptance in the Beloved (v. 6), the forgiveness of sins (v. 7), an understanding of Divine mysteries (vv. 8, 9), predestinated unto an inheritance (v. 11), sealed with the Holy Spirit (v. 13), and now the Spirit given to us as "the earnest of our inheritance" — a part-payment in promise and pledge of the whole. The dwelling of the Spirit in the believer's heart is the guaranty of his yet taking his place in that holy and joyous scene where all is according to the nature of God and where Christ is the grand Centre.

According to the literal meaning of the figure, an "earnest" signifies the clinching of a bargain, that it is a sample of what has been agreed upon, that it confirms and ensures the consummation of the contract. And that is what the operations and presence of the Spirit in the believer connote. First, they supply proof that God has made a covenant with him "ordered in all things and sure." Second, the present work of the Spirit in him is a real foretaste and firstfruit of the coming harvest. Is there not something of *the glorified eye* in that faith which the Spirit has implanted? Do the pure in heart see God face to face in Heaven? Well, even now, faith enables us to endure "as *seeing him* who is invisible" (Heb. 11:27). Is there not now something of that *glorified joy* wherein they in Heaven delight themselves in God: "In the multitude of my thoughts within me thy comforts *delight* my soul" (Ps. 94:19)? And is there not now a real though faint adumbration of that *glorified transformation of soul* into the image of Christ? (Compare II Cor. 3:18 with I John 3:2.)

The "earnest" ensures the consummation of that contract. It is so here. The first operations of the Spirit in the elect is the guaranty of the successful completion of the same: "being confident of this very thing, that he which hath begun a good work in you *will perform it* until the day of Jesus Christ" (Phil. 1:6). Thus, God has given us something in hand that we may confidently anticipate the promised inheritance. And this, in order that both our desire and our diligence may be stimulated. We are not asked to mortify sin, deny self, forsake the world, for nothing. If the "earnest" be so blessed, what shall the Inheritance itself be! O what lively expectations of it should be cherished in our hearts. O what earnest efforts should be made in "reaching forth unto those things which are before" (Phil. 3:13).

And *what is* the Inheritance of which the Spirit is the "earnest" unto the believer? It is nothing less than God Himself! The blessed God, in the trinity of His Persons, is the everlasting portion of the saints. Is it not written "If children, then heirs; heirs of God, and joint-heirs with Christ" (Rom. 8:17)? And what is Christ's "inheritance"? "The Lord is the portion of mine inheritance" (Ps. 16:5), He declared. The future bliss of believers will consist in the fulness of the Spirit capacitating them to enjoy God to the full! And has not the believer already "*tasted* that the Lord is gracious" (I Peter 2:3)? Yes, by the Spirit. The Spirit is the utmost proof to us of God's love, the firstfruit of glory: "Because ye are sons, God hath sent forth the Spirit of his Son into your hearts."

God, then, grants His people a taste in this world of what He has prepared for them in the world to come. The gifts and graces of the Spirit in the elect affirm *the certainty* of this glory awaiting them: as surely as an "earnest" guarantees the whole sum, so do the "firstfruits of the Spirit" (Rom. 8:23) the coming harvest of bliss. *The nature of* the Christian's "earnest" intimates both the character and the greatness of what is in store for him: even now He bestows a measure of life, light, love, liberty; but what shall these be in their fulness! One ounce of real grace is esteemed by its possessor more highly than a ton of gold: what, then, will it be like to bathe in the ocean of God's favor? If now there are times when we experience that peace which "passeth all understanding" (Phil. 4:7) and are made to "rejoice with joy unspeakable and full of glory" (I Peter 1:8), how incapable we are of estimating the full value of our inheritance, for an "earnest" is but a tiny instalment of that which is promised. O that the realization of this, faint though it be, may move us to look and long for the heavenly glory with greater vehemence.

30

The Spirit Fructifying

FAR more is said in Scripture on this aspect of our many-sided subject than is generally supposed: different figures being used, especially in the Old Testament, to express the graces and virtues which the Spirit imparts to and develops in the elect. A considerable variety of emblems are employed to set them forth. They are frequently referred to as flowers and gardens of them, to beds of spices, and unto trees and orchards. For example, in Solomon's Song we hear Christ saying to His Spouse: "A garden enclosed is my sister, my spouse; a spring shut up, a fountain sealed. Thy plants are an orchard of pomegranates with pleasant fruits; camphor, with spikenard. Spikenard and saffron; calamus and cinnamon, with all trees of frankincense; myrrh and aloes, with all the chief spices. A fountain of gardens, a well of living waters and streams from Lebanon" (4:12-15).

The figures used in the above passage are very beautiful and call for careful consideration. A "garden" is a piece of ground distinguished and separated from others, for the owner's use and delight; so the church of Christ is distinguished and separated from all other people by electing, redeeming, and regenerating grace. In a garden is a great variety of plants, herbs, and flowers; so in the church there are members differing much from each other, yet in all there is that which is delightful to their Lord. In a garden the plants and flowers do not grow up naturally of themselves, they do not spring forth spontaneously from its soil, but have to be set or sown, for nothing but weeds grow up of themselves; so in Christ's church, those excellencies which are found in its members are not natural to them, but are the direct product of *the Spirit's operations,* for by nature nothing grows in their hearts but the weeds of sin and corruption.

The commentators are not agreed as to whether Christ is speaking to His spouse in verse 15, or whether she is there heard replying to what He had said in verses 12-14. Personally, we strongly incline to the latter: that Christ having commended His church as a fruitful garden, she now ascribes it all to Him: "A fountain of gardens, a well of living waters, and streams from Lebanon." Yet, if we accept the former interpretation, it amounts to much the same thing, for He would there be explaining *what it was* that made His garden so fertile. To be healthy and productive a garden must be well watered, otherwise its delicate plants will quickly wilt and wither; the same being true of trees and all vegetation: a plentiful supply of water is indispensable. Consequently,

170

in keeping with the fact that believers are likened unto plants and trees, and their graces to flowers and fruits, the quickening, renewing, reviving, and fructifying operations of the Spirit are spoken of as "dew," as "showers," as "streams in the desert," etc.

The Holy Spirit not only *imparts* life and holiness, but He *sustains* the same in the soul; He not only communicates heavenly graces, but He cultivates and develops them. "That they might be called trees of righteousness, the planting of the Lord, that he might be glorified. . . . For as the earth bringeth forth her bud, and as the garden causeth the things that are sown in it to spring forth, so the Lord God will cause righteousness and praise to spring forth before all nations" (Isa. 61:3, 11). Yes, the same One who "planted" those "trees of righteousness" must also "*cause*" them" to "*spring forth*" to grow and bear fruit. While the tendency of the new nature is ever Godward, yet it has no power of its own, being entirely dependent upon its Creator and Giver. Hence, that fruit which is borne by the believer is expressly called "the fruit *of the Spirit*" so that the honor and glory may be ascribed alone unto Him. "From *me* is thy fruit found" (Hos. 14:8).

"For I will *pour water* upon him that is thirsty, and floods upon the dry ground: I will *pour my Spirit* upon thy seed, and my blessing upon thine offspring; and they shall spring up among the grass, as willows by the water courses" (Isa. 44:3, 4). Just as surely as a drought brings dearth, so the absence of the Spirit's working leaves all in a state of spiritual death; but just as heavy rains renew a parched vegetation, so an outpouring of the Spirit brings new life. Then shall it indeed be said, "The wilderness and the solitary place shall be glad for them, and the desert shall rejoice and blossom as the rose" (Isa. 35:1), which is expressly interpreted for us by the Spirit in "For the Lord shall comfort *Zion*: he will comfort all *her waste places;* and he will make *her wilderness* like Eden, and *her desert* like the garden of the Lord; joy and gladness shall be found therein, thanksgiving and the voice of melody" (Isa. 51:3). We have purposely added Scripture to Scripture because the spiritual meaning of these passages is commonly unperceived today, when carnal dispensationalists insist on the ignoring of all figures, and the interpreting of everything "literally."

"My little children, of whom I travail in birth again until Christ be formed in you" (Gal. 4:19) — that which the apostle did ministerially, the Spirit does efficiently. *This is how* the Spirit makes the Christian fruitful, or rather, it is how He first fits him to be fruitful: by forming *Christ* in him. The metaphor is taken from the shaping of the child in its mother's womb, so that as its natural parents communicated the matter of its body, it is then framed and shaped into their likeness, limb for limb, answering to themselves. In like manner, the Spirit communicates to the heart an incorruptible "seed" (I John 3:9) or spiritual nature, and then conforms the soul unto Christ's image: first to His graces, and then to His example: "That ye should *show forth* the virtue of him who hath called you" (I Peter 2:9) — which we could not do unless we had first *received* them. Ah, my reader, this is a solemn thing:

we pass among men for genuine Christians, but the only coins which will pass the eye of God are those which bear stamped upon them the image of His Son.

In other words, then, the Spirit's fructifying of the believer is the conforming of him *unto Christ*, first in his heart, and then in his life. By nature we are totally *unlike* Christ, being born in the image of Adam and dominated by Satan; or, to revert to the figure in the opening paragraph, so far from resembling a beautiful and well-kept garden, we are like a barren desert, where nothing but useless shrubs and poisonous weeds are found. "I went by the field of the slothful, and by the vineyard of the man void of understanding: and, lo, it was all grown over with thorns, and nettles had covered the face thereof, and the stone wall thereof was broken down" (Prov. 24:30, 31). *That* is how we appeared unto the holy eye of God in our unregenerate state! It is only when a miracle of grace has been wrought in our hearts that Christ begins to be formed in us, and that we (in our measure) reproduce His graces; and this is due solely to the sovereign and effectual operations of the Holy Spirit.

> "And every virtue we possess,
> And every victory won,
> And every thought of holiness,
> Are His and His alone.

"Even so every good tree bringeth forth good fruit, but a corrupt tree bringeth forth evil fruit. A good tree cannot bring forth evil fruit, neither can a corrupt tree bring forth good fruit. . . . Wherefore by their *fruits* ye shall know them" (Matt. 7:17, 18, 20). The fruit they bear is that which distinguishes the children of God from the children of the Devil. This "fruit" is the temper or disposition wrought in the elect by the Holy Spirit, which is manifested by them, severally, "according to the measure of the gift of Christ" (Eph. 4:7). The Spirit fructifies the regenerate by conforming them to the image of Christ: first to His graces, and then to His example. The lovely virtues found in them do not issue from the depraved nature of fallen man, but are supernaturally inwrought by God.

There are three leading passages in the New Testament on this subject. John 15 names the *conditions* of fruitfulness: union with Christ, purging by the Father, abiding in Christ, and Christ and His Word abiding in us. Galatians 5 furnishes a *description* of the fruit itself. II Peter 1:5-8 states the order of fruit or the *process* of its cultivation. "In the figure of the Vine, the Holy Spirit is not mentioned, but in comparing Himself to the Vine and His disciples to the Branches, the Tree corresponds to the Body, and the Life to His Spirit. The diffusion of life is the work of the Holy Spirit, and the fruit by which the Father is glorified is the fruit of the Spirit. Apart from Christ there is neither life nor fruit, but without the Spirit of Christ there can be neither union nor abiding. Our Lord does not specify the fruit. What He emphasises is the fact that it *is* fruit, and that it is fruit *directly from Himself*" (S. Chadwick).

The fruit of the Spirit is love, joy, peace, long-suffering, gentleness, goodness, faith, meekness, temperance" (Gal. 5:22, 23). These are *graces* of the Spirit as distinguished from the *gifts* of the Spirit, enumerated in I Corinthians 12, and which we hope to consider in our next chapter. They are holy and heavenly dispositions with the conduct which results therefrom. The apostle begins with the principal characteristics of the spiritual mind, and then passes on to its operation and manifestation in personal conduct, social virtues, and practical behavior. A threefold reason may be suggested why these spiritual graces are termed "fruit." First, because all grace is *derived* from the Spirit as fruit issues from the life of a plant. Second, to denote the *pleasantness* of grace, for what is more delightful than sweet and wholesome fruit? Third, to signify the *advantage* redounding to those who have the Spirit: as the owners are enriched by the fruit produced from their gardens and orchards, so believers are enriched by the fruits of holiness.

In the use of the singular number, "the fruit (rather than 'fruits') of the Spirit," emphasis is placed upon the *unity* of His operations: producing one harmonious whole — in contrast from the products of the flesh, which ever tend to discord and chaos. These virtues are not like so many separate flowers in a bouquet, as the variegated petals of one lovely flower exhibiting different shades and forms. A rainbow is one, yet in it all the primary colors are beautifully blended together. These graces which the Spirit imparts to a renewed soul are distinguishable, but they are inseparable. In some believers one grace predominates more than another — as meekness in Moses, patience in Job, love in John — yet all are present and to some extent active.

Galatians 5:22, 23 enumerates nine of the graces communicated by the Spirit. Some have suggested that the last eight are but varied expressions of the first. That "Joy is love exulting, Peace is love in repose, Longsuffering is love on trial, Gentleness is love in society, Goodness is love in action, Faith is love in endurance, Meekness is love at school, and Temperance is love in discipline" (A. T. Pierson). But while love is, admittedly, the greatest of all the graces, yet I Corinthians 13:13 shows that it is but one of several. Personally, we prefer the older classification which divided the nine graces into three threes: the first three — love, joy, peace — being Godward in their exercise; the second three — longsuffering, gentleness, goodness — being exercised manwards; and the last three — fidelity, meekness, temperance — being exercised self-ward.

"Love": the apostle begins with that which flows directly from God (Rom. 5:5), and without which there can be no fellowship with Him or pleasing of Him. "Joy" in God, in the knowledge of pardon, in communion with Christ, in the duties of piety, in the hope of Heaven. "Peace": of conscience, rest of heart, tranquillity of mind. "Longsuffering" when provoked and injured by others, exercising a magnanimous forbearance toward the faults and failings of our fellows. "Gentleness" rendered "kindness" in II Corinthians 6:6, a gracious benignity, the opposite of a harsh, crabbed, and brutal temper. "Goodness" or beneficence, seeking to help and benefit others, without expecting any return or reward. "Faith" or more accurately "faithfulness": being trustworthy, honest, keeping your promises. "Meekness" or yieldedness, the opposite of self-will and self-assertiveness. "Temperance" or self-control: being moderate in all things, ruling one's spirit, denying self.

"In newspaper English, the passage would read something like this: The Fruit of the Spirit is an affectionate, lovable, disposition, a radiant spirit and a cheerful temper, a tranquil mind and a quiet manner, a forbearing patience in provoking circumstances and with trying people, a sympathetic insight and tactful helpfulness, generous judgment and a big-souled charity, loyalty and reliableness under all circumstances, humility that forgets self in the joy of others, in all things self-mastered and self-controlled, which is the final mark of perfecting. This is the kind of character, that is the Fruit of the Spirit. Everything is in the word Fruit. It is not by striving, but by abiding; not by worrying, but by trusting; not of works, but of faith" (S. Chadwick). And, as our passage goes on to say, "Against such there is no law": that which the law enjoins the Spirit imparts, so that there is perfect harmony between the law and the gospel.

But here too there is to be a concurrence between the Christian and the Spirit: our responsibility is to cherish and cultivate our graces, and to resist and reject everything which opposes and hinders them. Fruit is neither our invention nor our product, nevertheless it requires our "diligence" as II Peter 1:5 plainly indicates. A neglected garden grows weeds in plenty, and then its flowers and fruits are quickly crowded out. The gardener has to be continually alert and active. Turn to and ponder Psalm 1 and see *what* has to be avoided, and *what* has to be done, if the believer is to "bring forth his fruit in his season." Re-read John 15 and note the conditions of fruitfulness, and then turn the same into earnest prayer. The Lord, in His grace, make both writer and reader successful horticulturalists in the spiritual realm.

31

The Spirit Endowing

FROM the *graces* which the Spirit works in God's children we turn now to consider the *gifts* which He bestows upon God's servants. This brings us to a comprehensive subject. We can but here single out one or two aspects of it — those which we consider most need our attention today. Broadly speaking, the fundamental principle underlying this branch of our theme may be expressed thus: when God calls any to the performance of special work in His service, He equips them by the gifts of His Spirit. For example we read "the Lord hath called thy name Bezaleel . . . and he hath filled him with the Spirit of God, in wisdom, in understanding, and in knowledge, and in all manner of workmanship; and to devise curious works, to work in gold . . ." (Exod. 35:30-32).

Now just as men have erred grievously concerning the *being* of God, grossly misrepresenting Him by images; and just as there have been the most horrible errors respecting the *person* of the Mediator; so there has been fearful confusion upon the *gifts* of the Spirit, in fact it is at this point there pertains the most serious mistakes with regard to Him. Men have failed to distinguish between His extraordinary and His ordinary gifts, and have sought to generalize what was special and exceptional. Urging the rank and file of professing Christians to *seek* "power from on High," the "baptism of the Spirit" or His "filling for service," the wildest extravagancies have been fostered and the door has been opened wide for Satan to enter and delude the souls and wreck the ·bodily health of thousands of people.

It was well said by John Owen nearly three centuries ago that, "the great *deceit* and *abuse* that hath been in all ages of the church under the pretence of the name and work of the Holy Spirit, make the thorough consideration of what we are taught concerning them exceedingly necessary." The most signal gift of the Spirit of God for the benefit of His people in Old Testament times was that of *prophecy*. The prophets were men who spoke in the name and by the authority of God, giving forth a Divinely inspired message from Him. It is not surprising, then, that many pretended unto this gift who were never inspired by the Holy Spirit, but rather were filled by a lying spirit, the Devil making use of them to accomplish his own designs (see I Kings 22:6, 7; Jer. 5:31, etc.). Those facts are recorded for *our warning!*

This same gift of prophecy occupied a prominent place in the early days of the Christian dispensation, before the New Testament was written. The gospel was at first declared from the immediate revelation of the Spirit, preached by His direct assistance, made effectual by His power, and accompanied in many instances by outward miraculous works, the whole of which is designated "the ministration of the Spirit" (II Cor. 3:8). Those extraordinary manifestations of the Spirit were then so obvious and so acknowledged by all Christians, that those who wished to impose and deceive found no more successful method than by claiming to be themselves immediately inspired by the Spirit. Consequently we find such warnings given by God as, "Despise not prophesyings. *Prove* all things: hold fast that which is good" (I Thess. 5:20, 21); "But there were false prophets also among the people, even as there shall be false teachers among you" (II Peter 2:1); "Beloved, believe not every spirit, but *try* the spirits, whether they are of God" (I John 4:1).

In order to preserve the church in truth and peace during those primitive times, and safeguard them from being imposed upon by the false prophets whilst there was a real communication of the extraordinary gifts of the Spirit (whereby the more occasion was afforded for charlatans to pretend unto the possession of them), God graciously endowed some of His people with the gift of *"the discerning of spirits"* (I Cor. 12:10). The saints were thereby provided with some who were enabled in an extraordinary manner to judge and determine those who claimed to be specially endowed by the Spirit; but when the extraordinary manifestations of the Spirit ceased, this particular gift was also withdrawn, so that Christians are now left with *the Word alone* by which to measure and try all who claim to be the mouthpieces of God.

"How shall we escape if we neglect so great salvation, which at the first began to be spoken by the Lord and was *confirm*ed unto us by them that heard: God also bearing witness, both with *signs and wonders,* and with divers miracles, and gifts of the Holy Spirit" (Heb. 2: 3, 4). This passage makes known to us God's *design* in the miraculous gifts of the Spirit at the beginning of this dispensation. They were for the purpose of confirming the *preached* Word — for none of the New Testament had then been written! They were for the establishing of the gospel: not to beget and strengthen faith, but to cause unbelievers to listen to the Truth (compare I Cor. 14:22, 24, 25).

In I Corinthians 12:8-10 we are supplied with a list of those extraordinary gifts of the Spirit which then obtained — we use the word "extraordinary" in contrast from His ordinary gifts, or those which obtain in all ages and generations. "For to one is given by the Spirit the word of wisdom; to another the word of knowledge by the same Spirit; to another faith by the same Spirit; to another the gifts of healing by the same Spirit; to another the working of miracles; to another prophecy; to another discerning of spirits; to another divers kinds of tongues; to another the interpretation of tongues." It will be noted that just as "the *fruit* of the Spirit" is divided into nine graces (Gal. 5:22, 23), so "the *ministration* of the Spirit" is here described under nine distinct gifts. A very few words must now suffice upon them.

"The word of wisdom" (I Cor. 12:8) was a special gift bestowed upon the apostles (hence it heads this list of gifts) for the defense of the gospel against powerful adversaries (see Luke 21:15)! "The word of knowledge" was a special gift bestowed on all then called of God to preach the gospel: it supernaturally qualified them to expound Divine mysteries without protracted study and lengthy experience (see Acts 4:13)! "To another faith," a special gift which enabled its possessor to trust God in any emergency, and to boldly face a martyr's death (see Acts 6:5). The "gifts of healing" and "the working of miracles" are seen in their exercise by the apostles in the Acts. "To another prophecy" or immediate inspiration and revelation from God. Upon "tongues" and their "interpretation" we shall have more to say a little later.

Now that all of these special impulses and extraordinary gifts of the Spirit were *not intended* to be perpetuated throughout this Christian dispensation, and that they have long since ceased, is clear from several conclusive considerations. Their non-continuance is hinted at in Mark 16:20 by the *omission* of Christ's "and, Lo, I am with you *alway*, even unto the end of the age" (Matt. 28:20). So too by the fact that God did *not* give faith to His servants to count upon the same throughout the centuries: it is unthinkable that the intrepid Reformers and the godly Puritans failed to appropriate God's promise if any had been given to that effect. "Love never faileth: but whether there be prophecies, they shall fail; whether there be tongues, they shall cease; whether there be *knowledge*, it shall *vanish away*" (I Cor. 13:8). The apostle *cannot* there be contrasting Heaven with earth, for those on High possess *more* "knowledge" than we have; so the reference *must be* to the cessation of the miraculous gifts of I Corinthians 12. The qualifying language "which *at the first* began to be spoken by the Lord and was confirmed unto us . . . with signs and wonders" (Heb. 2:3, 4) points in the same direction, and clearly implies that those supernatural manifestations had even then *ceased*. Finally, II Timothy 3:16, 17 proves conclusively that there is now no need for such gifts as prophecy and tongues: we are "throughly furnished" by the now completed Canon of Scripture.

These chapters on the person and work of the Holy Spirit would lack completeness if we ignored the fantastic and fanatical view which some have taken in regarding I Corinthians 12 and 14 as the Divine pattern and ideal for "the open meeting" of the local church today. We refer to those who decry a "one-man ministry" and who encourage an "any-man ministry" under the guise of allowing the Spirit full freedom to move and use any whom Christ has "gifted." It is insisted that here in I Corinthians 14 we behold different ones endowed with various gifts taking part in the same meeting, yet strange to say, these very people readily acknowledge that the gift of tongues has *ceased* — but this very chapter prescribes *how that gift* was and was not to be used!

Now in the first place there is not a single statement in all the New Testament that the practice which obtained at *Corinth* prevailed generally in other churches of that day, still less that the assemblies of the saints in all generations were to be patterned after *their* order. Rather is there much to show that what obtained at Corinth was *not* the regular mode established by Christ and His apostles. The fact is that not only were the conditions at Corinth merely *transitory and exceptional*, but they were *fraught with much evil*. In no other church of apostolic days was there such disorder and carnality. "Gifts" were valued there more highly than grace, knowledge than love, and the consequence was that the possessors of those miraculous gifts, by their pride and forwardness, neutralized whatever good those gifts accomplished. The reason for that is not far to seek: *they* had no governing head or heads and no Divinely authorized teacher or teachers. The *absence of elders* made them like an army without officers, or a school without masters. Where all were equal, none would submit; where all wanted to teach, none would learn.

So far from the Corinthian church supplying a pattern for all others to follow, it stands before us *a most solemn warning* and sample of what ensues when a company of Christians is left without a Divinely qualified leader. The most terrible laxity of discipline obtained: one member was living in adultery with his father's second wife (5:1), while others were getting drunk at the Lord's table (11:21). Those fearful sins (which would not be tolerated today in any Christian church worthy of the name) were winked at, because the assembly was split into parties through want of a controlling head (an under-shepherd of Christ), and because the sinning members belonged to the majority, the minority was powerless.

Besides the fearful laxity of discipline, the grossest irregularities prevailed at their public meetings for the worship of God. There was neither unity, order edifying ministry, nor decorum. One had his "psalm," another his "doctrine," another his "tongue," another his "revelation," and yet another his "interpretation" (I Cor. 14:26) — which is mentioned by the apostle *not* by ways of commendation, but as a *rebuke* for their disorder, as is quite evident from the final clause of that verse, as also from verse 40 (carefully compare the opening words of vv. 15 and 26)! As another has said, "Here, then, all were charged, as it were, to the muzzle, and each wanting to have the *first* say, the *longest* say, and the *loudest* say. They did not wish to edify, but to show off."

Now it was in view of *such* a situation that the apostle was moved of God to pen I Corinthians 14, in order to correct these abuses and to lay down rules for the regulation of those who possessed the extraordinary gifts of prophesying and speaking in tongues. But this very fact at once *overthrows* that theory which has been built on an erroneous conception of this chapter! Not only is there not a single statement elsewhere in the New Testament that the Holy Spirit *is the President over assemblies,* or that He is ever present in any other sense than that He dwells in individual believers, but I Corinthians 14 itself is very far from teaching that the Spirit presides over the local church, and requires those who have been "gifted" by Christ to wait on Him, and be governed entirely by His inward promptings. Surely it is perfectly obvious that inward promptings of the Spirit render quite needless such rules and regulations as are given here!

To affirm that "the spirits of the prophets are subject *to the prophets*" (v. 32), that is, their "gift" of prophecy is under the prophet's *own control*, is a vastly different thing from saying that the prophets were to be *subject to the Holy Spirit!* No matter how strong was the impulse to speak, he could not rightly defy the command given "Let the prophets speak two or three, and let the other judge" (v. 29) under the plea that the Spirit urged him *to* speak. So again, how easy it had been for the apostle to affirm, "If the Spirit impel any one to speak in a tongue, He will move some other brother to translate"; but so far from that, he commanded, "But if there be no interpreter, let him *keep silence* in the church" (v. 28), which utterly demolishes the idea that these Corinthians were being *presided over* by the Holy Spirit.

Nowhere in I Corinthians 14 is it stated that the Spirit conducted (or ought to conduct) their meetings, nor were the Corinthians *rebuked* for failing to look to Him for guidance. There is not a hint of their sinfulness in limiting His sovereign freedom among them! Instead, the apostle says "*I would* that ye all spake with tongues, *but rather* that ye prophesied" (v. 5), and "*I had rather* speak five words with my understanding . . . then ten thousand words in an unknown tongue" (v. 19), which he most certainly had *not* said if his theme here was the Spirit's *superintendence*, for in *that* case the apostle would have gladly and entirely subjected himself to His control. Throughout the entire chapter the apostle presents action as coming from *the side of the possessors* of the gifts, and not from the side of the Spirit. It is *not* "when ye come together the Spirit will move one to speak in a tongue, another to prophecy. . . ." No, they are bidden to use good sense, to show their love to one another by subjection, and to beware of shocking visitors (vv. 20, 23). But enough.

As there were *offices* extraordinary (apostles and prophets) at the beginning of our dispensation, so there were *gifts* extraordinary; and as successors were *not* appointed for the former, so a continuance was never intended for the latter. The gifts were *dependent upon the officers* (see Acts 8:13-21; 10:44-46; 19:6; Rom. 1:11; Gal. 3:5; II Tim. 1:6). We no longer have the apostles with us and therefore the supernatural gifts (the communication of which was an essential part of "the *signs* of an apostle" (II Cor. 12:12) are absent. None but a prophet can "prophesy"! Let it be definitely noted that the "prophet" and the "teacher" are *quite distinct* (I Cor. 12:28, 29; Eph. 2:20; 3:5) — the one is no more, the latter still exists. A prophet was inspired by God to give out an infallible communication of His mind (II Peter 1:21).

Surely it is a manifest absurdity, then, to take a chapter which was given for the express purpose of regulating the exercise of the extraordinary gifts of the Spirit, and apply it to a company today where none of those gifts exist! Furthermore, if I Corinthians 14 sets forth the Spirit's superintendence of the local assembly in worship, why is it that there is *not a single mention of Him* throughout the whole of its forty

verses? *That* is indeed a hard question to answer. Obviously there has
been read into it *what is not there*. But do we not still have the
"word of wisdom" and "the word of knowledge?" Certainly not: they
too were among the spiritual gifts of I Corinthians 12:1, and that word
"spiritual" is *not* used there in contrast from "carnal" (as is clear from
I Cor. 3:1, for they were *not* spiritual in that sense), so that it *must*
mean *inspired*, and "inspired" men ceased when the Canon of Scripture
was closed!

It is true the Spirit *acts today*, but it is *in secret*, and not in open
manifestation as in the days of the apostles; and *by mixed agency*. The
Truth is taught, but not perfectly as the apostles and their delegates
preached it. The best sermon now preached or article written, is not
a standard (as it *would be* if inspired by the Spirit), for it has blemishes
in it; yet the Spirit is not responsible for them. What the Spirit does
now is to bestow ordinary ministerial gifts, which the possessor must
improve and develop by study and use. To *"seek* power from on High"
or a special "filling of the Spirit" is to run the serious risk of being controlled by evil spirits posing as angels of light.

32

Honoring the Spirit

IT seems fitting that we should close this discussion upon the person, office, and operations of the Holy Spirit, by dwelling upon what is due Him from those in thom He was wrought so graciously, for it is very evident that some *recognition and response* must be made Him by us. There is, however, a need for us to write something thereon, because there are some who belong to a company which refrains from all direct worship of the third Person in the Godhead, deeming it unscriptural and incongruous to do so. It seems strange that the very ones who claim to give the Spirit a freer and fuller place in their meetings than any branch of Christendom, should, at the same time, demur at prayer being immediately directed to Him. Yet it is so: some of them refuse to sing the Doxology because it ends with "Praise Father, Son, and Holy Ghost."

People have, from time to time, taken exception to occasional statements made by me, such as "what praise is due the Spirit for His grace and goodness unto us!" challenging us to point to any definite passage wherein we are bidden to worship or pray to the Spirit distinctively. First, let us point out that there are many things clearly *implied* in Scripture which are not formally and expressly stated, and to assert we must for that reason reject them is absurd — some have refused the canonicity of the book of Esther because the name of God is not found therein, yet His superintending providence, His overruling power, His faithfulness and goodness, shine forth in each chapter. We build not our faith on any isolated texts, but on the Word of God as a whole, rightly and spiritually interpreted.

We have begun thus not because we are unable to find any definite statements in the Word which obviously warrant the position we have taken, but because we deemed it well to refute an erroneous principle. Even if there were no clear cases recorded of prayer and praise being offered immediately to the Holy Spirit, we should surely require some *strong positive proof* to show that the Spirit is *not* to be supplicated. But where, we ask, is there anything in Holy Writ which informs us that one Person in the Godhead must be *excluded* from the praises that we make unto the Lord? Here we are meeting the objector on his own ground: if what we are about to advance fails to convince him, he must at least allow that he knows of no texts which refute or condemn us, no verse which warns us *against* rendering to the blessed Spirit that recognition and honor to which we consider He is fully entitled.

181

"Thou shalt fear ["worship" — Matt. 4:10] the Lord thy God, and serve him" (Deut. 6:13). Now the Lord our God is a Unity in Trinity, that is, He subsists in three Persons who are co-essential and co-glorious. Therefore the Holy Spirit, equally with the Father and the Son, is entitled to and must receive devout homage, for we are here commanded to render the same to Him. This is confirmed by the "holy, holy, holy" of Isaiah 6:3, where we find the seraphim owning separately and worshipping distinctively the Eternal Three. The words that follow in verse 8, "Who will go for us?" make it quite clear that the threefold "holy" was ascribed to the Blessed Trinity. Still further confirmation is found in Acts 28:15, 16, where the apostle prefaces his quotation of Isaiah 6:9 with "well spake *the Holy Spirit* by Isaiah the prophet." If, then, the angels ascribe glory and render worship to the Holy Spirit, shall we, who have been regenerated by Him, do less!

"O come, let us *worship* and bow down; let us kneel before the Lord our Maker" (Ps. 95:6). *Who is* our "Maker?" Perhaps you answer, Christ, the eternal Word, of whom it is said, "All things were made by Him, and without Him was not anything made that was made" (John 1:3 and cf. Col. 1:16). That is true, yet Christ is not our "Maker" (either naturally or spiritually) *to the exclusion* of the Holy Spirit. The third Person of the Godhead, equally with the Father and the Son, is our "Maker." In proof of this assertion we quote, "The Spirit of God hath made me, and the Breath of the Almighty hath given me life" (Job 33:4). Let the reader carefully compare Job 26:13 with Psalm 33:6. Let it also be duly noted that Psalm 95 (vv. 7-11) is quoted in Hebrews 3:7-11 and prefaced with "Wherefore as the Holy Spirit saith." Thus not only *may* we worship the blessed Spirit, but here in Psalm 95:6 we are *commanded* to do so.

It does indeed seem strange that any professing Christian should raise any objection and question the propriety of worshipping the Spirit. Are we not to acknowledge our dependence upon and obligations unto the Holy Spirit? Surely! surely! He is as much the Object of faith as is the Father and the Son: He is so in His Being and perfections, His Deity and personality, His offices and operations. Moreover, there are particular acts of trust and confidence to be exercised on Him. As He is God, He is to be worshipped, and that cannot be done aright without faith. We are to trust Him for His help in prayer and the discharge of every duty! We are to exercise confidence that He will complete the good work which He has begun in us. Especially should ministers of the Word look to Him for His help in and blessing upon their labors.

"Then said he unto me, prophesy unto the wind [breath], prophesy, son of man, and say to the wind, Thus saith the Lord God; Come from the four winds, O Breath, and breathe upon these slain, that they may live" (Ezek. 37:9). We sincerely trust that none of our readers will suppose that the Lord bade His servant to perform an *idolatrous* act by invoking the *literal* "wind." No, a comparison of verses 9 and 10 with verse 14 shows plainly that it was *the Holy Spirit* Himself who was referred to (see John 3:8). Nor does this passage stand alone. In Song of Solomon 4:16 we find the spouse praying to the Spirit for renewal and revival: "Awake, O north wind; and come, thou south; blow upon my garden that the spices thereof may flow out." She expressed her desires metaphorically, but this is what she breathed after. It is the Spirit of life, then, we should always apply to for quickening, for the enlivening and exciting of His graces in us.

Honoring the Spirit is (alas) new to many. Not a few seem to have been misled through a wrong understanding of that word concerning the Spirit in John 16:13, as though, "He shall not speak of himself" signified He shall never occupy the saints with His own person and work, but always direct them to Christ. It is true that the Spirit is here to glorify Christ, yet *that* by no means exhausts His mission. His first work is to direct the attention of sinners to God *as God,* convicting them of rebellion against their Creator, Ruler, and Judge. Then, too, He occupies the saints with the Father: His love, grace, and providential care. But John 16:13 no more means that the Spirit does not magnify Himself than Christ's "I have not spoken of myself" (John 12:49) meant that He never occupied people with His own person — His "come unto *me*" (Matt. 11:28; John 7:37) proves otherwise.

Others create difficulty out of the fact that, in the economy of redemption, the Spirit now occupies the place of *Servant* of the Godhead, and as such it is incongruous to *worship* Him. Such a cavil hardly deserves reply. But lest some of our readers have been misled by this sophistry, let it be pointed out that during the days of His flesh, Christ occupied the place of "Servant," the One who came here not to be ministered unto, but to minister: nevertheless, even during that season of His humiliation we are told "Behold there came a leper and *worshipped* Him" (Matt. 8:2). And have we not read that when the wise men from the east entered the house where He was, they "fell down and *worshipped* Him" (Matt. 2:11)? Thus, the fact that the Holy Spirit is the Executive of the Godhead by no means debars Him of His title to our love and homage. Some say that because the Spirit is *in* us, He is not a suitable Object of worship, as the Father and Son without us. But is the Spirit within the *only* relation He sustains to us? Is He not omnipresent, infinitely above us, and as such an appropriate Object of worship?

That the Holy Spirit *is to be* publicly owned and equally honored with the Father and the Son is very evident from the terms of the great commission, "Go ye therefore, and teach all nations, baptizing them in the name of the Father, and of the Son, *and of the Holy Spirit*" (Matt. 28:19). Now to be baptized in the name of the Holy Spirit is either a real act of *worship,* or otherwise it would be a mere formality — which of the two is not difficult to determine. In view of this verse, no one need have the slightest hesitation in rendering the same homage to the Spirit as he does to the Father and the Son. This is not a case of reasoning on our part, nor of drawing an inference, but is a part of Divinely-revealed truth. If we praise and revere the Son for what He has done *for* us, shall not the Spirit be adored for what He has wrought *in* us! The Spirit Himself loves us (Rom. 15:30), by whose authority, then, are we to stifle our love for Him!

"The grace of the Lord Jesus Christ, and the love of God, and the communion of the Holy Spirit, be with you all. *Amen*" (II Cor. 13:14). Here again the Holy Spirit is honored equally with the Father and the Son — the apostles certainly did not slight Him as do some of our moderns. Let it be duly weighed that "communion" is a *mutual* thing, a giving and receiving. In our communion with the Father we receive from Him, and then return to Him love and obedience. From the Son we receive life, and acknowledge it in our praises. From the Spirit we receive regeneration and sanctification, shall we render Him nothing in return? We understand this verse to signify. "O Lord Jesus Christ, let thy *grace* be with us; O God the Father, let thy *love* be manifested unto us; O Holy Spirit, let thy saints enjoy much of thy *communion*." This invocatory benediction revealed the longings of Paul's heart unto the Corinthian saints, and those longings prompted his petition on their behalf.

"And the Lord direct your hearts into the love of God, and into the patient waiting for Christ" (II Thess. 3:5). What could be plainer? Here each of the three Divine Persons are distinguished, and the apostle prays directly *to the Lord the Spirit* — obviously "the Lord" here cannot refer to the Son, for in such case it would signify "The Lord (Jesus) direct your hearts into . . . the patient waiting for Christ." As it is the Spirit's office to "'guide' us into all truth" (John 16:13), to "'lead' us into the paths of righteousness" (Ps. 23:3), so to "direct" our hearts into the love of God and longings after Christ. He it is who communicates God's love to us (Rom. 5:5), and He it is who stirs us up to the performance of duty by inflaming our hearts with apprehensions of God's tenderness toward us; and for this we are to pray to Him. It is just as though the apostle said, "O Thou Lord the Spirit, warm our cold hearts, with a renewed sense of God's tender regard for us; stabilize our fretful souls into a patient waiting for Christ."

"John to the seven churches which are in Asia: Grace be unto you and peace, from him which is, and which was, and which is to come; and from the seven Spirits which are before his throne; and from Jesus Christ, who is the faithful witness" (Rev. 1:4, 5). This is as much a prayer — an invocation of blessing — as that recorded in Numbers 6: 24-26. The apostle John desired and supplicated God the Father ("Him who is," etc.); God the Holy Spirit in the plenitude of His power ("the seven Spirits"); and God the Son, that the seven churches in Asia might enjoy *their* grace and peace. When I say "The Lord *bless* you, dear brother," I should utter empty words unless I also *pray* the Lord *to* bless you. This "grace and peace be unto you," then, was far more than a pleasantry or courtesy: John was making known to the saints his deep *longings* for them, which found expression in ardent supplication for these very blessings to be conferred upon them. In conclusion let us say that every verse in the Bible which bids us "Praise the Lord" or "worship God" has reference to *each* of the Eternal Three.

"Pray ye therefore the Lord of the harvest, that he will send forth laborers into his harvest" (Matt. 9:38). Here is something very plain and expressive, the only point needing to be determined is, *Who is* "The Lord of the harvest?" During the days of His earthly ministry, Christ Himself sustained that office, as is clear from His calling and sending forth of the Twelve; but after His ascension, *the Holy Spirit* became such. As proof thereof, we refer to "The Holy Spirit said, separate *me* Barnabas and Saul, for the work whereunto *I* have called them . . . so they, being sent forth by the Holy Spirit, departed" (Acts 13:2, 4). So again we read, "Take heed therefore unto yourselves, and to all the flock over the which *the Holy Spirit* hath made you overseers" (Acts 20:28). It is the Holy Spirit who now appoints the laborers, equips them, assigns their work, and blesses their efforts. In I Corinthians 12:5 and II Corinthians 3:17 the Holy Spirit is expressly designated "Lord."

Textual Index